Discussing Economics

Dedicated to Basil O'Leary whose use of class discussion stimulated a lifelong desire to do it well. (Michael Salemi)

Dedicated to Victor Moeller and Ed Moldof, of the Great Books Foundation, for introducing me to the glories of classroom discussion, and to my Monroe Street Library (Madison, Wisconsin) Great Books Discussion Group for helping me hone my skills over the past three decades. (W. Lee Hansen)

Discussing Economics

A Classroom Guide to Preparing Discussion Questions and Leading Discussion

Michael K. Salemi
University of North Carolina at Chapel Hill, US

W. Lee Hansen
University of Wisconsin Madison, US

Edward Elgar
Cheltenham, UK • Northampton, MA, USA

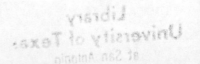

Published by
Edward Elgar Publishing Limited
Glensanda House
Montpellier Parade
Cheltenham
Glos GL50 1UA
UK

Edward Elgar Publishing, Inc.
136 West Street
Suite 202
Northampton
Massachusetts 01060
USA

A catalogue record for this book
is available from the British Library

Library of Congress Cataloguing in Publication Data

Salemi, Michael K.
    Discussing economics : a classroom guide to preparing discussion questions
and leading discussion / Michael K. Salemi, W. Lee Hansen.
      p. cm.
    Includes bibliographical references.
      1. Economics—Study and teaching. I. Hansen, W. Lee. II. Title.

HB74.5.S25 2005
330'.071—dc22

                                                   2004063371

ISBN 1 84376 449 0 (cased)

Printed and bound in Great Britain by MPG Books Ltd, Bodmin, Cornwall

Contents

Preface

This book is about discussion as a learning strategy in economics. By discussion, we mean a formal consideration of a set of questions about a reading that is conducted during a class session with the instructor present and generally serving as discussion leader. We do not mean a spontaneous, loosely planned exchange of ideas. For us, discussion is a highly structured and carefully planned activity in which students investigate the meaning of a reading.

Our intention is to provide our readers everything they need to use our discussion strategy in their classrooms. It is our experience that students learn to think deeply about economics by preparing for and participating in classroom discussions. We also find that students like discussions. They frequently tell us that they value the opportunity that discussion provides them 'to do' economics and to work with the original writings of important economists. We hope that readers will find our handbook to be a resource that they come back to term after term.

We recommend that instructors take a gradual approach to adding discussion to their courses. Instructors who are trying out discussion for the first time might choose one topic where discussion fits well and one or two readings for that topic. Subsequently, they can add topics and readings until they judge that the mix of discussion, lecture and other activities is right.

The book develops in much greater detail themes that we first introduced in Hansen and Salemi (1998). In Chapter 1, we explain why discussion is an effective learning strategy and provide suggestions for getting the most out of classroom discussions. In Chapters 2 and 3, we define and describe interpretive questions and question clusters – lynchpins of our approach to discussion. In Chapter 4, we suggest to the reader how they can prepare for and conduct successful discussions in their economics courses.

Parts Two through Five of the book provide discussion suggestions for more than sixty economics readings. A list of the readings follows this preface. So that readers can easily find readings for their courses, we collect them into 15 chapters by topics such as 'Incentives and Markets', 'Economic Growth', and 'International Financial Institutions'. We then group chapters into parts: Discussing Economic Principles, Discussing Macroeconomics, Discussing Microeconomics, and Discussing Financial Economics. Our groupings are meant solely to help readers locate readings and should be taken with a grain of salt. Readings that we associate with one part of the economics curriculum would frequently be useful in others.

For each reading we provide several resources. First, we provide an abstract of the article. Second, to aid in course planning, we explain what students can learn by reading and discussing the article. Third, we provide question clusters that instructors can use to discuss each reading. We hope that readers will eventually write discussion questions of their own but understand that they may find it useful to have good questions available as they begin to use our approach. Fourth, we make a number of suggestions that are specific to each reading and are based on our own classroom experiences.

Complementary on-line resources are available from Aplia, the learning company whose web address is www.aplia.com. Three kinds of companion resources are available. First, the Aplia site provides some of the readings referred to in this book. Second, it provides discussion questions for those readings. Third, it includes a tutorial for users who wish to learn how to create discussion questions using the methodology we explain in this book.

List of Discussion Readings

We provide a guide to discussing the following readings in Parts Two through Five of this book.

Akerlof, George A. (1970), 'The Market for "Lemons": Quality Uncertainty and the Market Mechanism', *Quarterly Journal of Economics*, **LXXXIV** (3), August, 488-500.

Ball, Laurence and N. Gregory Mankiw (1995), 'What Do Budget Deficits Do?', in Federal Reserve Bank of Kansas City (ed.), *Budget Deficits and Debt: Issues and Options: A Symposium Sponsored by the Federal Reserve Bank of Kansas City, Jackson Hole, Wyoming, August 31-September 2, 1995*, 95-119.

Barnett, A. H. and David L. Kaserman (1995), 'The "Rush to Transplant" and Organ Shortages', *Economic Inquiry*, **XXXIII** (3), July, 506-15.

Feige, Edgar L. (1990), 'A Message to Gorbachev: Redistribute the Wealth', *Challenge Magazine*, **33** (3), May-June, 46-53.

Fisher, Irving (1930), *The Theory of Interest*, reprinted in (1974), *The Theory of Interest*, Clifton, NJ: Augustus M. Kelley Publishers.

Friedman, Benjamin M. (1991), 'U.S. Fiscal Policy in the 1980s: Consequences of Large Budget Deficits at Full Employment', in James M. Rock, (ed.), *Debt and the Twin Deficits Debate*, Mountain View, CA: Mayfield Publishing Company, 149-72.

Friedman, Milton (1962), 'The Relation between Economic Freedom and Political Freedom', *Capitalism and Freedom* Chicago: University of Chicago Press, Chap. 1, 7-21.

Friedman, Milton (1977), 'Nobel Lecture: Inflation and Unemployment', *The Journal of Political Economy*, **85** (3), 451-72.

Friedman, Milton and Rose Friedman (1980), 'The Tide Is Turning', *Freedom to Choose: A Personal Statement*, New York: Avon Books, Chap. 10, 119-39.

Galbraith, J. K. (1946), 'Reflections on Price Control', *Quarterly Journal of Economics*, **LX** (4), 475-89.

Galston, William A. (2004), 'Thinking about the Draft', *The Public Interest*, **154** (Winter), 61-73.

Goldman, Marshall (2000), 'Reprivatizing Russia: Two Views on Europe', *Challenge Magazine*, **43** (3), May-June, 28-43.

Gorbachev, Mikhail (1987), *Perestroika: New Thinking for Our Country and the World* New York: Harper and Row, Chap. 1, 17-38.

Hammond, Bray (1957), *Banks and Politics in America*, Princeton, NJ: Princeton University Press, 89-143.

Hansen, W. Lee and Robert J. Lampman (1983), 'Basic Opportunity Grants for Higher Education: Good Intentions and Mixed Results', in Robert H. Haveman and Julius Margolis (eds), *Public Expenditure and Policy Analysis*, Boston: Houghton Mifflin Co., 493-512.

Harris, Ethan and Charles Steindel (1991), 'The Decline in U.S. Saving and its Implications for Economic Growth', Federal Reserve Bank of New York *Quarterly Review*, **15** (3-4), 1-19.

Haveman, Robert (2000), 'Poverty and the Distribution of Economic Well-Being since the 1960s', in George L. Perry and James Tobin (eds), *Economic Events, Ideas, and Policies: The 1960s and After* Washington DC: Brookings Institution, 243-98.

Hayek, F. A. (1945), 'The Use of Knowledge in Society', *The American Economic Review*, **35** (4), 519-30.

Heilbroner, Robert L. (1970), 'On the Limited Relevance of Economics', *The Public Interest*, **21** (Fall), 80-93.

Heilbroner, Robert L. (1989), 'Reflections: The Triumph of Capitalism', *The New Yorker*, **LXIV**, January 23, 98-109.

Heilbroner, Robert L. (1990), 'Reflection: After Communism', *The New Yorker,* **LXVI**, September 10, 91-100.

Hewitt, Ed. A. (1989), 'Economic Reform in the USSR. Eastern Europe, and China: The Politics of Economics', *American Economic Review, Papers and Proceedings*, **79** (2), May, 16-20.

Hoffmann, Carl, and John Shelton Reed (1981), 'Sex Discrimination? The XYZ Affair', *The Public Interest*, **62** (Winter), 21-39.

Jefferson, Gary H. and Peter A. Petri (1990), 'From Marx to Markets', *Challenge Magazine*, **33** (5), September-October, 4-16.

Johnson, Robert A. (1995), 'Commentary: What Do Budget Deficits Do?', in Federal Reserve Bank of Kansas City (ed.), *Budget Deficits and Debt: Issues and Options: A Symposium Sponsored by the Federal Reserve Bank of Kansas City, Jackson Hole, Wyoming, August 31-September 2, 1995*, 121-8.

Keynes, John Maynard (1936), 'Concluding Notes on the Social Philosophy Towards Which the General Theory Might Lead', *The General Theory of Employment, Interest, and Money*, London: Macmillan, Chap. 24, 372-84.

Kotlikoff, Laurence J. (1998), 'Privatizing U.S. Social Security: Some Possible Effects on Intergenerational Equity and the Economy', Federal Reserve Bank of St. Louis, *Review*, **80** (2), 31-7.

Kotlikoff, Laurence J. and Scott Burns (2004), 'The Perfect Demographic Storm: Entitlements Imperil America's Future', *The Chronicle of Higher Education*, **L** (28), March 19, B6-B10.

Krugman, Paul (1994), 'Past and Prospective Causes of High Unemployment', Federal Reserve Bank of Kansas City, *Economic Review*, Fourth Quarter, 23-43.

Lucas, Robert E. Jr. (1996), 'Nobel Lecture: Monetary Neutrality', *Journal of Political Economy*, **104** (4), 661-82.

Lucas, Robert E. Jr. (2000), 'Some Macroeconomics for the 21st Century', *Journal of Economic Perspectives*, **14** (1), 159-68.

Mankiw, N. Gregory, David Romer, and David N. Weil (1992), 'A Contribution to the Empirics of Economic Growth', *The Quarterly Journal of Economics*, **107** (2), 407-37.

Marx, Karl (1844), 'Wages of Labour', and 'Estranged Labour', in *Early Writings*, Introduced by Lucio Colletti (1974), Translated by Gregor Benton (1974), London: Penguin Group (Penguin Classics Reprint 1992), 282-88, 322-34.

Marx, Karl, and Friedrich Engels (1848), 'The Manifesto of the Communist Party', in *The Communist Manifesto*, introduced by Gareth Stedman Jones (2002), Translated by Samuel Morse (1888), London: Penguin Group (Penguin Classics Reprint 2002), 218-58.

Meltzer, Allan H. (1995), 'Commentary: What Do Budget Deficits Do?', in Federal Reserve Bank of Kansas City (ed.), *Budget Deficits and Debt: Issues and Options: A Symposium Sponsored by the Federal Reserve Bank of Kansas City, Jackson Hole, Wyoming, August 31-September 2, 1995*, 129-37.

Meyer, Laurence H. (2001), 'Inflation Targets and Inflation Targeting', Federal Reserve Bank of St. Louis *Review*, **83** (6), 1-14.

Mishkin, Frederic (1999), 'Global Financial Instability: Framework, Events, Issues', *Journal of Economic Perspectives*, **13** (4), 3-20.

Morris, Charles R. (1993), 'It's *Not* the Economy, Stupid', *Atlantic Monthly*, **272** (1), July, 49-62.

Obstfeld, Maurice (1998), 'The Global Capital Market: Benefactor or Menace?', *Journal of Economic Perspectives*, **12** (4), 9-30.

Okun, Arthur (1975), 'Rights and Dollars', in *Equality and Efficiency: The Big Tradeoff*, Washington, DC, The Brookings Institution, Chap. 1, 1-31.

Okun, Arthur (1975), 'The Case for the Market', in *Equality and Efficiency: The Big Tradeoff*, Washington, DC, The Brookings Institution, Chap. 2, 32-64.

Okun, Arthur (1975), 'Equality of Income and Opportunity', in *Equality and Efficiency: The Big Tradeoff*, Washington, DC, The Brookings Institution, Chap. 3, 65-87.

Okun, Arthur (1975), 'Increasing Equality in an Efficient Economy', in *Equality and Efficiency: The Big Tradeoff*, Washington, DC, The Brookings Institution, Chap. 4, 88-120.

Radford, R. A. (1945), 'The Economic Organization of a P.O.W. Camp', *Economica*, **XII** (48), November, 189-201.

Redish, Angela (1993), 'Anchors Aweigh: The Transition from Commodity Money to Fiat Money in Western Economies', *Canadian Journal of Economics*, **XXVI** (4),777-95.

Rogoff, Kenneth (1999), 'International Institutions for Reducing Global Financial Instability', *Journal of Economic Perspectives*, **13** (4), 21-42.

Sargent, Thomas J. (1986), 'Reaganomics and Credibility', in *Rational Expectations and Inflation*, New York: Harper & Row, 19-39.

Sargent, Thomas J. (1986), 'The Ends of Four Big Inflations', in *Rational Expectations and Inflation*, New York: Harper & Row, 40-109.

Schelling, Thomas C. (1984), 'Economics and Criminal Enterprise', *Choice and Consequence: Perspectives of an Errant Economist*, Cambridge, MA: Harvard University Press, Chap. 7, 158-78.

Schumpeter, Joseph A. (1949), 'Prologue', and 'The March into Socialism', *Capitalism, Socialism, and Democracy*, New York, Harper, Third Edition, 61, 415-25.

Shatalin, S. (1990), 'Man, Freedom, and Market: On the Program Developed by the Task Force Headed by Academician S.S. Shatalin', in G. Yavlinsky, B. Federov, S. Shatalin, N. Petrakov, S. Aleksashenko, A. Vavilov, L. Grigoriev, M. Zadornov, V. Machits, A. Milhailov, and E. Yasin, *500 Days: Transition to the Market*, New York: St. Martin's Press, vi-xxi.

Smith, Adam (1776), 'Of the Division of Labour', 'Of the Principle which gives Occasion to the Division of Labour', 'That the Division of Labor is limited by the Extent of the Market', and 'Of the Origins and Use of Money', *The Wealth of Nations* (Cannan Edition, 1937), Introduction by Robert Reich (2000), New York: The Modern Library Paperback Edition (2000), Book I, Chap. 1-3, 3-23; Chap. 4, 24-26.

Smith, Adam (1776), 'On the Real and Nominal Price of Commodities, or of their Price in Labour, or their Price in Money', and 'Of the Component Parts of the Price of Commodities', *The Wealth of Nations* (Cannan Edition, 1937), Introduction by Robert Reich (2000), New York: The Modern Library Paperback Edition (2000), Book I, Chaps. 5-6, 33-61.

Smith, Adam (1776), 'Of the Natural and Market Price of Commodities', *The Wealth of Nations* (Cannan Edition, 1937), Introduction by Robert Reich (2000), New York: The Modern Library Paperback Edition (2000), Book I, Chapter 7, 62-72.

Smith, Adam (1776), 'Of the Wages of Labour', *The Wealth of Nations* (Cannan Edition, 1937), Introduction by Robert Reich (2000), New York: The Modern Library Paperback Edition (2000), Book I, Chapter 8, 73-99.

Smith, Adam (1776), 'Inequalities arising from the Nature of the Employments themselves', *The Wealth of Nations* (Cannan Edition, 1937), Introduction by Robert Reich (2000), New York: The Modern Library Paperback Edition (2000), Book I, Chapters 10, Part I, 114-36.

Smith, Adam (1776), 'Of the Expense of the Institutions for the Education of Youth', *The Wealth of Nations* (Cannan Edition, 1937), Introduction by Robert Reich (2000), New York: The Modern Library Paperback Edition (2000), Book V, Chap. 1, Part III, Article 2d, 819-46.

Solow, Robert M. (1970), 'Science and Ideology in Economics', *The Public Interest*, **21** (Fall), 94-107.

Tawney, R. H. (1931), 'Equality', in Edward C. Budd (ed.), *Inequality and Poverty*, New York: Norton 1967, 27-37; based on excerpts from 1929 Halley Stewart Lecture originally published in *Equality*, London: George Allen and Unwin (1931).

Taylor, John B. (1993), 'Discretion versus Policy Rules in Practice', *Carnegie-Rochester Conference Series on Public Policy*, **39** 195-214.

Taylor, John B. (1995), 'The Monetary Transmission Mechanism: An Empirical Framework', *Journal of Economic Perspectives*, **9** (4), 11-26.

Van Lear, William (2000), 'A Review of the Rules Versus Discretion Debate in Monetary Policy', *Eastern Economic Journal*, **26** (1), 29-39.

Warner, John T. and Beth J. Asch (2001), 'The Record and Prospects of the All-Volunteer Military in the United States', *Journal of Economic Perspectives*, **15** (2), Spring 2001, 169-92.

Webb, Roy H. (1993), 'Personal Saving Behavior and Real Economic Activity', Federal Reserve Bank of Richmond *Economic Quarterly*, **79** (2), 68-94.

Wolf, Charles Jr. (1979), 'A Theory of Non-market Failure', *The Public Interest*, **55** (Spring), 114-33.

Woodward, Bob (2000), *Maestro: Greenspan's Fed and the American Boom*, New York: Touchstone, Simon and Schuster.

Yavlinsky, G., B. Federov, S. Shatalin, N. Petrakov, S. Aleksashenko, A. Vavilov, L. Grigoriev, M. Zadornov, V. Machits, A. Milhailov, and E.

Yasin (1991), 'The Logic and Stages of the Transition to a Market Economy', *500 Days: Transition to the Market*, New York: St. Martin's Press, Part 1, Chap. 4, 27-45.

Acknowledgments

We thank William E. Becker for encouraging publication of this book and Denise Hazlett, Mark Maier, KimMarie McGoldrick, and Scott Simkins for insightful comments and helpful suggestions.

We are grateful to Alan Sturmer, our editor at Edward Elgar, for guiding us as we prepared the manuscript. We thank Paul Romer and Nicholas Smith for partnering with us to create the complementary materials available at www.aplia.com. We are especially grateful to Lisa Gaines who skillfully and painstakingly helped us revise our manuscript.

We thank Blackwell Publishing for permission to reprint the Radford article and McGraw Hill Companies for permission to re-publish passages from the Walstad-Saunders Handbook.

Finally, we thank the many discussion workshop and seminar participants with whom we have worked over the years. Without their enthusiasm and suggestions, this book would never have been written.

1. Why Discussion

I asked a student what St. Thomas had to say about the order of the passions. He quite correctly told me that love, according to St. Thomas, is the first of all the passions and that the other emotions, which he named accurately, follow in a certain order. Then I asked him what it meant to say this. He looked startled. Had he not answered my question correctly? I told him he had, but repeated my request for an explanation. He had told me what St. Thomas *said*. Now I wanted to know what St. Thomas *meant*. The student tried, but all he could do was to repeat, in slightly altered order, the same words he had used to answer my original question. (Adler and Van Doren, 1972, p. 36)

Mortimer Adler, one of the great philosophers and educators of the twentieth century, was largely self-educated. He dropped out of school at 14 and began working toward a career in journalism. Adler's interest in the great thinkers began when he learned that John Stuart Mill had read Plato as a child. Adler went on to study philosophy at Columbia which refused him a bachelors's degree because he had not completed a required physical education course but later awarded him a doctorate on the strength of his command of classic literature. Adler served on the faculty of Columbia, the University of Chicago, and the University of North Carolina at Chapel Hill. He is perhaps best known as co-founder of The Center for the Study of The Great Ideas and for his role in the publication of 'The Great Books of the Western World'. Mortimer Adler died in 2001. Many of our ideas about discussion have origins in Adler's approach to Great Books discussion.

WHAT IS DISCUSSION?

We use the term 'discussion' in a very specific way and at the outset it is a good idea to say what we mean and what we do not mean. By discussion, we do not mean an informal exchange of ideas or 'bull session'. We do not mean an invitation to students to exchange undisciplined opinions. We do not mean a class session devoted to the spontaneous exchange of ideas. We do not mean shouting matches or debates in which students argue positions without listening carefully to others. We do not mean an oral quiz where instructors put pointed questions to students and then 'play' off their answers. Our meaning is close to the American Heritage Dictionary definition of discussion as 'Consideration of a subject by a group...an earnest conversation'. For us, discussion is a highly structured and carefully planned activity in which students investigate the meaning of a reading.

Interpretation is the cornerstone both of Mortimer Adler's approach to literature and of our approach to discussing economic ideas. Discussion provides students an opportunity to say what a reading means. As they form and revise their interpretations, students use the concepts that the authors used in ways that deepen their understanding, lengthen their retention, and enable them to transfer their mastery to new contexts. Put another way, discussion helps students become literate in economics.

In this chapter, we make the case for discussion as a productive, cost-effective pedagogy. Skeptics complain that discussion takes a lot of class time and involves loss of control over the flow of ideas. They doubt the value of allowing students to offer imprecise answers to questions. They prefer that instructors provide students with concise and 'correct' interpretations. Part of our job is to answer the skeptics.

We make a three-part case for discussion. First, discussion helps students master economic ideas at higher cognitive levels. It helps them think more deeply about economics. Second, discussion motivates students to recognize that economics is important and to work harder at it. It helps students see that economics is an interesting, relevant, and important discipline in which they can participate. Third, discussion improves economic literacy. Through discussion, students gain a practical understanding of economics that they can apply throughout their lives. We take up each of these claims in the sections that follow. We also suggest a set of strategies that help instructors maximize the benefits of discussion and minimize its cost.

DISCUSSION PROMOTES DEEPER UNDERSTANDING

Like Adler, we want our students to understand what economists mean, not just what they say. Most of us agree that the overarching goal of economic education is to help students 'think like economists' (Siegfried *et al.*, 1991, p. 199). Hansen, Salemi and Siegfried (2002) contend that helping principles students think like economists requires many in-class opportunities to practice using basic economic ideas. Hansen (2001, pp. 232-3) implies that, to think like economists, economics majors should attain six proficiencies including command of existing knowledge and the ability to interpret and apply it. Discussion helps principles students and majors think like economists because it provides them opportunities to interpret, and thereby better understand, the writing of economists

Bloom (1956) sets out a taxonomy with six levels of cognition: knowledge, comprehension, application, analysis, synthesis, and evaluation. Through discussion, students have an opportunity to practice using economic ideas at higher taxonomic levels. We explain why this is so in the context of a specific economic writing, 'The Economic Organisation of a P.O.W. Camp' (Radford, 1945), which is reproduced as an appendix to this volume. Radford page references refer to pagination in the original article. We ask readers to re-familiarize themselves with Radford's article before proceeding further.

Radford explains how and why cigarettes came to be used as money in World War II prisoner camps and describes an attempt to replace cigarettes with a paper money called the Bully Mark. Discussing Radford provides an excellent opportunity for students to work with the concepts of money and inflation at higher cognitive levels. To show what it means to master money at different levels of Bloom's taxonomy, we provide questions that permit students to demonstrate mastery.

The lowest level of the taxonomy is 'knowledge' which requires students to remember previously learned material. Answering a question like 'What are the three functions of money?' would indicate that students know what money is. Asking this question is asking students what Radford said – he lists the functions of money on page 194.

The next level of Bloom's taxonomy is 'comprehension' which requires students to grasp the meaning of material. Students demonstrate comprehension by interpreting the meaning of a concept and translating that meaning into a new context. Answering a question such as 'What behavior of the prisoners show that cigarettes functioned as a store of value?' would demonstrate that students comprehended the store-of-value function of money.

The next taxonomic level is 'application' which requires students to use concepts in a new, concrete situation. By reading their text and listening to lectures, students encounter statements, explanations, and examples of the three functions of money. By discussing Radford, students transfer their understanding of the functions of money to a new context – cigarette money in a P.O.W. camp. The question 'Why, according to Radford, did cigarettes function well as money in the P.O.W. camp?' prompts students to apply what they have learned. Radford provides many examples that show how cigarettes were used in the camp. By answering the question, students demonstrate that they understand the functions of money well enough to sort the examples into those that show that cigarettes are a medium of exchange, those that show cigarettes are a unit of account, and those that show cigarettes are a store of value. Radford never explicitly answers this question himself. When students answer it, they demonstrate that they know what Radford meant as well as what he said.

Still higher on the Bloom taxonomy is 'analysis'. Students can analyze if they can break down material into its component parts and understand its organizational structure. To analyze, students must understand individual concepts and how they fit together in an argument. A discussion question that asks students to analyze the use of cigarettes as money is: 'What does Radford mean when he says of cigarettes that "It was this intrinsic value which gave rise to their principal disadvantage as money...a strong demand for non-monetary purposes?"'. To answer the question students must recognize that a cigarette could be either consumed or used as money and explain why the fact that cigarettes could be smoked made them work less well as money. As part of their answer, students could cite Radford's examples of what happened to prices immediately before and after Red Cross cigarette allotments were distributed. They could also explain what would have happened to prices if no one smoked.

A second question that prompts students to work at the level of analysis is: 'Does Radford's camp experience support Milton Friedman's claim that inflation is always and everywhere a monetary phenomenon?' To answer this question students must understand the theoretical connection between money growth and inflation, must be able to recognize events in camp life that can be viewed as changes in the stock of money, and must be able to find evidence that prices responded as Friedman predicts.

The penultimate level of Bloom cognition is 'synthesis'. Students synthesize when they put together economic ideas to form a new whole and communicate the new whole to others. Analysis requires students to decompose an argument and identify its working parts. Synthesis requires that students understand the parts well enough to be able to build something new with them. When students master economic concepts at the synthesis level they achieve Hansen's sixth proficiency – the ability to create new knowledge in economics.

A discussion question that invites students to work at the synthesis level is: 'Why did the Bully Mark work for a while but ultimately fail as a camp currency?' To answer this question, students must understand why prisoners were initially willing to exchange goods for Bully Marks even though cigarettes were still widely accepted. They must explain why a shortage of Red Cross parcels and bombing of the camps led prisoners to stop accepting the Bully Mark even though they continued to accept cigarettes. They must apply the concepts of self interest to explain the rise and the fall of the second camp currency. What makes this question synthesis rather than analysis is that it requires students to use their understanding of what makes for an acceptable money to create a new idea – an explanation of what could lead self-interested agents to refuse to accept a formerly acceptable money.

A second question that would invite students to work at the synthesis level with the Radford article is: 'What are the parallels between the creation of the Bully Mark in Radford's P.O.W. camp and the Free Silver movement in the late nineteenth century United States?' For instructors who cover the Free Silver movement, the question provides an attractive opportunity to ask students to use what they learned about one dual currency arrangement to investigate another. To answer the question, students would first break their analysis of the Bully Mark into parts such as 'Why did some prisoners favor creation of a second currency when cigarettes already functioned well as money?' Then, students must answer the question again for the Free Silver movement and consider whether the same sort of forces were at work. Drawing out the parallels between the two dual currency episodes requires students to put together their part-by-part comparisons to form a new whole.

The highest level of Bloom's taxonomy is 'evaluation'. Students can evaluate if they can judge the value of material for a given purpose with criteria that they choose. To evaluate, students must undertake 'what if' thought experiments and evaluate marginal costs and benefits. They must understand the consequences of policy actions and market shocks, must apply criteria such as equity and efficiency, and must make policy recommendations. To think like an economist is to evaluate.

A discussion question that invites students to work at the level of evaluation is: 'If you were senior officer in the P.O.W. camp, would you prohibit the use of cigarettes as money?' This question invites a full exploration of what Radford means about the use of cigarettes as money. It invites students to think about the costs and benefits of having cigarettes serve as money given the view of the medical officer that some smokers suffered from malnutrition. It invites them to consider the wisdom of reported attempts to fix prices in ways that promoted healthy behavior. It asks students what Radford means when he says '...prices moved with the supply of cigarettes, and refused to stay fixed in accordance with a theory of ethics' (p. 200). The question also challenges students to identify criteria on which to base their decision. Camp morale, preservation of individual freedom, and the health of the weakest prisoners are all possibilities.

Hopefully, our examples make clear that discussion based on the right kind of questions can promote deeper thinking by asking students to master economic concepts at higher cognitive levels. What the right kind of questions are is a matter that we take up in Chapters 2 and 3. For now, let us say that the right kind of questions are those that ask students what an author means rather than what the author says.

DISCUSSION IMPROVES STUDENT ATTITUDES ABOUT ECONOMICS

Economists lecture. Surveys show that economics instructors, at all types of institutions, spend over 80 percent of class time lecturing and make little use of other pedagogies (Becker and Watts, 2001). New instructors mimic their own instructors (Krueger, 1991, p. 1049).

When instructors overuse lecture, students are deprived of the benefits that derive from interactive strategies (Chickering and Gamson, 1987; Bonwell and Eison, 1991; Bartlett, 1998; and McKeachie *et al.*, 2002). Johnston *et al.* (2002) find that students understand concepts better, enjoy economics classes more and value their tutors more highly when they engage in collaborative learning. Chizmar and Ostrosky (1998) report that learning improves when students interact with their instructors via 'one-minute papers'. Taylor and Emerson (2004) find that principles students who participated in a series of classroom experiments scored substantially and significantly higher on the Test of Understanding of College Economics (TUCE) than students who were taught by lecture. Smith and Kolb (1986) show that women and minorities are more likely to be 'concrete' than 'abstract' learners and Bartlett and Ferber (1998) explain why interactive strategies are more effective for concrete learners. Respondents to the Harvard Assessment Seminars survey recommend that students take courses with in-class interaction and work in teams on structured learning tasks (Light, 1992).

In this section, we explain why participating in discussion improves student attitudes toward economics and economic ideas.

Through discussion, students gain the satisfaction of creating their own answers with course concepts. Imagine a discussion of Radford centered around the question: 'If you were senior officer in the P.O.W. camp, would you bar the use of cigarettes as money?' As discussion leader, you might first canvas initial views so that students can see where they stand as a group. Next, you might ask for a list of the costs and benefits associated with prohibiting exchange with cigarettes. You might then ask whether the restriction would be effective, that is, whether camp inmates would continue to use cigarettes as money even if doing so was prohibited. Next, you might ask students what criteria the senior camp officer should use to make a decision. Finally, you would ask students to put the parts together and answer the question.

In our experience, the 'class answer' to a discussion question, the answer agreed upon by students toward the end of a discussion, is much better than answers that even the best students had in mind when discussion began. This occurs even though we require students to read the assigned article and answer assigned questions before discussion and monitor compliance with a start-of-class quiz. The class answer is better because, through discussion, the class combines the best parts of individual responses into one that is more complete, precise, and insightful. Students indicate in course evaluations that they find the discussion process valuable and satisfying.

Students value discussion because it is part of a joint learning effort. As we argue throughout this book, the best discussions are those where the discussion leader truly does not know in advance the answers the class will arrive at. That is not to say that anything goes. A good discussion leader should challenge responses that do not make sense. But students frequently interpret economic readings in valid ways that we had not anticipated.

On one occasion, my (Salemi's) intermediate macro students were discussing Robert Lucas's article 'Some Macroeconomics for the 21st Century', one of the articles that we recommend in Part Three of this book. Lucas sets out a variant of the Solow growth model in which countries start to grow at different times. Spillovers are important. Lucas assumes that the probability that a non-growing country starts to grow increases with the average level of world income.

During discussion, I asked students why Lucas's probability assumption made sense. One student suggested that as the world grows, citizens in non-growing countries place increasing pressure on their leadership to remove political and institutional impediments to growth. I had never contemplated this line of attack. It sparked an interesting round of give and take along political economic lines. At the end, I could truthfully say that I had learned something important about the Lucas article.

We routinely tell our students that ownership of and responsibility for answers to discussion questions are jointly-held properties. As instructors, we are responsible through the questions we ask for helping students examine their understanding of a reading. Students are responsible for putting their interpretations on the table and for responding to the answers offered by others. The answers themselves are not as important as the process that produces them. Through discussion, we help students take responsibility for learning. Many students work harder to bear their responsibility than they would if we treated learning as a private good.

Students value discussion because it provides them an opportunity to talk about course concepts with their peers using familiar language. The language of economics is highly specialized. As specialists, we have spent years refining our understanding and usage of economic terms. Our proficiency is potentially a barrier to student participation. It need not be.

Instructors can encourage students to offer initial answers using informal language. For example, instructors can ask students to develop their discussion responses as part of a small group. In the group setting, students will feel more comfortable in trying to get their ideas out using whatever language they have available. Initially, they may have only part of an answer and the informal setting encourages them to say something like 'I am not sure about the whole thing but I think this is partly what is going on'. As students exchange ideas, they begin the process of revising their understanding and refining their use of economic language.

The instructor may help students to refine their use of economic language by offering gently worded suggestions. By allowing students to begin talking about economics with their own voices and then helping them improve their language proficiency, instructors send a powerful signal that students are expected to be practitioners of economics. In course evaluations, students say that they value the signal and the development it leads to.

Students value discussion because it provides them with feedback about how well they understand course concepts. Frequently, students who do poorly on examinations say something like: 'I don't know what happened. I understood everything. But I didn't know what you wanted.' I used to think that such laments were generic attempts to transfer blame. Now I believe that students who say the above mean that course concepts and examples made sense when the teacher explained them but that they became confused when it was time to use the concepts.

Because students use course concepts in answering discussion questions, discussion provides feedback to students on how well they understand the concepts. The feedback can take lots of forms. One sort of feedback occurs when students, whose ideas are only partially formed, have trouble saying what they mean. Another occurs when students respond to a question in different ways. Subsequent responses may support an initial response, may oppose it, or may appear to be unrelated. In each case, respondents benefit by thinking about how other responses fit together with theirs.

Of course, some of the most valuable feedback is provided to students by instructors. When a student's answer does not make sense, the discussion leader should gently say so. For example, if a student were to say that there was no discussion of inflation in Radford's article, an instructor might respond: 'I am not sure that I agree. What form would inflation take when a commodity is used as money?' The instructor might then ask others whether there were inflation episodes in the camp. We postpone further recommendations for leading discussion until Chapter 4.

Through discussion, students learn which ideas they understand and which they do not. Good discussion questions prompt students to use economic ideas. As they formulate and communicate their answers, students are confronted with their misunderstandings. Since discussion questions make excellent examination essays, discussion gives students precise feedback about how to prepare for exams. In our experience, students value this feedback and benefit from it.

Instructors benefit from feedback as well. If students show unexpected mastery, the instructor can decide to raise the bar. If students have unexpected problems with a concept, the instructor can decide to depart from the syllabus and provide students with more opportunities to master the concept.

Instructors learn student tendencies. They may learn that a certain student favors free markets and use that knowledge later to provoke a debate about a recommended government intervention in the marketplace. 'Sal, how would a proponent of free markets respond to the senior camp officer who proposes to ban the use of cigarettes as money?' Or the instructor might learn that a student has certain relevant experiences. 'Jorge. You lived in Argentina during a period of high inflation. How did your family cope?'

By giving students a stake in the production of knowledge, by allowing them to begin working with ideas even though their mastery of economic language is incomplete, by signaling to students that we expect them to be practitioners of economics, and by providing them with feedback about how well they are doing, instructors who use discussion improve student attitudes toward learning economics. Students respond by working harder and by placing higher value on their economic studies and on economic ideas.

DISCUSSION PROMOTES LITERACY

Hansen, Salemi and Siegfried (2002) point out that Americans have little practical knowledge about economics. Survey after survey has revealed shocking misunderstandings about how our economic system works. Respondents know that demand and supply matters but they do not know what that means. They know what inflation is but they do not know who benefits and who loses when inflation suddenly rises, what inflation risks they face, or what they could do to hedge inflation risks. They know that the Federal Reserve undertakes monetary policy but they do not understand the practical significance of changes in the real rate of interest.

Walstad and Rebeck (2002) report that taking a high-school or college economic course has little impact on economic literacy. Those who take a course score only slightly higher than those who do not on tests of economic understanding. Hansen, Salemi, and Siegfried argue that the proper response to low economic literacy is to target literacy in the economic principles course.

Literacy is the ability to apply concepts years after formal study, in situations that are different from those originally contemplated. To be literate is to master concepts well enough to use them at the analysis, synthesis, and evaluation levels of Bloom's taxonomy. Re-orientation of the principles course toward literacy means teaching fewer concepts and teaching students to use the concepts that are retained. Discussion is a good way to help students learn concepts well enough to use them for the rest of their lives.

Consider the Radford article again. A basic economics principle is that trade creates wealth. A literacy-targeted course would help students gain an understanding of what this principle means.

Imagine teaching the trade principle with a discussion centered around the question: 'What, according to Radford, accounts for the development of an exchange system in the P.O.W. camp?' To answer this question, students must consider what Radford had to say about why prisoners traded. They must explain what Radford means when he says that the padre at the transit camp was able to acquire an entire Red Cross parcel because the market was not yet perfect.

Further discussion might be centered around the question: 'In your view, did the P.O.W. exchange system produce a just distribution of goods?' To respond, students must understand the trade principle at the level of evaluation. That is, they must adopt a definition of 'just', contemplate alternative allocation mechanisms, weigh tradeoffs, and reach a conclusion.

Further work with the trade principle might ask students to transfer what they learned from Radford to a current public policy issue. For example, they could read the article on transplant organs by Barnett and Kaserman described in Part Four of this book and discuss whether they support market allocation of cadaveric organs.

Through discussion, students prepare themselves to think like economists later in life. They better understand the costs and benefits of tariffs and quotas, free trade treaties such as NAFTA, and policies concerning allocation of scarce health resources. They understand that there are good reasons to allow the price of gasoline to rise after an oil shock and the price of generators to rise after a power failure. They recognize the perverse incentives created by price ceilings and floors. They become more literate.

Discussion is not the only pedagogy that promotes literacy. Becker and Watts (1998) and Walstad and Saunders (1998) describe other strategies that help students gain a working knowledge of economic ideas. McGoldrick and Ziegert (2002) describe service-learning models where students use economics in real world settings. In our experience, however, classroom discussion has a very high benefit cost ratio.

MAXIMIZING BENEFITS AND MINIMIZING COSTS

So far, we have focused on the advantages of classroom discussion. Of course, there are disadvantages. Part of our case is that there are remedies to ameliorate the disadvantages. We will discuss our recommended remedies briefly here and return to them in Chapter 4.

Discussion takes too much time. We do not recommend exclusive use of discussion in undergraduate economics courses. Instead, we recommend that instructors use discussion to help students achieve more complete mastery of only the most important course ideas. In a principles course, opportunity cost is a key concept and we have students discuss an article where they apply opportunity cost. Proper construction of a price index is a less important idea and we would not have students read an article about it.

Discussion involves a loss of control. Our answer is yes and no. It is true that we can not control what students say in discussion. We can, however, guide discussion by asking the right kinds of questions as we explain in Chapters 2 and 3. We can use follow up questions to have students clarify their meaning and correct their mistakes. We can create incentives that improve student preparation and increase their participation in discussion.

Getting students to respond is difficult. At the beginning of a course, many students are reluctant to speak up in class. We believe they are reluctant because they do not yet believe that the classroom is a friendly environment where they can venture ideas without risk of humiliation. We address this problem in several ways.

First, we tell students why we employ discussion in our courses. We explain that we want them to benefit in a lasting way from the course and that economics provides a useful lens through which they can look at challenging problems. We say that discussion is interesting and fun. In our experience, students respond positively once they understand why we are asking them to prepare for and participate in discussion.

Second, we model behavior that characterizes a friendly learning environment. We show respect to students whether or not we agree with what they say. We listen hard and take pains to understand what students mean. We praise students for their contributions. When necessary, we raise objections – but take care to maintain a respectful tone when we do.

Third, we sometimes alert students before class that we will ask them a question so that they can get ready.

Fourth, we allow students to prepare small-group responses to discussion questions. We explain our group strategy more fully in Chapter 4 and simply point out here that the strategy works well. Students who were prepared but reluctant to speak in front of the entire class will often speak willingly in a small group. After a couple of group-based discussions, students are more willing to speak up.

Some students talk too much. We have all taught classes where certain students seem to need a lot of air time. One remedy that works well is to assign a talkative student to a group where another student is spokesperson.

A second is to say gently but firmly: 'I see your hand. Thanks for volunteering but I have not yet heard from other students. I will come back to you later.' A third is to take talkative students aside, applaud their energy, and ask their cooperation in providing opportunities for other students to speak. In our experience, these approaches open opportunities for less talkative students to speak up.

Students can't take notes during discussion. Taking notes should not be a priority during discussion. Instead, students focus on what others are saying and on identifying passages that are relevant to the discussion. Even so, students can come away from a discussion with a good overview of what they have learned. How? First, the discussion leader can write out short statements of student answers as they are contributed. For example, suppose we have asked students whether there were inflationary episodes in Radford's camp. After asking some follow up questions to make sure the answer was clear, the leader might summarize Fran's answer as: 'Radford says that prices rose after the Red Cross delivered cigarettes to camp.' In this way, the discussion leader writes a running commentary of student contributions on the board.

Another strategy that provides an overview is the class answer. After students have fully explored a core discussion question (which we will call a basic question in Chapter 3), the discussion leader can ask what the class answer to the question is. The leader might say: 'We seem to have fully explored the issues raised by this question. You have contributed lots of different ideas and have seemed to have reacted fully to one another. At this point, what would you say is the class answer to the question?' Sometimes one student will offer a class answer that all the others approve. More often, several students will contribute parts of the class answer. Having the class summarize what their answer is to the question provides everyone with an overview. Students who wish to take notes can easily do so at this point.

Finally, the discussion leader can pause the discussion to provide students an opportunity to write. For example, the leader might ask students to write a one-minute paper describing the most important thing they learned and the most important unanswered question they have. The leader could then review the papers and decide whether or not to reprise the discussion next class.

Some students are confused by the responses of others. It is true that discussion produces both wheat and chaff and that it is sometimes hard for students to separate them. This sorting is an important benefit of discussion rather than a cost. To be literate with economic concepts is to understand them well enough to recognize when they are being used incorrectly and to be able to disagree in an informative, constructive, and respectful way. Discussion allows students to practice sorting the good from the bad and offering constructive criticism. It prepares students to use their economics later in life when no instructor is present.

CONCLUSION

In this chapter we have made the case for discussion. We explained why discussion promotes deeper understanding and higher cognitive mastery of economic ideas, why it motivates students to think economics is important and to work harder at it, and why it helps students use economic ideas in their lives. We also explained that there are remedies for some of the standard objections to discussion. If we were to summarize our case in the briefest way, we would say simply that we have students discuss economic writings because what matters is not what we cover but what they learn.

In the remaining chapters of Part One, we set out our discussion technology in more detail. Chapter 2 explains the interpretive question and why it is the cornerstone of our strategy. Chapter 3 explains how to bundle questions together into a plan for discussion. Chapter 4 provides suggestions for leading discussions.

In the remainder of the book, we provide abstracts, learning objectives, question clusters and tactical suggestions for discussing over sixty classic and contemporary economic writings.

PART ONE

Preparing for and Leading Discussion

2. Interpretive Questions

Advancing the learning of students through discussion depends on having something worthwhile to discuss. Productive discussions are not vehicles for checking factual knowledge, as in oral examinations. Nor are they opportunities for participants and instructors to trade opinions and value judgments, as in bull sessions. The only way to avoid these common traps is to center classroom discussion around questions of interpretation. Interpretive questions help students probe the meaning of a reading selection. The larger purpose is to help students gain a deeper understanding of the reading and its economic content.

This chapter has several goals. One is to demonstrate the importance of interpretive questions in gaining an understanding of what an author means by what he says. A second is to describe the characteristics of good interpretive questions. A third is to give instructors guidance in identifying reading selections that are rich enough in content to support interpretive questions and sustain productive discussions. The last is to explain how to write interpretive questions that are well coordinated with learning objectives and provide structure to discussion.

To illuminate the role of interpretive questions, we draw on the classic article by R. A. Radford, 'The Economic Organisation of a P.O.W. Camp' which appeared in *Economica* in 1945. The paper is included as an appendix and page references refer to pagination in the original article.

TYPES OF QUESTIONS

Good questions are a necessary starting point for successful discussions. But what is a good discussion question? To answer that question, it is essential to understand the types of responses that discussion questions elicit. We distinguish among questions of fact, interpretation, and evaluation.

Factual Questions ask for specific information that can be found in the reading assigned for discussion. The facts of the reading are the words used by the author. Sometimes these facts may differ from the facts as they are understood by participants. In discussion, it is necessary to focus on the facts as the author presents them. In effect, factual questions are all versions of the question 'What did the author say?'

Sometimes factual questions seek to clarify the meaning of an obscure word or phrase from the reading. Sometimes, they concern the location or wording of a passage in the reading. A participant may want to check the passage before responding to a question or posing one. Sometimes, factual questions concern background material that provides a context for the reading.

Several examples from the Radford article illustrate factual questions that deal with terminology: 'What is the Atlantic Charter?' (p. 189) 'What is Gresham's Law?' (p. 194) 'What is a treacle ration?' (p. 194) 'What is arbitrage?' (p. 191). The meanings of these terms can be found in most dictionaries. Students should be encouraged to note words they encounter in the reading but do not understand and then look them up. Ideally, students will have done this before the discussion begins. More frequently, at least at first, they will have skipped over difficult words.

If a student asks for a definition, the leader should call upon someone in the class to provide it. If no one can respond, the leader should provide the definition so that discussion can move ahead but should do so sparingly so that participants do not come to depend on the leader for this kind of help. Another possibility is for the instructor to provide a glossary. Doing so ensures that students understand the terminology but it fails to develop their responsibility for looking up unfamiliar words.

Other factual questions about the Radford reading concern economic activity in the camp. Here are several examples. 'Where in the reading does Radford explain what happened to prices when Red Cross parcels arrived?' 'What are the three functions of money?' 'What was the Bully Mark?'

Whatever form Factual Questions take, responses to them help establish the common basis on which participants can discuss the reading selection.

Interpretive Questions help discussion participants gain a deeper understanding of the reading by exploring the meaning of what the author says. Frequently, the meaning of a passage is unclear because the issue under discussion is abstract, the author's prose has ambiguous meaning, or there is no general agreement about an issue raised by the passage. Interpretive questions help participants resolve any lack of clarity.

Interpretive questions can range widely in scope, from encompassing an entire reading to focusing on an important idea within the reading. An example of an interpretive question that focuses on the entire Radford reading is: 'What, according to Radford, accounts for the development and success of the exchange system in the P.O.W. camp?' A less encompassing question is: 'According to Radford, how well did the P.O.W. camp exchange system work?' Some interpretive questions focus on more specific issues. One example is: 'What does the author mean by saying that "...cigarettes rose from the status of a normal commodity to that of currency"?' (p. 190) Still another type of interpretive question might ask: 'How can Radford's description of the P.O.W. camp, as providing a "living example of a simple economy", be reconciled with the complexity of making the camp shop operate?' (pp.190, 198). Thus, interpretive questions take a variety of forms.

The objective of discussion is to probe an author's meaning, in the hope that participants arrive at some deeper shared understanding of the text. Interpretive questions help launch the search for that understanding. As the discussion evolves, participants may come up with different interpretations of the meaning of a specific passage or the whole reading. Further discussion can often reconcile these differences and produce a common, though not necessarily unanimous, interpretation of what the author means.

At this point, it is useful to distinguish between readings that are literary and those that are scientific. Ambiguity of meaning is the essence of literature. Through discussion, participants attempt to resolve the ambiguity and discover the author's meaning. The playing field is level – no one has an edge because discussion is confined to the author's words.

With scientific readings, ambiguity and the potential value of discussion derive from a different source. Scientific authors take great pains to state their conclusions clearly so that questions about those conclusions are typically factual rather than interpretive. With scientific writing, interpretive questions focus on how the author reached the stated conclusions and what the conclusions mean. Interpretive questions can focus on how the author constructed his argument, how he used economic theory in the argument, how he supported the argument with evidence, and the practical implications of his conclusions. Initial student perceptions will differ because of the complexity of the reading. Through discussion, students come to better understand the argument, why it is important, and how the author supported it.

With scientific writing, the playing field is not level. The instructor and others with more advanced economic training are more likely than students to understand how the author's argument works. This means that interpretive questions that work well in an intermediate course may not work well in an advanced course. Interpretive questions must take the background of the participants into consideration. For example, asking students in an intermediate macroeconomics course how Benjamin Friedman explains the connection between high federal fiscal deficits and slow wage growth is asking for an interpretation. Asking graduate students the same question is asking a factual question because graduate students are well versed in the standard models used in open-economy macroeconomics.

To sum up, interpretive questions, in contrast to factual questions, require participants to use higher-order cognitive skills together with the facts reported in the reading to comprehend what an author means. Interpretive questions are the backbone of successful discussions precisely because they require students to practice using not only the skil! of comprehension but also the higher-order skills of application, analysis, synthesis, and evaluation.

Evaluative Questions ask participants for judgments. They invite participants to consider the reading in light of their own experience and to determine whether and how they agree with the author's point of view. Evaluative questions may also ask participants how to reconcile the discussion reading with an earlier selection that touched on similar issues. Or, they may ask how the author's views bear on some current problem or issue.

Questions of evaluation are asked on the assumption that participants possess a sufficient understanding of the author's meaning to think beyond it and judge the significance of the author's ideas. When evaluative questions call on participants to relate the material to their own experience, they should invite them to use the reading as a frame of reference. For example, suppose the leader asks: 'In your view, did the P.O.W. exchange system produce a just distribution of goods?' The leader should invite respondents to use information from the reading in supporting their opinion. Put another way, the leader should remind students that an evaluative question is not an invitation to provide unsupported opinions. Rather, it is an invitation for students to offer responses that draw on their own values as well as the shared understanding of the author's meaning that has resulted from discussing earlier interpretive questions.

What are some examples of evaluative questions that might be prompted by reading and discussing the Radford selection? Here are several.

1. In what sense could the exchange system operating within the P.O.W. camp be viewed as fair to the prisoners?
2. Was the German high command wise in allowing a market system to operate within its P.O.W. camps?
3. In a modern-day P.O.W. camp, is it likely that cigarettes could serve as a standard of value?

Depending on what prior selections have been discussed, the leader might ask participants to compare the reading with an earlier selection. The leader might say: 'Compare the description of the P.O.W. camp's market system with the market system described by Adam Smith in his chapter "On the natural and market Price of Commodities"'. A similar cross-cutting evaluative question is: 'Explain what connection you see between what Radford describes as "...the universality and spontaneity of this economic life..." and Adam Smith's famous reference to "a certain propensity in human nature . . . to truck, barter, and exchange one thing for another"'.

A visitor to a college economics classroom would observe all three kinds of questions in use. Instructors regularly pose factual questions as a means of finding out whether students are learning the facts. For example: 'What is the current unemployment rate?' Or, 'What happens to price when the supply curve shifts?' There is nothing wrong with this practice but it is not discussion. Students sometimes ask their instructor to repeat or elaborate on some point. Again, there is nothing wrong with this practice but whatever exchange occurs can hardly be described as discussion.

Students sometimes ask what could be considered interpretive questions, such as the meaning of some recent action by the Federal Reserve Board or the implications of a recent change in the price of oil. Without a context for these questions, such as a shared reading, instructors and students alike have difficulty responding. The reason: they are unlikely to be familiar with the outside material that prompted the question. Still, it is important for students to develop an ability to pose factual and interpretive questions, and instructors should respond to such questions in the normal course of their teaching. But the interchanges that such questions stimulate should not be mistaken for discussion as we mean the term.

Students are also prone to ask questions of evaluation, such as what the instructor thinks about a particular policy or about the views expressed in a reading. Again, without a context, framing a response is difficult. Depending on the circumstances, some instructors enjoy responding to such questions while others do not. Whether or not such interchanges are enjoyable, they are not discussion.

Though questions of fact, interpretation, and evaluation are often asked in the classroom, they rarely generate discussion or help students reach a deeper, shared understanding of the relevant ideas.

INTERPRETIVE QUESTIONS

Interpretive questions are the linchpin of effective discussions. By asking good interpretive questions, the discussion leader transfers responsibility for critical thinking to students and makes the discussion more challenging for all participants, including the leader. The challenge to students is both to sift through the facts of the reading to frame a response to the question and to assess and react to responses from others.

A good interpretive question satisfies four criteria. First, a good interpretive question can be answered from the reading. We presume the instructor has chosen a particular reading because it is rich enough to sustain productive discussion. The test comes in being able to write interpretive questions about the reading.

It is important that information in the reading is sufficient to answer the question. Discussion can degenerate to lecture when instructors recognize, in the midst of a discussion, that to answer the posed question students require more information than given in the reading. Of course, the instructor should treat course material covered before the date of the discussion as shared background.

Second, a good interpretive question asks students to explain the meaning of the entire reading or some important part of it. It asks for more than a quotation of the author's conclusions. For literary selections that deal with complex human issues, the need for interpretation is apparent because the author's meaning may differ for different readers. For scientific writing, the complexity of the author's argument makes the reading difficult to understand and interpretive questions help establish both agreement about what the author means and understanding of how the author reached his view.

Third, a good interpretive question is interesting and stimulating. To the extent the discussion leader is curious about the author's meaning, students are also likely to be curious. Curiosity is a powerful motivator.

Fourth, a good interpretive question is, above all, a question that appears to permit more than one answer. Literary selections are inherently ambiguous. The discussion leader will sense the ambiguity and formulate questions to probe it. The leader must remain open to the possibility that participants will come up with differing interpretations, each of which gives added insight into the reading. While students should be encouraged to cite the evidence, the leader should take care not to 'lock onto' a single answer.

In the case of scientific writing, the problem is different – understanding a complex argument. Scientific authors try hard to make their arguments clear. Nevertheless, students may experience difficulty grasping how the detailed arguments fit together and how they are supported by evidence. In both literary and scientific writing, the lack of clarity makes students more willing to contribute their own interpretations and to demand explanations of interpretations advanced by their fellow participants.

CHOOSING READING SELECTIONS

Discussion can be exciting and rewarding for leaders and participants provided that all fulfill their responsibilities. The most important responsibilities of instructors who want to incorporate discussion into their teaching are to choose suitable readings and to prepare interpretive questions for them. Neither of these responsibilities should be taken lightly. By suitable materials, we mean readings that are rich enough to generate several good interpretive questions. Instructors should write interpretive questions for prospective discussion readings before the semester begins and choose only those readings for which they were able to write good questions. A reading is appropriate for discussion only if an instructor can answer 'yes' to the following five questions.

First, will the reading advance and extend student understanding of an important course idea, concept, or theory? To answer in the affirmative the instructor must understand the content knowledge of the reading and agree that such knowledge is an appropriate focus for the course.

Second, does the reading contain a sufficient number of ideas to warrant discussion? To test whether a particular piece is sufficiently rich and hence worth discussing, the instructor should be able to formulate several interpretive questions about it. These interpretive questions should be interesting, require students to explain what the author has written, and support more than one reasonable response.

Third, is the reading self-contained? The reading should be able to stand on its own so that discussion does not require the introduction of supplementary information. Discussion participants should be able to come to the discussion equally well prepared. Discussion is cut off when participants introduce information that is not commonly held because others cannot judge the meaning of the outside material and its relevance to the reading under discussion. Discussion of the reading can and should build on knowledge acquired earlier in the course from textbooks, lectures, and readings already discussed. Being able to link the current reading to earlier ones is an important 'spillover' benefit that enhances student learning.

Fourth, is the reading selection reasonably well written? Reading material that is poorly written or organized will cause the discussion to get bogged down in attempts to determine exactly what the author said. Material that is well written, by contrast, permits the discussion to focus on the deeper issues of interpretation. To qualify, the reading material need not apply economic logic faultlessly. Straightening out a confused or incorrect presentation of economic ideas is a good discussion outcome, but such a discussion should focus on intellectual rather than stylistic confusion.

Fifth, is the reading selection interesting to both the instructor and the students? It is essential that the instructor find the reading selection interesting because instructor enthusiasm is an important source of student motivation. A helpful check is to ask whether the reading takes up important issues, offers new insights, or helps resolve some puzzle.

WRITING INTERPRETIVE QUESTIONS

The most challenging task is writing good interpretive questions. Having identified material as possible reading selections, instructors must be able to develop several interpretive questions that probe students' understanding of the author's meaning. Here is how to proceed.

The first step is to read the selection carefully. A initial reading gives a general overview of the selection. A second reading helps identify key ideas and questions. A third or even fourth reading stimulates the development and refinement of interpretive questions.

During the first reading, it is important to have a pencil at hand to mark words, sentences, and paragraphs that need to be looked at more closely. As questions about the selection come to mind, it is useful to note them in the margin. During the second closer reading it is essential to systematically underline key words and sentences that pose questions, as well as longer passages that students may have difficulty understanding. It is also helpful to note the repetition of certain phrases or ideas even if their significance may not be immediately apparent. Special effort should be given to noting passages that have multiple meanings or that students might be asked to react to. By the end of the second reading, ideas for several interpretive questions will have emerged.

During the third and subsequent readings, efforts should be directed toward refining the interpretive questions and formulating additional questions that help participants respond to them.

What kinds of interpretive questions emerge from a close reading of the Radford selection? Here are three.

1. 'What, according to Radford, accounts for the development of an exchange system in the P.O.W. camp?' (Hansen and Salemi, 1998, p. 214)
2. How effectively did the exchange system operate within the P.O.W. camp?
3. Why, according to Radford, did prices fluctuate in the P.O.W. camp, and what effect did these fluctuations produce?

Once instructors have identified several interpretive questions, they should test their richness. The best test is whether, for each interpretive question, the instructor can write related questions that help participants respond to the main question. In Chapter 3, we call the main question a basic question and the related questions supporting questions. Supporting questions help break down the interpretive question into smaller chunks that are easier to grasp and respond to. They are typically interpretive questions.

Ideally, a discussion is keyed around the broadest possible interpretive question. To remind participants that they are to answer using evidence from the reading, it is useful to begin interpretive questions with the words 'Why, according to the author' or 'What does the author mean by'. We use this device in the earlier-mentioned Radford question: 'What, according to

Radford, accounts for the development of an exchange system in the P.O.W. camp?'

The responses that will come from participants can never be fully anticipated. One student may cite the 'unity of the market and the prevalence of a single price' as evidence. Another might mention differences in supplies, or differences in preferences among the prisoners. Still another might mention the ascendence of cigarettes as a numeraire. Multiple responses challenge participants to understand each response and to investigate what they have in common. Multiple responses challenge the leader to ask probing questions designed to move the discussion forward.

How many questions are required to produce a shared understanding of an author's meaning? There is no surefire answer.

Consider the question: 'What, according to Radford, accounts for the development of an exchange system in the P.O.W. camp?' This is an overarching question that requires consideration of many aspects of the reading. But, the instructor can guide participants by asking them to interpret passages in the reading. For example, the instructor might ask: 'What does Radford mean by the statement "...through his economic activity, the exchange of goods and services, his standard of material comfort is considerably enhanced"?' (p. 189)

Other interpretive questions that support the overarching question ask participants to consider different aspects of economic life in the P.O.W. camp.

1. How can development of an exchange system be explained by the equality or lack of equality in the distribution of supplies?
2. What, according to Radford, was the connection between the composition of Red Cross parcels and development of an exchange system?
3. How, according to Radford, did differences in preferences gave rise to exchange?
4. Of what significance is Radford's statement about the 'universality and the spontaneity of this economic life'? (p. 190)
5. In what sense, according to Radford, is development of a camp exchange system a sociological phenomenon? (p. 190)
6. Which force does Radford think was most important in accounting for the evolution of the exchange system?

In Chapter 3, we explain how to combine a list of questions like that above into a coherent plan for discussion which we call Question Clusters.

3. Question Clusters

A successful discussion requires a well thought-out questioning strategy, one that helps participants achieve a shared understanding of the reading. The strategy guides discussion from beginning to end and keeps students focused on the learning objectives set by the instructor. In this chapter, we call such a strategy a question cluster, a carefully constructed set of interpretive, factual and evaluative questions.

This chapter has three purposes. The first is to explain four roles that questions play in a discussion. Question clusters begin with a basic question, continue with supporting questions, and end with a concluding question. During a discussion, a leader uses follow-up questions to probe the meaning of participant responses. The second purpose is to show how understanding of question roles guides construction of question clusters. The third is to suggest how to target question clusters to specific learning objectives.

QUESTION ROLES

A Question Cluster is composed of a basic question, one or more supporting questions, and a concluding question. The instructor should distribute question clusters in advance to guide students as they prepare for discussion.

Basic Questions are used to launch discussion. A basic question should focus on a key issue in the reading and should stimulate participant responses. Participants should find a basic question interesting and perceive it to be substantive rather than rhetorical. Basic questions are what discussion is all about.

Supporting Questions organize discussion of the basic question. Supporting questions are essential because basic questions are too rich to be answered instantly or easily. Once the discussion begins, the leader asks supporting questions to move the discussion forward and to make sure that participants consider all aspects of a basic question.

What makes good supporting questions depends on the reading and on the basic question. We will provide specific examples later in this chapter. Often good supporting questions break the basic question into smaller, more manageable chunks. For example, if the basic question asks about a chain of reasoning, supporting questions might ask about the links in the chain. If the basic question hinges on a particular passage in the reading, a supporting question might ask for an interpretation of the passage. If some facts in the reading bear importantly on the basic question, a supporting question can draw attention to those facts. If the basic question asks about different sides of an issue, supporting questions can help participants understand the separate sides before they attempt to relate them.

Supporting questions are important to a discussion. If the instructor finds that the supporting questions are not necessary, it may be that the basic question (or the reading itself) is not sufficiently rich to support the kind of discussion that develops student thinking.

Concluding Questions are used by the leader to draw a line of discussion to a close. There comes a time in any discussion when the leader perceives that participants have done as much as they can to address the issues raised by a basic question. At that point, the leader introduces a concluding question to end the discussion. Or, if more time is available, a concluding question can serve as a bridge to starting a discussion on another basic question. For the instructor, asking a concluding question is an alternative to providing students with a summary or overview of the discussion. By asking a concluding question, the instructor makes students responsible for bringing a line of inquiry to a close.

Concluding questions take various forms. One asks participants to provide the 'class answer' to the basic question, as a way of solidifying what has emerged from the discussion. Another asks participants whether the discussion has sufficiently resolved the meaning and interpretation of the basic question and, if not, what dissatisfaction with the collective response remains. Still another seeks to illuminate the discussion's meaning for a related issue or policy debate.

Follow-Up Questions perform a different function, probing participant responses to the basic question, to supporting questions, and to the concluding question. They ask participants to clarify their responses, support their comments, maintain the focus of the discussion, and react to responses of other participants. The instructor uses follow-up questions to elicit additional responses from participants, to ensure that responsibility for the substance of the discussion remains with the participants, and to encourage participants to think more deeply about the questions and responses. Through follow-up questions, the instructor helps participants stretch their minds and their understanding of the reading.

The instructor can also use follow-up questions to move discussion along its most productive channels. Student responses often include several ideas. The instructor can use follow-up questions to focus subsequent discussion on the parts of the response that appear most promising. However, the instructor must take care to allow the discussion to evolve fully. If students perceive the instructor is 'sheep-dogging' the discussion, they will learn to take less responsibility for it.

To use follow-up questions effectively, the leader must be thoroughly acquainted with the reading selection. The leader must listen carefully to the flow of the discussion, watching for opportunities to seek clarification and make connections among participant responses.

Unlike basic, supporting, and concluding questions, follow-up questions cannot be formulated beforehand because they depend on what students say. The instructor creates follow-up questions on the fly and uses them as the occasion demands. But there are some rules of thumb that leaders can follow.

One is to prompt participants to make additional contributions to the discussion, such as 'Can you elaborate on your response?' A second is to ask participants to support their response: 'Why does your answer make sense?' A third is to ask for clarification: 'Exactly what do you mean? Please respond with different words so that we can better understand you.' A fourth is to ask one participant to react to another: 'Ms. Smith, how does your response differ from Mr. Williams' response?'

Another important rule of thumb is to use follow-up questions to make sure that participants focus on the question under discussion and support their responses with evidence from the reading: 'Please explain how your response bears on the question we are investigating? Or 'What evidence from the reading supports your interpretation?'

Sometimes, the leader uses follow-up questions to direct 'traffic' during a discussion. 'Mr. Hernandez, why don't you respond first, and then we can hear from Ms. Wong?' 'Fred, we have heard from you once already on this question. Would you kindly hold your answer until we have heard from other volunteers?' Or 'Mr. Smith, does your answer relate to what Ms. Martin has said or do you wish to take a new tack?'

In summary, the leader uses follow-up questions to prompt deeper responses, to link the responses made by different participants, to keep the discussion focused on the proper questions, and to move the discussion along.

QUESTION CLUSTERS

We now have the ingredients needed to construct the question clusters that give discussion shape and structure. A question cluster is essential for two reasons. First, it is a plan that helps discussion achieve its educational objectives. Second, it is the best indicator we know for whether or not a reading is rich enough to support discussion.

To construct a good question cluster, an instructor must understand the question types – interpretive, factual, and evaluative – explained in Chapter 2 and the question roles – basic, supporting, concluding and follow-up – explained in the previous section. A good question cluster satisfies three criteria. First, it addresses an important and interesting idea in the reading. Second, it is organized around a basic question, supporting questions, and a concluding question. Third, it uses the right type of question for each question role.

For the basic question, the discussion leader should select an interpretive question that addresses a key idea or issue in the reading. Supporting questions are frequently interpretive questions that help break discussion of the basic question into manageable chunks. Supporting questions are usually more narrowly focused than the basic question. Some supporting questions are factual questions that the leader asks to raise awareness of important facts in the reading or to clarify the meaning of language. For a concluding question, the discussion leader can choose either an evaluative or interpretive question depending on the situation. One sort of concluding question asks participants their views about the importance or relevance of the reading and its argument. Another asks participants to relate the reading to another reading.

The relationship between question types and roles in a question cluster is illustrated in the following figure, reprinted from Hansen and Salemi, 1998 (p. 213). The three types of questions are shown in the columns, and the four roles that questions play are shown in the rows.

Table 3.1 Two-Way Classification of Questions in a Question Cluster

		Question Types		
		Interpretive	Factual	Evaluative
Question Roles	Basic	Yes	No	No
	Supporting	Yes	Possibly	No
	Concluding	No	Possibly	Yes
	Follow-Up	Yes	Yes	Yes

Two principles guide our assignment of question types to question roles. The first is that participants earn the right to evaluate a reading by interpreting it. To achieve the educational benefits of discussion, participants must show understanding of what the author means before they evaluate the author's arguments and evidence. Participants demonstrate the requisite understanding by answering interpretive questions. We use evaluative questions as concluding questions but not as basic or supporting questions.

The second principle is that asking factual questions too early converts a discussion from an inquiry to a drill. We use interpretive questions as basic questions to draw participants into discussion. We use factual questions as supporting questions when certain facts are crucial to a reading. We use factual questions as follow-up questions when we want participants to relate their responses to the facts of the reading.

The question-cluster approach differs markedly from what often passes for classroom discussion. Too frequently, instructors and students move immediately to evaluative questions, such as: 'What do you think of Radford's conclusion?' or 'Do you agree that we can learn something about the outside economic world from the behavior of prisoners in a P.O.W. camp?' In our experience, responses to such questions reveal that some students do not yet understand what Radford means and that others have not read the selection. In this case, trying to evaluate the author's arguments is unproductive – it serves no educational purpose.

This is not to say that evaluative questions are less important than interpretive questions. Both play an important role in helping students learn and understand. However, interpretive questions must be the central focus of a shared quest for deeper understanding. By first interpreting a reading, participants better understand how the author uses economic ideas and, as a result, better understand those ideas. By interpreting a reading, participants develop the higher-order cognitive skills we want them to have.

With the deeper understanding that interpretation provides, participants have a firm basis on which to address the normative issues raised by a reading. We want participants to make judgments but we want those judgments to be disciplined by a correct understanding of economic ideas and arguments. Evaluative concluding questions ask participants to bring their understanding of a reading to bear on the larger world. Interpretation followed by evaluation is 'thinking like an economist'.

Instructors should prepare question clusters as a guide to selecting readings and planning discussion. They should also distribute their question clusters to students in advance. In our experience, students find it helpful to know what will be asked as they prepare for a discussion. If the discussion questions are good, distributing them in advance does not reduce the energy in a discussion. In our experience, quite the opposite is true. Discussion is more lively when students have had an opportunity to prepare and reflect on their answers.

Question clusters are likely to change. The instructor will gain new insights into a reading and students will raise new issues and questions during discussion. The instructor should re-work question clusters in light of these insights and new issues. Also, times change and the context in which the reading is read may evolve in ways that alter student interpretations. Again, the instructor should revise the question clusters. The best time for revision is either immediately after discussion when ideas are fresh or after the relevant assessment when the instructor will better understand how well students have understood the reading.

In summary, the basic question of a question cluster is an interpretive question that gets at what the instructor believes to be a key idea of the reading. In choosing the reading for discussion, the instructor will have written several interpretive questions and can often recast many of them as supporting questions. The instructor should include, as supporting questions, factual questions that prompt students to answer the basic question in light of important facts in the reading. The concluding question is typically an evaluative question on the principle that participants earn the right to evaluate an article by first showing that they can interpret an author's meaning.

EXAMPLES OF QUESTION CLUSTERS

To illustrate our ideas about question clusters, we present two clusters for the Radford reading. The first addresses the reading selection as a whole as is reprinted from Hansen and Salemi, 1998, p. 214. The second focuses on the rise of a commodity money in the camp.

First Radford Question Cluster

Basic question
What, according to Radford, accounts for the development of an exchange system in the P.O.W. camp?

Supporting questions
1. Can the development of the system be explained by the equality or lack of equality in the distribution of supplies? Why or why not?
2. Were prisoners generally unhappy with their particular allotment of supplies and thereby motivated to develop an exchange system? Why or why not?
3. Could the supplies received by the prisoners have been repackaged so that the initial distribution would have left everyone happy? If so, how? If not, why not?
4. What forces does Radford think were most important in accounting for the evolution of the exchange system?
5. Does Radford believe that prisoners might have developed an exchange system because they were used to living in an exchange economy?

Concluding question

What weights would you assign to the various forces Radford notes as having
contributed to the development of the exchange system?

Second Radford Question Cluster

Basic question

According to Radford how well did cigarettes function as money in the
P.O.W. camp?

Supporting questions

1. According to Radford, was the fact that cigarettes had intrinsic value
   important to their use as currency?
2. Why would individuals re-roll their machine-rolled cigarettes?
3. Why were high quality cigarettes, such as Churchman's No. 1, rarely used
   in trading?
4. What is the significance for cigarette 'prices' of the halving of Red Cross
   parcels?
5. What, according to Radford, accounted for the development of the 'Bully
   Mark'? What contributed to its later decline in value?

Concluding question

What are the implications of Radford's article for circulation of the recently
issued US state quarters?

LINKING CLUSTERS TO LEARNING OBJECTIVES

While discussions are exciting for both instructors and students, the main
purpose of discussion is the intellectual development of students. To achieve
that purpose, readings must be selected and group discussion conducted so that
they contribute to the content learning and the proficiencies expected of
students in the course. While the ability to read closely and argue effectively
should not be ignored, the central purpose of any economics course is mastery
of its economic content. In each course, we must ask what students must learn
to advance their knowledge and skills and become literate in economics.

As already noted, the first question cluster is only one of several
possibilities for the Radford reading. The first cluster focuses on interpersonal
trade, an appropriate topic for the introductory course. While we may feel
confident about the structure and substance of the question cluster, we should
be explicit about the learning objectives that discussion of the reading is
intended to reinforce. Thus, we face another test. Just as a reading selection

should be rich enough to generate a discussion centered around a basic interpretive question, the question cluster should contribute to advancing student learning of this particular component of the course.

To make certain the reading and its discussion contribute to the learning that instructors hope their students will achieve, it is important to make explicit the learning objectives for each question cluster. While writing out these learning objectives can be a tedious exercise, making them explicit helps to produce the kind of learning the course is intended to produce.

Formulating learning objectives and question clusters is frequently an interactive process. The instructor selects a reading because it illustrates a key idea. The instructor prepares learning objectives to indicate precisely what the key idea is and how students should demonstrate mastery of it. The instructor prepares a question cluster to help students achieve the desired learning. Often preparing a question cluster will help an instructor refine the relevant learning objective.

Much has been written about what constitutes good learning objectives and how to frame these objectives. Our purpose is not to involve readers in the details of learning objectives but to illustrate how learning objectives fit with question clusters. Making learning objectives explicit tells us what we want students to take away from discussion and guides us in the selection of readings and in the construction of question clusters. The learning objectives we set out in what follows are one example of what students could accomplish by reading and discussing Radford. Other instructors may have different objectives in mind. What is important is the match between the objectives, the reading, and the questions, rather than the objectives themselves.

We begin by setting out learning objectives for the two Radford question clusters.

Learning Objectives

The objectives that match the first question cluster can be stated as follows. After reading and discussing the Radford paper, students should be able to:

1. Explain why a system of exchange develops among the prisoners.
2. Describe factors that complicate the workings of the P.O.W. camp market.
3. Explain how external events affect the P.O.W. camp market.
4. Describe the parallels between the prison economy and the outside economy.

The learning objectives for the second question cluster differ.

After reading and discussing the Radford paper, students should be able to:

1. Explain the advantages and disadvantages of a barter system of exchange.
2. Describe the functions of money and determine whether cigarettes and the Bully Mark performed these functions.
3. Explain what internal and external conditions affected the price of cigarettes.
4. Explain how the time horizon of prisoners affected prices.

The structured approach to group discussion outlined in this chapter – preparing for discussion by constructing question clusters, using the clusters as a plan for discussion, and relating the clusters to explicit learning objectives – offers rich possibilities for enhancing student learning and student learning skills. Discussion engages students more directly in their own learning, deepens their understanding of the economic issues posed in readings, and sharpens their skills of inquiry. It also helps them learn how to respect and respectfully critique the discussion responses of others. Students who learn by discussion are, in our experience, better equipped to benefit from subsequent courses, better able to find productive employment after graduation, better able to demonstrate their knowledge in the ordinary business of life, and better able to engage in lifelong learning long after specific content acquired in a course has faded from memory.

4. Leading Discussion

My discussion section never really had much discussion. The instructor asked a few questions but we never got into any meaty issues.

The instructor in this course (a small upper division course) spent almost 100 percent of the time lecturing. The few times he tried to get a discussion going, it failed completely. I thought small classes were intended to permit discussion that can't occur in large principles courses.

Our discussion[s] in this course have been boring and a waste of time. Neither the instructor nor the students know much about how to have good discussions. (Hansen and Salemi, 1998, p. 207)

Many instructors believe that discussion is a risky instructional strategy. They fear that students either will not prepare or not volunteer answers. They worry that aggressive students may persuade others by the force of their personality rather than the quality of their argument. They are concerned that students will be confused by the hodgepodge of conflicting opinions that surface during a discussion. Some think that discussion amounts to pandering where students talk about half-formed ideas instead of listening to and thinking about a carefully crafted lecture.

In this chapter, we suggest how instructors can create an environment where students benefit from discussion. We explain how instructors can make sure that students are prepared. We suggest discussion leading strategies that achieve the potential benefits of discussion. We recommend ways to integrate discussion with other instructional strategies. We conclude with ideas for testing whether students learn through discussion what we want them to learn.

GETTING READY FOR DISCUSSION

Before the first day of class, instructors should choose discussion readings, revise their syllabus so that it describes discussion assignments and expectations, and put in place incentives for students to prepare discussion assignments well.

Choosing Discussion Readings

Instructors should select discussion readings before their course begins. Because discussion requires considerable class time, instructors should be confident that its educational benefits will outweigh its costs. This calculus requires that instructors assess what students will gain by discussing a reading and judge how the reading illuminates and reinforces key course concepts. It also requires instructors to verify that the reading is meaty enough to support discussion by preparing at least one cluster of discussion questions (Chapter 3) or by choosing readings that others have used successfully like those we describe in Parts Two through Five.

Because discussion requires considerable advanced planning, we recommend that instructors add reading selections gradually. Instructors who are trying out discussion for the first time might choose one topic where discussion fits well and one or two readings for that topic. In subsequent terms, they can add topics and readings until they judge that the mix of discussion, lecture and other activities is right. From that point on, instructors would revise discussion questions as needed and replace old readings when they find superior alternatives.

Discussion and the Syllabus

Students should know on the first day of a course that discussion is an important part of the course plan and that they have specific discussion responsibilities. A careful reading of the course syllabus should make clear when discussions will occur, what readings will be discussed, what student responsibilities are, and why discussion is an important part of the course. While instructors should reinforce their expectations as the course goes on, the right place to start is the syllabus.

On the first day of a course instructors should familiarize students with the rules and expectations for class discussion. The course syllabus should include a list of discussion readings and a calendar that identifies days on which discussions will occur. Instructors who are teaching a course for the first time may find it difficult to pinpoint discussion days on their first try. In that case, the syllabus should point out where discussions will occur and the instructor should tell students the specific days of discussion at least one week in advance. To signal the importance of discussion on the first day, we often distribute a relevant news article and ask students to read and discuss it.

In the syllabus and at the beginning of the course, instructors should explain their expectations for discussion. For first year students, we recommend an explicit 'contract for discussion'. An example appears at the end of this chapter. For more senior students, it is sufficient to list expectations in the syllabus. The most important of these expectations are that students will: (1) Read discussion readings carefully. (2) Prepare, in advance, answers to discussion questions. (3) Contribute their own ideas to discussion. (4) Listen carefully when others speak. (5) Ask questions when they do not understand. (6) Disagree constructively when they disagree with a response. (7) Bring the reading to class. It is a good idea to remind students about these expectations once or twice as they prepare for the first discussion assignment.

Instructors should communicate their expectations about attendance. Discussion only provides an opportunity for students to use economic ideas and create answers if they are present and participate. We tell our students that we expect regular attendance.

Creating Incentives for Full Participation in Discussion

Instructors should create incentives for students to prepare for and participate in discussion and explain them in their syllabi. We have several recommendations.

On a discussion day, instructors can give a short quiz that asks one of the assigned discussion questions. We expect answers to be better after discussion and assign 'full marks' to a quiz answer that shows that students read the article and thought about the question.

Alternatively, instructors can use a Just-in-Time approach (Clerici-Arias, Maier, and Simkins, 2002) and require students to submit preliminary responses to discussion questions in advance, via email or the web. By reading preliminary answers, instructors can better understand what parts of the reading students found difficult and which questions will spark more interesting and productive exchanges in class.

A second, more important, incentive for energetic participation in discussion is to test student understanding of discussion articles on course examinations. Good discussion questions make excellent examination essay questions. By the time of the exam, instructors will expect more complete and thoughtful answers than they did on the pre-discussion quiz.

We are of two minds about discussion participation grades. On one hand, assigning participation grades signals that discussion is important. On the other hand, it is a full time task to monitor the discussion process and keep track of the flow of ideas. In addition, participation grades create an incentive for students to speak, whether or not they have something to say.

We promote participation by explaining to students our view of education. We explain that through discussion students can practice using economic ideas and gain the satisfaction of analyzing readings that were written by economists for economists. We say that we want students to learn how to challenge constructively a response with which they disagree. We acknowledge that discussion can be messy, explain that it gives students practice in sorting out strong ideas from weak ones, and point out that such sorting skills will be valuable later in life when students are on their own. In our experience, students respond by preparing better and by working harder.

Should instructors hand out discussion questions in advance?

When we first started using our discussion strategy, we did not pass out discussion questions in advance. We feared that, if students had questions in advance, they would show up at class with 'right' answers, give them, and that would be it. We quickly learned otherwise and revised our plan. We learned that there is no single interpretation of an author's meaning that will satisfy all discussants. We learned that discussion is more lively when students have questions in advance because they prepare better and feel more comfortable knowing where the focus will be. We distribute our discussion questions one or two classes before discussion and post them on our web page so that students can find them easily.

Should students prepare discussion questions?

Instructor control of discussion questions is a two-edged sword. It permits the instructor to ensure that discussion focuses on the issues that are part of the course plan. But, it fosters dependency of students on the instructor. If one of the objectives of education is that students learn how to educate themselves, they should learn how to identify the important issues that an article raises and ask intelligent questions about them.

We take a pragmatic view. In courses where instructors assign few readings, we recommend they keep control of discussion questions. Once instructors are satisfied that a class has fully answered the assigned discussion questions, they can ask students whether there are other issues raised by the reading they would like to address.

In courses where instructors rely on discussion as the chief instructional strategy, we recommend a gradual transition toward student responsibility for preparing questions. In the beginning of the course, instructors can write questions and control the discussion agenda. Once students become accustomed to volunteering answers, to explaining themselves further when asked, to listening to one another, and to responding constructively to suggestions, the instructor can train students to prepare discussion questions.

To train students to prepare questions, instructors could assign Chapter 2 of this book as a companion to a course reading and ask students to write interpretive questions. After editing the questions, instructors could combine them and their own questions into clusters and distribute the clusters as the discussion agenda. The agenda should identify the author of each question. By comparing edited and original versions, students will better understand how to write good questions. By sharing preparation of discussion questions, students will learn how to identify important issues raised by a reading and how to prepare for their own discussions. An example of an assignment in which students are asked to prepare their own questions is included at the end of this chapter. Once students get the hang of writing discussion questions, instructors can routinely invite them to submit discussion questions.

In our experience, few courses provide an opportunity for students to become skilled discussion-question writers. In courses where students discuss 10-12 readings during a term, we have begun the process of training them to write discussion questions. A single question writing exercise is not sufficient but students do learn to write good questions after several attempts.

Two reminders. First, while we distribute discussion questions one or two classes before discussion, we need to prepare questions before the beginning of the term to be sure that the readings we have chosen are rich enough to support discussion. Second, students should come to class with preliminary answers to assigned questions. The quality of ideas that surface in discussion is far better when students have tried to answer the questions themselves beforehand. In our experience even talented and well prepared students leave discussion with better answers than they came with.

Class Size

We have experience in using our approach to discussion in classes with enrollment as small as 15 and as large as 80. The chief difference is how frequently individual students get to offer responses. With 25 or fewer students, a good objective is to have each student respond at least once in each discussion. With 40 or more students, this is not possible.

The small-group approach that we explain later is valuable in larger classes because it permits many mini-discussions to occur simultaneously. In a class of 80, 10-12 groups can simultaneously work on their responses to a discussion question. Group spokespersons would report their groups' responses and comment on the responses of other groups. Subsequently, the instructor would call the class together to debrief the reports.

One of us (Hansen) has successfully led discussion in a class of 80 without using groups. The chief difficulty is making sure that all students are engaged and that the discussion is not dominated by a few.

In a large-enrollment principles course, discussions can be held during weekly teaching-assistant sessions. In our experience, it is important to train teaching assistants before asking them to lead discussions. For additional strategies to use in large-enrollment classes, the reader can see Mazur (1997).

LEADING DISCUSSION

Although being well prepared for discussion is more than half the battle, some instructors may worry that they do not know what to do during the discussion itself. How should they react if students seem unwilling to participate? How can they keep the discussion focused on the questions they prepared without destroying spontaneity? How can they make discussion an inclusive activity instead of one focused on the few students who are most willing to talk? What can they do to make sure that students get the big picture without slipping back into a lecture that tells the students what to think? In this section, we do our best to answer these and related questions.

Promoting Student Participation in Discussion

It has happened to all of us. We choose a great reading. We prepare questions carefully. The time for discussion comes and we ask our best question. The response is – silence. And not just a few seconds of silence but a silence that goes on and grows more awkward as the seconds pass. What can we do?

Calling on students

Should we call only on volunteers or on others as well? There are tradeoffs but, on balance, we prefer to call on non-volunteers and volunteers alike. Different students have different personalities and different learning styles. While some are less willing to volunteer answers, it is important to check their thinking.

One technique that works well is to take answers from volunteers and then, before giving volunteers a second opportunity, to say to the class: 'I want to hear from those of you who have not yet offered your views'. Some quiet students will now volunteer. Others will not. At that point, instructors can call on quiet students and ask their views. Some will acknowledge that they are not prepared and can be encouraged to mend their ways. Others will say they have nothing to add but can be probed.

Not infrequently, a quiet student will respond to the instructor's invitation by saying that they are confused on a point. These are valuable opportunities. Often, a point that confuses one, confuses many. When students say they are confused, the instructor should ask them what is confusing and then invite the class to help. The instructor might say: 'Heads up, class. One of your colleagues is confused on a point and is asking you for clarification and assistance. What help can you offer?'

Sometimes, quiet students respond to an invitation by saying they have nothing to add. That is fine. We think that students should be allowed to 'pass' without consequences provided they do not do so habitually.

Calling on students signals to the entire class that they are expected to prepare for and contribute to discussion. Most students respond by preparing and by volunteering their answers. Quiet students remain. But they come to understand that they will sometimes be called on to give their views. From time to time, the quiet students hold the key to important insights. The benefits from calling on them, in our view, far outweigh the costs.

Small group discussion
It is beyond the scope of our book to explore fully the educational benefits of small groups and cooperative learning. We refer the interested reader to Bartlett (1998). We have found that using groups in discussion promotes student participation and explain our approach in this subsection.

At the beginning of a course, students may have answers to offer but be reluctant to offer them because they fear speaking out in class. To help students become comfortable in discussion, instructors can break the class into groups and assign discussion questions as small-group work. We create groups with four to eight students and make one student the spokesperson. The instructor can assign the spokesperson role randomly, say, choosing the student who has the next birthday.

Instructors can then go to each group and clarify the group assignment. The instructor assignment to each group could be something like the following.

To begin, I would like you to come up with your group's answer to discussion question one. Please make sure that your answer takes into account each of the indented questions below question one. You may wish to answer these first and then step back and frame your answer to the larger question. Spokesperson, your job is to make sure you have heard from everyone and have combined their contributions into a group answer. Others, your job is to make sure that you have given your ideas to the spokesperson, have listened carefully to other group members, and have reacted to their ideas in constructive ways.

After giving each group its assignment, the instructor can make the rounds to monitor progress and to help resolve impasses. Instructors must be careful to facilitate a group's progress but stop short of 'feeding it' answers.

In our experience, placing students in groups has a dramatic effect. Earlier classroom silence is replaced by a hum of activity as students begin to form their answers. This is not surprising. Small groups provide a low-threat environment for students to try out their ideas. Frequently, they begin by saying something like. 'I am not sure what the answer is but I think it has something to do with ... Do any of you feel the same way?' Often students who begin tentatively are on to something interesting and other group members will respond. Students gain confidence that their ideas have value and, through the group process, revise their answers and polish their language.

Once groups have their answers, the instructor asks for reports. One good way to debrief groups is to ask the first group for its answer. As the spokesperson gives the answer, the instructor can summarize it on the board. The instructor then asks other members of the group whether they have anything to add. Once the first group has responded, the instructor can move on to the second group asking its spokesperson to focus on those parts of their answer that differ from the responses given by the first group. The instructor might say: 'What does your group have to add to the answer? Would your group disagree with anything that has been said so far?'

In similar manner, the instructor calls for the reports of the remaining groups. Typically, the reports will grow shorter because earlier groups will have anticipated parts of the answer that later groups want to offer. The instructor should encourage groups to report only what is new, should praise them when they do, and should assure them that they will have a chance to go first in later discussions.

Once all the reports are in, the instructor can begin the process of reconciling responses. If responses conflict, the instructor can raise awareness and ask the class how to resolve the conflict. If two groups have provided answers that address different aspects of the question, the instructor can ask the class how the two answers fit together. If two groups have offered essentially the same answer using different language, the instructor can ask the class whether the answers are fundamentally different or the same. In each case, the instructor uses group reports to delve more deeply into the issues raised by the article and the discussion questions.

The small-group approach is particularly helpful in courses with first year students who have yet to gain sufficient confidence in their own abilities to be willing to speak in front of the class. For courses that target more mature students, the small-group approach may not be necessary. The instructor can begin by putting an assigned question to the class and seeing what happens. If students volunteer readily, the instructor can keep the class together. If students are reticent, the instructor can use groups to break the ice. Once students become comfortable offering answers to the whole class, the instructor can drop the small-group approach. While some students would benefit by remaining in groups, progress toward good interpretation is more rapid when the entire class participates simultaneously.

Maintaining a receptive and respectful posture
One of the most important things an instructor can do to promote student participation in discussion is to maintain a respectful posture toward students

and their contributions. Sometimes students give answers that seem ridiculous or that seem bent on provocation. We should not rise to the bait.

Several realizations help us maintain a respectful posture. First, we should recognize that what is obviously wrong to an experienced economist may not be obviously wrong to a novice. An important benefit of discussion is that it confronts students with their misunderstandings and helps them gain understanding. If students are worried about making fools of themselves, they will not venture answers until they are sure they are right. That is too late! Students benefit most from discussion when they stretch their understanding of economic ideas in order to figure out what an author means. We should remember that we once were novices and made plenty of mistakes. We must maintain a respectful stance toward students if we want them to take chances and stretch their minds.

Second, we should recognize that our behavior is a model. If we want students to listen carefully to one another and to offer criticism in a constructive way, we must do the same. If we show disrespect to students through what we say, through our intonation, or through our body language, we cannot expect them to do differently.

Some students may end up feeling too comfortable and may not think carefully before offering an answer. If this occurs, instructors can firmly but kindly point out that the answer does not make sense without signaling that it was unwelcome. The occasional half-thought-through answer is a small price to pay for a rich flow of contributions and the insights it brings.

Before concluding that we worry too much about preserving student egos, the reader should reflect on how often students have said: 'I know this may be a stupid question, but....' Students are concerned with seeming to be inept before their peers and instructors. We are convinced that student fear gets in the way of learning. We like to tell our students: 'In this course, no honestly asked question is stupid. A stupid question does not exist. As your instructor, I realize that you can approach an issue in a different way than I do and become confused as a result. My job is to help you find answers for your questions, not to judge them.'

Respectful disagreement

Respecting students and student answers does not mean surrendering the responsibility to disagree. Suppose during discussion that a student misuses an economic concept or offers an interpretation that seems wrong. A discussion leader has two choices. First, the leader can wait for other students to disagree with the response. This is the better option because it signals to students that it is important to listen carefully and offer constructive criticism. Second, the leader can raise an objection. This option may be better than letting the response go unchallenged. The instructor can say: 'I think Jan may have misstated what it means for money to function as a store of value. Is there someone who agrees and can help us out here?' Instructors should understand that there is no essential conflict between encouraging student participation and disagreeing respectfully with answers that do not make sense.

The keys to balancing these two responsibilities are to keep focused on ideas and to ask others in the class to participate in the processing of vetting answers. Suppose the discussion assignment is 'The Economics of a P.O.W. Camp' and we have asked 'Why, according to Radford, did cigarettes function as money in the Camp?' Suppose Jim answers that cigarettes were an inferior money and were quickly replaced by the Bully Mark that was accepted in the camp store and supported by the camp officers. This response contradicts Radford. Cigarettes functioned as money before, during, and after the brief existence of the Bully Mark. But what do we say to Jim?

A discussion leader who was very concerned about promoting participation might thank Jim for his contribution and move on hoping that other students hadn't paid much attention. A better response would be to thank Jim for reminding us about the Bully Mark and then asking the class whether Jim's claim that the Bully Mark supplanted cigarettes is true. 'Thanks, Jim, it is important to remember that there was a second camp money. But I am not sure that the Bully Mark replaced cigarettes. Class, what does Radford say about this? Do you agree or disagree with Jim?'

While it is important to make discussion an inclusive activity and the classroom a friendly environment in which students can try out ideas without bearing undue costs, the discussion leader must remember that a higher priority is helping students strive for the best possible answers. Students agree and realize that out of disagreement comes better understanding.

Before winding up the section on student participation, we want to remind the reader of one additional reason that students may not volunteer answers during a discussion. It may be that we have chosen a reading that, given their background, is beyond student comprehension. Once we conclude that the reading is beyond the grasp of our students, the long term solution is to replace it with another better suited to our purpose. Several short term solutions are possible. The instructor may decide to use the class to provide students with the missing background information and then reschedule the discussion for a later time. The instructor may break the class into small groups, ask each to come up with a list of things that they do not understand about the article, and then provide the needed information before moving on. Because these 'recovery' strategies use a good bit of class time, it is important to plan well and make sure we choose suitable articles for discussion.

Helping Students Think More Deeply Through Discussion

When students offer preliminary answers to discussion questions, the instructor has a valuable opportunity to help students deepen their understanding of economics by probing their answers. During a discussion the most important thing an instructor can do is probe well.

Summarize student answers

A good way to begin probing is to write a summary of the student's answer on the board. Writing helps the instructor understand the answer better by extracting its essential components. When the instructor cannot write a summary, it may mean that the answer is not coherent and the instructor can probe the student to obtain more clarity. 'Jim, I can't seem to finish my summary of what you are saying. How would you finish the sentence I have started?' Even if the instructor understands a student's answer, it is useful to check that understanding. 'Jules, please read my summary of your answer. Have I got it right? If not, please tell me how to revise what I have written.'

Writing a summary provides a record that the instructor can use to promote student interaction. 'Jean, you appear to disagree with what Jim said earlier. Please explain to Jim why you disagree.' Writing a summary also helps other students keep track of the flow of discussion. As discussion winds down, the instructor will have on the board a summary of different student answers to the question and can ask the class to combine the contributions into a class answer. 'OK. We have heard a number of interesting answers to our question. The summaries on the board help us to remember what has been said. How will we now answer the question as a class? What should be our class answer to the question?'

Probing strategies

Another probing strategy is to always be on the lookout for ways to ask students why they think as they do. Sometimes a simple 'why' will do. Other times, one link in the chain requires particular attention. 'Fran, I hear you say clearly that using cigarettes as money contributed to the perfection of the camp market. That is a very interesting idea. But I am not sure everyone understands you fully. What do you mean by market perfection?' Still other times, the instructor may think the class will benefit from an alternative explanation. 'Frank, not everyone has understood you. I think you make sense but would like you to explain your answer in a different way.'

Probing is a good way to encourage students to support their views with evidence from the reading. Probes can be direct. 'Cite a passage from Radford that supports your interpretation and then explain why it does.' Probes can be less direct. 'What in the article leads you to believe that

Radford would support your view?' Or, 'What evidence from Radford would strengthen your case?'

Probing for evidence is particularly important in a scientific article. In a scientific article, the author is likely to have stated conclusions clearly with the implication that discussion is better focused on how the author reached the conclusions than what the conclusions are. Often, discussion promotes deeper understanding by asking students to explain what information is contained in tables, charts, and figures and how that information fits into an author's argument. 'Jean, you have said that Benjamin Friedman believes that high budget deficits led to low investment. How would Friedman use Table 1 and Figure 1 to argue his case?' Or, 'Stacy, what feature of the regression results presented in Table 5 would the author consider to be crucial?' Or, 'Fred, what feature of the graph presented in Figure 6 would the author most want you to remember? Why?'

Students sometime find probing uncomfortable. They may believe that they have prepared well and given a good answer to the assigned question and resent receiving a string of follow up questions that seems to stop only when they run out of answers. It is useful for the instructor to remind students that the purpose of discussion is to deepen their understanding and stretch their minds. Nevertheless, it is important for instructors to learn how far they can go. When students feel too uncomfortable, they focus on their discomfort and not on economics.

Concluding a discussion
With discussion, as with all active learning, it is important for the instructor to debrief the exercise. Sometimes students get caught up in one facet of a discussion. They may get so involved with arguing their point that they lose sight of the bigger picture. It is the instructor's responsibility to provide an opportunity for all students to reflect on what they have learned. Our favorite debriefing strategy for discussion is to ask for a class answer to discussion questions. Maier (2000) gives other suggestions for debriefing.

Discussion begins by asking students for individual answers. Students offer different answers, clarify their positions, react to one another, disagree, modify their answers, and so forth. Once activity slows and marginal product falls, the instructor can ask the class for its answer to the question. The instructor might say: 'Suppose one of your colleagues missed today's class due to illness and asked you later what the answer to the discussion question was. What answer would you give them? Keep in mind the answer should reflect the important insights of all members of the class. It should also hang together and be supported by evidence from the reading.' The instructor can ask for a volunteer to give the class answer or can request the same of a quiet student. Once someone has contributed their version of the class answer, the instructor should ask 'Class, are you satisfied? Should something else be part of the class answer?' Of course, if the contributed class answer is incomplete or incorrect, the instructor should respectfully raise objections and ask for more. 'Thank you, Ernie, for starting us off. But it seems to me the class answer should say more about why the camp prisoners used cigarettes as money. Let's get some help from other class members.'

During discussion, the job of the instructor is to press for answers – not to give answers. Instructors should concentrate on what a student is saying – how to summarize it, how to relate it to what others have said, and how to probe. They should pay attention to who has spoken and who has not and how to get students to react to one another. They should monitor the flow of ideas so that they can move on at an appropriate point. There is plenty to do without being a discussion participant. The instructor's job is to promote and monitor the process – not to manufacture the product.

INTEGRATING DISCUSSION AND OTHER STRATEGIES

Discussion is not the be-all and end-all of 'hands on' learning. It is one of many strategies available to help students master course content. Students get more out of discussion when they understand how it fits with other course activities and how discussion readings fit together with other course resources. In this section, we offer instructors several suggestions on how to tie discussion together with other activities.

Find More Recent Readings

Some of the readings we assign for discussion are timeless. Others are written about issues that, for a time, have captured public consciousness. The articles by Benjamin Friedman and Thomas Sargent on deficits during the Reagan administration (Chapter 12), were written as analyses of current public policy issues. Others, such as the articles by Maurice Obstfeld and Kenneth Rogoff (Chapter 20) were written in response to economic crises like the Asian financial crises of the late 1990s. We first assign these articles because we want our students to be current on important issues and controversies. We continue to assign them, after the topic they address fades from the headlines, because they are well written applications of economics to interesting questions.

One good follow-on activity is asking students to find more current readings that address the same issue. For example, Benjamin Friedman argues that the current account deficit was the twin of the fiscal deficit during the 1980s. He has in mind a standard result from open economy macroeconomics.

A tax cut at full employment raises domestic real rates and leads to an appreciation of the home currency as foreign savers redirect funds toward high yield opportunities. The currency appreciation lowers exports, raises imports, and moves the current account toward deficit. After discussion of the Friedman article, instructors might ask students to research whether tax cuts during the G. W. Bush administration had the effects that Friedman predicts. The instructor could have students search for articles about the effects of the Bush deficits and analyze them in the light of the Friedman article. Alternatively, the instructor could simply ask students to locate and bring to class current relevant literature and let them decide which aspects of the issue deserve additional attention.

Why not simply assign readings about the Bush tax cuts in the first place? While editorials and short articles covering recent events and issues may be available, a full analysis may not be. Also, transferring their understanding of the Friedman analysis to a new situation should deepen student understanding. For example, students should recognize that Friedman assumes a full employment economy whereas the economy was in recession during the first part of the Bush administration. Students should also recognize that the US current account was in balance at the beginning of the Reagan administration and deeply in deficit at the beginning of the Bush administration. So, while the economic forces that attend a tax cut certainly apply in both situations, students should come to understand that they can not apply the Friedman analysis in a cookie-cutter way.

Gather Data

Another strategy that ties discussion together with other activities is to have students gather recent data that bears on a question raised by a discussion article. For example, in the article about unemployment included in Chapter 10, Paul Krugman argues that rising unemployment in Europe and rising inequality in the US were both caused by a shock to labor markets that favored workers with the skills to take advantage of computers. In Europe where unemployment benefits are relatively generous, low skilled workers who were disadvantaged by the shock were more likely to opt for the dole. In the United States where unemployment benefits are less generous, low skilled workers hurt by the shock simply earned less.

Krugman uses data from the 1970s, 1980s and early 1990s to support his conclusions. Instructors might ask students whether current data continue to support Krugman's explanation for relatively high unemployment in Europe. They might ask students to find current data on unemployment and wage inequality and to write a paragraph explaining whether or not the data support the view that Krugman's skill-based technological change is still at work.

Another example focuses on the relationship between the real rate of interest and fiscal deficits. Economists like Benjamin Friedman point to higher real interest rates as the mechanism through which fiscal deficits crowd out investment and slow growth. Instructors can ask students to collect time series data on fiscal deficits, interest rates, and inflation. With that data, students can create an estimate of the real rate of interest and investigate whether or not it appears to be correlated with deficits.

Write

A natural follow-on activity to discussion is writing. After discussion, instructors can ask students to write an essay that answers one of the discussion questions. When students have discussed more than one article on a topic, the instructor can assign an essay that requires students to compare the arguments in the readings. For example, the reading by Harris and Steindel in Chapter 11 argues that low saving in the 1980s will translate into lower capital, lower output, and lower consumption after 2000. The reading by Webb disagrees, offering as evidence the fact that household wealth continued to rise even though NIPA saving measures declined during the 1980s. After discussing the two articles, an instructor might give students the following assignment. 'Write a one page essay arguing whether or not low rates of saving should be remedied by public policy. Along the way, support your view with evidence from readings by Harris and Steindel and Webb.'

Instructors can also assign an essay as a follow-on to discussion of a single article. Instructors might ask students to write an essay that answers the basic discussion question. The assignment could specify that students must cite evidence from the reading to support their interpretations. It could also invite students to include as part of their essay a paragraph on 'unanswered questions.'

Instructors can use the completed essays in a variety of ways. They can read and grade them using student feedback about unanswered questions to guide class preparation. In a large class, instructors could pair students, have pairs swap essays and provide feedback to one another, and read only a sample of the essays to monitor compliance and gather information about issues that students find troubling. Instructors could also ask students to keep a course journal and write their essay as a journal entry. See Petr (1998) for more information about student journals.

Many other complementary writing assignments are possible. For example, after a discussion an instructor could assign a one-minute paper that asked students the most important thing they learned during the discussion and the most important unanswered question they have about the article.

Tie the Reading and the Text Together

Frequently, instructors will assign a reading because it illustrates important ideas raised in the text. In such cases, a natural follow-up to discussion is asking students how the article relates to the relevant text material. For example, many intermediate macro texts include models of large open economies where domestic shocks to saving and investment have world-wide effects on interest rates and lead to changes in the flow of funds from the rest of the world to the domestic economy. After discussion of the Benjamin Friedman article, instructors might ask their students how Friedman's predictions about the effects of deficits compare with the predictions of the model.

Chapter 11 of this book includes a selection of readings on economic growth. After discussion of the article by Lucas or that by Mankiw, Romer and Weil, the instructor could ask students how the model of growth used by the authors compares to the model of growth presented in the text. Comparing issues and models from readings and the text provides students with the opportunities to obtain a bird's eye view of the text material and helps them understand that texts often present models and issues that are relevant for thinking about the world.

ASSESSMENT

Economists believe in incentives. Economic educators believe that students will work harder to achieve educational outcomes if doing so improves their grade. To provide students with an incentive to seek excellent answers to discussion questions, we recommend testing discussion outcomes in a formal way. We have already explained that we use pre-discussion quizzes to provide our students with an incentive to read discussion articles and prepare discussion questions. Here we explain how to test whether or not students have mastered the important content of the articles they have read and discussed as described by the learning objectives.

Our strategy is simple. Good discussion questions are easily transformed into good essay questions. Earlier, we described the article by Paul Krugman that accounts for differences in unemployment and inequality in Europe and the United States. One of the basic questions we assign for the Krugman article is: 'What economic forces explain, according to Krugman, why the natural rate of unemployment has risen in Europe but not in the US?' While the basic question focuses on how Krugman explains differences in the natural rate of unemployment in Europe and the United States, the follow-up questions (p. 137) help students explore the components of Krugman's argument.

We can test understanding of the Krugman article with the following essay question:

What economic forces explain, according to Krugman, why the natural rate of unemployment has risen in Europe but not in the US?
1. What does Krugman mean when he says that '...a likely explanation for this rise is the collision between welfare state policies that attempt to equalize economic outcomes and market forces that are pushing toward greater inequality.'?
2. Why does Krugman believe there is a connection between rising inequality in the US and rising unemployment in Europe? What does he mean by inequality?
3. What evidence does Krugman provide to explain why a technology shock provides a better explanation of rising inequality in the US than does 'globalization'. Along the way, explain what Krugman means by globalization.

The essay question requires that students explain what we consider to be the three most important facets of Krugman's argument. What the example makes clear is that students who strive for answers during discussion of the Krugman article are gaining insights that will help them do well in the examination. We believe that aligning the examination with discussion in this way provides clearer signals to students about where to focus their energy and thus enhances their learning.

For a second example, consider again Lucas' essay on growth. To prepare for discussion we ask students to prepare answers for the following two basic questions:

1. What, according to Lucas, accounts for the extraordinarily high rate of growth that occurred in the world between 1960 and 1990?
2. Why, according to Lucas, are growth rates of nations highly unequal in each year in the 1960 through 1990 period?

The basic question goes to the heart of the article while the supporting questions (pp. 143-44) help students consider the separate chunks of Lucas' argument. The first question asks students to explain how Lucas accounts for high average levels of world growth. The second asks students to explain how Lucas accounts for the fact that growth is highly unequal across nations. To test student mastery of the Lucas article we ask:

This question is about 'Some Macroeconomics for the 21st Century.'

1. What, according to Lucas, accounts for the extraordinarily high rate of growth that occurred in the world between 1960 and 1990?
2. Why, according to Lucas, are growth rates of nations highly unequal in each year in the 1960 through 1990 period?
3. What does Lucas mean when he says that his model is a 'model of spillovers'?
4. Do you agree with Lucas when he describes his model as an 'economic' model?

The examination question requires students to account for the two features of recent growth experience that Lucas considers to be important and to explain how he accounts for each. It also requires them to explain the spillovers that differentiate the Lucas model from the textbook Solow model. Again in this example, it is clear that the objectives of the examination are in line with the objectives of discussion.

It bears emphasis that instructors should set higher standards for student essays that are based on discussion questions than on essays that are not. The discussion process should deepen student understanding of the underlying concepts and issues and it is reasonable to expect them to demonstrate higher mastery in an examination essay.

CONCLUSION

In this chapter, we have indicated how instructors can create an environment where students will reap the educational benefits of discussion without bearing needless costs. There are several keys to our strategy.

1. Plan for discussion in advance of the course. Choose discussion readings wisely, make sure that the syllabus explains discussion responsibilities, and put into place incentives for students to prepare for discussion and participate energetically.
2. Keep in mind a strategy for getting discussion started.
3. Press for responses. Instructors should probe students and refrain from offering answers of their own.
4. Assess discussion outcomes. Good discussion questions make good examination questions.
5. Connect discussions to other activities by having students gather data, find and comment on related articles, or write about what they have read.
6. Link end-of-course examinations to the learning objectives for discussion course components.

A CONTRACT FOR DISCUSSION

Discussion is an important part of our course and I have chosen readings that are rich, interesting, and central to the course's main ideas. During discussion, I ask you to fully answer the questions of interpretation I pose before you judge the importance and relevance of a reading. Doing so will help you gain a deeper understanding of the economic ideas used by authors we read. I ask you to agree to the following contract, and pledge to abide by it myself.

As discussion leader, I agree to.
1. Read the material carefully.
2. Prepare well-thought out questions and distribute them in advance.
3. Pose questions carefully during class.
4. Develop the discussion fully.
5. Avoid difficult and technical terms unless they are essential.
6. Listen intently to students.
7. Involve each and every student.
8. Confine myself to asking questions and resist the temptation to lecture.
9. Evaluate the discussion in a formal way.

As a discussion participant, you agree to:
1. Read the material carefully.
2. Offer evidence from the reading to support your responses.
3. Refer only to outside sources that everyone has access to.
4. Listen carefully to others and to the questions being asked.
5. Ask for clarification of points you do not understand.
6. Respectfully challenge answers you do not agree with.
7. Be willing to change your mind if someone shows you to be off the mark.
8. Respond to the questions posed by the leader before making other points.
9. Be as brief as possible and not repeat what others have said.

DISCUSSION QUESTION WRITING ASSIGNMENT

Discussion of articles has been an important part of our learning strategy. My discussion strategy focuses on discussion of interpretive questions. I believe that students gain a deeper understanding of articles and concepts when they work together to figure out what authors mean by the things they say.

To learn the strategy, it is necessary to understand that there are three types of questions. Interpretive questions ask for an interpretation of the author's meaning. Factual questions ask for facts. Evaluative questions ask for judgments. Earlier in the semester, we discussed Benjamin Friedman's article

'US Fiscal Policy in the 1980s: Consequences of Large Budget Deficits at Full Employment.' Here are examples of the three question types for the Friedman article.

Interpretive: 'What, according to Friedman, is the connection between high budget deficits of the 1980s and the decline in weekly paychecks that occurred during the same period?' Factual: 'What exactly is the US deficit on current account?' Evaluative: 'In your view, does Friedman's analysis provide a valid framework with which to assess the economic consequences of fiscal deficits during the G. W. Bush Administration?'

A well-written interpretive question has four characteristics. First, the question asks for an interpretation. It asks discussion participants to explain the author's meaning and not merely to quote the author's words. Second, the question is interesting. The question writer is curious and thinks that participants will be too. Third, the question can be answered with evidence from the reading. The question writer should make sure that evidence is available in the reading. The discussion leader should encourage participants to cite evidence from the reading. Fourth, the question appears to permit more than one answer. The question should be sufficiently meaty that participants will perceive that there is room for their interpretations. If the author of the article states conclusions clearly, a good interpretive question will ask participants how the author reaches conclusions, supports them with evidence, or explains why they are important.

Your assignment is to write a factual question, an interpretive question, and an evaluative question for 'Privatizing U S Social Security: Some Possible Effects on Inter-generational Equity and the Economy' by Laurence Kotlikoff. Check to make sure your questions have the properties listed above and revise if necessary. Email your questions to me no later than 5:00 p. m. on Friday. Your questions will count as a quiz. I will select the best questions submitted to guide our discussion of Kotlikoff on Tuesday and email selected questions to the class list on Friday afternoon.

5. Discussion Modules

As they begin to incorporate discussion into their teaching, instructors may find it useful to have available articles and companion questions that others have successfully used in their economics courses. We offer these in Parts Two through Five of our book.

We believe that most instructors who try our approach to discussion will sooner or later want to write their own discussion questions. As they plan their courses, instructors will have specific learning objectives in mind and will want to target those objectives with discussion questions. We also believe that, with a bit of practice, any economics instructor can write good interpretive questions and question clusters. Indeed, our intent in chapters 1 through 4 is to help instructors become independent practitioners of our approach to discussion.

We also realize that many instructors will want to take a gradual approach to employing our discussion technology. In that spirit, we offer the specific discussion resources in the remainder of this book. We suggest that instructors begin experimenting with our approach to discussion by assigning articles and questions that we recommend. After gaining some experience, instructors might use the same articles but revise the questions as their classroom experience dictates. Finally, instructors should choose their own readings and write questions for them.

We have chosen over sixty classic and contemporary readings that span much of the undergraduate economics curriculum. For each, we provide a synopsis of the article, a list of suggested learning objectives, one or more question clusters designed to help students meet the given objectives, and specific ideas about how to lead discussion using the article. We have used many of the readings and questions in our own courses but have included others to broaden the reach of our book.

Some of the readings we have chosen are from books, others from journals. Many are in the public domain. We treat one (or several) book chapters as a separate reading when it is sufficiently rich and cohesive to stand alone. *The Wealth of Nations* is the source of several different readings in our book. On the other hand we treat *Maestro: Greenspan's Fed and the American Boom* as a single reading.

We collect readings into chapters by themes so that instructors can more easily find readings that they will find useful in their courses. In some cases, we include a reading in more than one chapter because it treats more than one theme. For example, we include Radford's 'The Economics of a P.O.W. Camp' in Chapter 13, Thinking about Markets, and in Chapter 18, The Evolution of Money. Whenever we use a reading in more than one chapter, we try to strike a balance between avoiding unnecessary repetition and making the chapter a convenient, stand-alone resource.

We collect the chapters of the remainder of our book into four parts. Part Two, Discussing Economic Principles, includes a chapter devoted to discussion of *The Wealth of Nations* and additional chapters on the triumph of capitalism, and transition economics. Part Three, Discussing Macroeconomics, includes chapters on monetary policy, unemployment and inflation, economic growth, and deficits. Part Four, Discussing Microeconomics, includes chapters on introductory ideas about markets, the connection between markets and incentives, labor economics, income distribution, and the future of economic thought. Part Five, Discussing Financial Economics, includes chapters on the evolution of money, the theory of interest, and international financial institutions.

We caution our readers not to map Parts Two to Five of our book into specific economics courses. Many, but not all, readings suitable for discussion in a first course appear in Part Two. For example, several of the readings on the evolution of money fit nicely into both pre-principles and principles courses. When a reading seems well suited to a particular economics course, we say so under the heading of Discussion Suggestions.

PART TWO

Discussing Economic Principles

6. *The Wealth of Nations*

Students can profitably discuss *The Wealth of Nations* in many parts of the undergraduate economics curriculum. Pre-principles students benefit from discussing Smith's ideas about economic coordination and the connection between division of labor, trade, and the use of money. Principles students benefit, in addition, from discussing what Smith has to say about the 'Invisible Hand' and the connection between self-betterment and the betterment of society. Intermediate micro students better understand the division of labor after discussing Smith's description of a pin factory. They also benefit from comparing Smith's views on natural prices and the concept of long-run equilibria. Intermediate macro and finance students better appreciate social costs of inflation after they discuss Smith's ideas about how best to preserve the real value of rents over long periods of time.

We have divided *The Wealth of Nations* into four parts. Part one comprises Chapters 1-3, part two is Chapter 4, part three is Chapter 5, and part four comprises Chapters 6-7. While it is reasonable for students to read and discuss a later part without reading the parts that precede it, a superior alternative would be to assign earlier parts as background reading.

At the end of the chapter, we suggest questions that help students explore connections among the ideas presented in the first seven chapters.

CHAPTERS 1-3

In Chapters 1-3, Adam Smith defines, illustrates, and discusses the economic benefits associated with 'the division of labor', today commonly referred to as 'specialization'. In Chapter 1, he sets out his now famous example of a pin factory where the manufacture of straight pins entails about 18 separate operations often performed by eighteen different workers. Through specialization, Smith says that pin factory workers can produce 4000 pins per day. Working alone, he surmises that each worker could make between one and 20. Smith argues that the division of labor increases efficiency because it leads to increased manual dexterity, it saves the time needed to pass from one task to another, and it facilitates labor-saving inventions.

In Chapter 2, Smith links the division of labor to a particularly human trait, 'the propensity to truck, barter, and exchange one thing for another' (p. 14).

He argues that trade is an appeal to the self interest of our fellow humans through which we endeavor to gain their cooperation. Self interest gives rise to the division of labor. The skilled bow maker quickly realizes that he may have more venison by making bows and trading than by using time to hunt.

In Chapter 3, Smith explains that 'the division of labor is limited by the extent of the market' (p. 19). He argues that workers will specialize only if they have access to a market large enough to absorb the output of their specialized labor. Smith explains that development of water transport has been important to specialization and suggests that nations that developed more rapidly were those with access to navigable rivers and seas.

Learning Objectives

After reading and discussing Chapters 1-3 of *The Wealth of Nations*, students should be able to

1. Define 'division of labor' and 'extent of the market'.
2. Give modern examples of division of labor.
3. Give a modern example showing that the extent of the market limits the division of labor.
4. Explain how Smith accounts for higher quality and lower price of manufactured goods in England in comparison to France and Poland in 1776.
5. Explain how Smith connects three concepts: self-interest, trade, and specialization.

Question Clusters

1. Why, according to Smith, does the division of labor account for 'the greatest improvement in the productive power of labor'?
   a. What does Smith mean by the division of labor? How is the division of labor illustrated by the pin factory?
   b. Why, according to Smith, are 'the hard-ware and the coarse woollens of England...superior to those of France, and much cheaper too in the same degree of goodness'?
   c. Why, according to Smith, is the invention of labor-saving machinery enhanced by the division of labor?
2. What, according to Smith, is the connection between the division of labor and the highly social nature of the human species?
3 Why, according to Smith, is the division of labor limited by the extent of the market?
   a. What does Smith mean by 'the extent of the market'?

   b. What, according to Smith, are the connections among geography, transportation, and the extent of the market?
4. What modern examples support Smith's views on the connection among the division of labor, the extent of the market, and the availability of cheap transport? Are there modern examples that contradict Smith's views?

Discussion Suggestions

A discussion assignment based on Chapters 1-3 of *The Wealth of Nations* fits well into both Principles and Pre-Principles courses. Our students have been able to work past the archaic language of the text but we find it useful to check their understanding (say, of the term 'corn') and provide them with opportunities to check the meaning of dated terms. It is important for students to consider whether Smith's ideas about labor efficiency and market extent are valid today. We also think that students appreciate Smith's 'invisible hand' much more when they discover it for themselves in *The Wealth of Nations*.

CHAPTER 4

In Chapter 4, Adam Smith argues that because the division of labor greatly increases trade among individuals, it gives rise to the use of money. He goes on to provide an overview of the evolution of money from commodity forms, through the use of metals in bar form, to the types of coinage that were used in his era. He explains that coinage obviates the need to weigh and assay metal money but creates an incentive for 'princes and sovereign states' to diminish the real quantity of metal contained in coins. He closes the chapter by explaining the difference between 'value in use' and 'value in exchange'.

Learning Objectives

After reading and discussing Chapter 4, students should be able to

1. Explain the connection between the division of labor and the use of money.
2. List the costs and benefits to individuals of an economy with coined money.
3. Explain how 'inflation' is the modern equivalent of the debasement of coins by princes and sovereign states. Explain how inflation benefits some and harms others.
4. Explain how money evolved from something that had value in use to something that has little value in use but great value in exchange.

Question Clusters

1. Why, according to Smith, does the division of labor lead to the use of money?
   a. Do you agree with Smith that the division of labor accounts for the use of money? Why?
2. What, according to Smith, are the costs and benefits to society of money use?
   a. Why, according to Smith, do metals make better money than other commodities?
   b. What, according to Smith, gives rise to coinage?
   c. What does Smith mean when he says 'The inconvenience and difficulty of weighing those metals with exactness gave occasion to the institution of coins...[which] were received by tale as at present, without the trouble of weighing'?
   d. What does Smith mean when he says the 'avarice and injustice of princes and sovereign states, abusing the confidence of their subjects, have by degrees diminished the real quantity of metal, which had been originally contained in their coins'?
3. Why according to Smith, does money have 'value in use' as well as 'value in exchange'? Why?
   a. What, according to Smith, is the difference between value in use and value in exchange?
   b. How, according to Smith, has the value of money evolved over time?

Discussion Suggestions

It works well to combine Chapters 1-4 into one long reading, which, in our experience, can be discussed in a 75 minute class.

CHAPTER 5

In Chapter 5, Adam Smith presents his own version of the labor theory of value. He argues that the real value of a commodity is the quantity of labor that may be commanded by possession of it. 'The real price of everything...is the toil and trouble of acquiring it' (p. 33).

Smith acknowledges, however, that the value of a commodity is not commonly reckoned in labor. It is difficult to determine the quality-adjusted labor content of a commodity and to measure the quantity and value of effort and ingenuity. Thus, society most often measures the value of commodities in money.

Smith argues, however, that if one wanted to enter into an extremely long-term contract, and to specify payment far in advance in a way that preserved the value of future payments, one would be better off specifying payment in commodities rather than in money because of variation in the metallic content of money and in the value of precious metals. He concludes that '[e]qual quantities of labour will at distant times be purchased more nearly with equal quantities of corn, the subsistence of the labourer, than with equal quantities of gold and silver' (p. 39).

Smith goes on to discuss the various metals that have been used as money by different civilizations. He explains that legal tender status tends to be reserved for the metal that a society originally uses as money and explains that gold was not legal tender in Britain until many years after it was first coined there. The last third of the chapter concerns issues associated with bimetallism that most instructors will not wish to emphasize.

Learning Objectives

After reading and discussing Chapter 5 of *The Wealth of Nations*, students should be able to

1. Explain the difference between the real and nominal price of a commodity.
2. Provide a modern day example of the practical importance of the real price of commodities.
3. Discuss the impact of the green revolution in agriculture on stability of the 'corn' prices of commodities.
4. Explain why Smith believes that 'labour...[is] the only standard by which we can compare the values of different commodities at all times and at all places'.

Question Clusters

1. What, according to Smith, is the difference between the nominal price of a commodity and the real price of the commodity?
   a. Why is labor the 'real measure of the exchangeable value of all commodities'?
   b. What is the significance of Smith's observation that the 'labor content' of some commodities is difficult to measure?
   c. What, according to Smith, determines the real price of gold and silver money?
   d. Why is it important to understand the difference between nominal and real price?

2. Why, according to Smith, is corn a better measure of value from century to century while silver is a better measure of value from year to year?
   a. Using Smith's criterion, what are modern examples of the practical significance of the distinction between the real and the nominal price of commodities?
   b. Is there a modern counterpart to Smith's example of the 'corn rents' of Oxford, Cambridge, Winchester and Eton?
   c. How would Smith regard corn as a measure of value had he lived to see the decline in agricultural prices caused by the 'green revolution' in the twentieth century?

Discussion Suggestions

Most instructors will want to focus attention on the first two-thirds of the chapter and skip the complicated material on coining more than one metal. In a course with a history focus, students could profitably discuss the relevance of Smith's observations on coining gold and silver to the Free Silver movement in the United States.

The questions that Smith raises about preserving value into the far distant future are fascinating and provide a good opportunity for students to consider the practical problems of saving for their own retirement that is 50 years ahead. Smith's observations about fluctuation in the value of gold and silver provide an opportunity to debunk the commonly held notion that any nation would be better on the gold standard than on any other standard.

CHAPTERS 6-7

In Chapter 6, Adam Smith explains why the price of every commodity is accounted for by the sum of three components: the wages of the labor that produces the commodity, the profit of the entrepreneur who owns the capital (including raw materials and advanced wages) used to produce the commodity, and the rent of the land used to produce the commodity. Smith explains that profit is different from the wages of the person who oversees and directs production. He argues that profit is determined by a market rate of return and is proportional to the amount of stock invested by the entrepreneur. Smith allows that some commodities such as ocean fish have prices that resolve only into wages and profits. He points out that a gardener who owns his own garden receives compensation for labor, rent, and profit even though common usage would confound the three and describe them all as the gardener's wages.

In Chapter 7, Smith defines the 'natural price' of a commodity and compares it to the market price. The natural price is just sufficient to pay land, labor, and entrepreneurship their natural rates of return. Smith defers discussion of natural rates of return to Chapters 8, 9 and 11. Smith argues that market price gravitates to the natural price because self-interested owners of stock, land, and labor will commit more resources to production of a commodity whose market price exceeds natural price, and will remove resources from production of a commodity whose price falls below natural price. He argues that fluctuations in market price tend to affect either wages or profits depending on whether the market tends to be 'over-stocked or under-stocked with commodities or with labour; with work done or with work to be done' (p. 67). To illustrate, he says that a public mourning raises the profits of merchants who have stocks of black cloth and the wages of tailors who can make garments from it, but not the wages of weavers since the black cloth is wanted immediately. He goes on to discuss the effect of a trade secret or a granted monopoly on market price.

Learning Objectives

After reading and discussing Chapters 6 and 7, students should be able to

1. Explain the difference between the market price and the natural price of a commodity.
2. Explain why some commodities vary in price more than others.
3. Describe the forces that tend to drive market price to natural price.
4. Explain why self-interested merchants and laborers will try to block others from participating in sale and manufacture of certain commodities.
5. Discuss the costs and benefits of granting patents to new inventions.

Question Clusters

1. What, according to Smith, is the difference between natural and market price of a commodity?
   a. What, according to Smith, is the difference between the natural price of a commodity and the real price of a commodity ?
   b. What accounts for cases where the market price differs greatly from the natural price?
   c. Why do fluctuations in market price 'fall chiefly upon those parts of its price which resolve themselves into wages and profits.'? What forces explain whether wages or profits are more affected by the fluctuations?
   d. How is Smith's distinction between natural and market prices useful for understanding how prices are set in a modern market economy?
2. Why, according to Smith, does the market price of a commodity gravitate toward the natural price of that commodity?

a. What does Smith mean by the natural price? The market price?
b. Why, according to Smith, does the market price of a commodity sometimes exceed the natural price? What happens when it does?
c. Why, according to Smith, does the natural price of a commodity sometimes exceed the market price? What happens when it does?
d. What forces, according to Smith, keep market price from reaching natural price?
e. Why, according to Smith, is it important that market price tends toward natural price?

Discussion Suggestions

The most challenging part of these two chapters is the section that discusses whether wages or profits are more affected by a departure of commodity price from its natural level. It is important to use follow-up questions until students understand clearly that a public mourning required people to wear black immediately, and so that they were not willing to wait for new black cloth to be woven.

Discussion of the force that makes market price tend toward natural price is particularly useful for helping students understand the workings of the invisible hand. The agents who respond to high market prices do so out of self interest, but nevertheless promote efficiency.

OVERVIEW

After students discuss the individual parts of *The Wealth of Nations*, instructors may want to provide them with an opportunity to explore how the parts fit together. The following questions would provide opportunities to explore connections linking themes that Smith raises separately.

1. What, according to Smith, are the important differences in economic life that occur as societies evolve from collections of relatively independent households to highly interdependent communities?
2. What, according to Smith, determines society's valuation of a good or service? What determines which workers will receive high wages and which will receive low?
3. If Smith were alive today, would he favor a return to the gold standard? Why?
4. What would Smith think of a taxation scheme that taxed profits at a much higher rate than wages?

5. How would Smith regard interference by government in the free working of the marketplace? When and why?

We leave the reader with two final thoughts. First, it is especially important when asking overarching questions like those above to insist that students support their contributions with specific references to the text. It is not nearly as important that students form answers that agree with what we believe than that they learn the process of inferring an author's meaning from the words the author spoke. Also, students may come to a course with a pre-conceived notion about the nature of Adam Smith's economics. It is part of our job to separate students from the uninformed parts of their beliefs.

Second, answering overarching questions such as those above provide opportunities for students to work with Smith's ideas at very high cognitive levels. For example, to decide whether Smith would favor a gold standard today, students would have to make a list of the costs and benefits and support their ideas with specific references to the text. They then would have to decide what Smith's criteria would be, again by consulting the text for hints as to Smith's values. Finally, they would draw conclusions.

Writing this book has reminded us of the richness of *The Wealth of Nations*. We believe that discussing it is a high value opportunity for college seniors and even for graduate students.

7. Triumph of Capitalism

With the fall of the Berlin Wall in 1988 and the subsequent rapid disintegration of the Soviet Union, the world witnessed the evaporation of Communism's hoped-for benefits from what had become a broken, inefficient command economy. Western style capitalism had triumphed. This triumph occurred in the face of Marx's prediction that because of its own internal contradictions, capitalism would collapse and scientific socialism would triumph. This prediction never materialized, notwithstanding the optimism that greeted the Soviet Union's establishment of a centralized planned economy in the late 1920s and early 1930s. This optimism continued, manifesting itself with Premier Khrushchev's 1960 Cold War threat that by 1970 the Soviet Union would 'bury' the United States economy. By the early 1980s, Soviet leaders came to realize the failures of its economic system and the need for change. Attempts at internal reform within the old structure unleashed a host of repressed forces that quickly caused both the Soviet political structure and its economic system to come crashing down.

This group of readings tries to capture the high points of the struggle between the capitalism and other forms of economic organization, and the tensions created by capitalism. It offers snapshot views on eminent economists regarding the state of capitalism, beginning with Adam Smith, continuing to Marx and Engels' Communist Manifest, moving on to Keynes in the 1930s, Schumpeter in the 1940s and early 1950s, Friedman in the 1960s, and then skipping on to Heilbroner, who, shortly after the Soviet Union began to implode, offered a brilliant synthesis of the contest between capitalism and socialism.

This chapter begins with the first four chapters of Adam Smith's 1776 book, *The Wealth of Nations*. With their focus on the division of labor, the forces giving rise to the division of labor, the extent to which the division of labor is limited by the extent of the market, and real and nominal prices, these chapters help characterize the nature and strength of capitalism

The second selection contains excerpts from Marx and Engel's 1848 publication, *The Communist Manifesto*. This famous statement offers a ringing critique of capitalism, ending with the call: 'Working men of the world, unite!' Marx and Engels criticize the conditions of production and property relationships that exploit the worker and lead to periodic crises in capitalistic countries. The *Manifesto* provides a list of recommendations that among other things call for abolishing private property, centralizing production, reducing the extent of income inequality, and changing the conditions of work. In the years that followed, other forms of economic organization were proposed, but the most prominent of them, socialism, never gained a firm foothold. However, in the aftermath of the Russian Revolution of 1917, Lenin and later Stalin seized the opportunity to implement scientific socialism, *à la* Marx, and it produced the command economy under which Russians lived for decades.

The seeming success of the Soviet system and the Great Depression of the 1930s fueled discontent with capitalism. Keynes' 1936 book, *The General Theory,* revolutionized thinking about macroeconomics with its focus on stimulating aggregate demand through fiscal policy. This chapter from Keynes' book expresses concern about the ability of capitalistic economies, while seeking to maintain full employment, to ensure a fair distribution of income. Keynes discussed what could be done to promote greater income equality but in so doing notes some of the serious tradeoffs that are involved in doing so.

Schumpeter, writing shortly after World War II, worried that the very success of capitalism, rather than its failures, would be its downfall. He argued that the destructive forces inherent in capitalism would weaken it and lead to its demise. In this particular selection, he also expresses concern about the growing power of unions and their role in undermining capitalism.

Friedman revived interest in capitalism in his early 1960s book, *Capitalism and Freedom*. In the selection included here, Friedman emphasizes the importance of capitalism's continued success to maintaining political and economic freedom. Without political freedom, economic freedom will be threatened. At the same time, economic freedom is essential in maintaining political freedom.

Finally, Heilbroner, writing in early 1989 when it was already clear that the Soviet Union had changed in fundamental ways and could never reconstitute itself as it had been, synthesizes the long-running competition between capitalism and socialization as only he could do. He highlights the evolution of economists' thinking about the prospects for capitalism, describing capitalism's sustaining and enduring attributes, detailing why centralized economic systems could not succeed, and finally giving his assessment of the challenges capitalism faces after its triumph over socialism.

CHAPTERS 1-3, *THE WEALTH OF NATIONS*, ADAM SMITH

Adam Smith, in his 1776 treatise, *The Wealth of Nations*, not only spelled out the essentials of capitalism, but also made a persuasive case for it as a successor to Mercantilism. Ever since then no discussion of capitalism can be considered complete without reference to Smith and his classic work. Here, we focus on Chapters 1-3 where Smith illustrates and discusses the economic benefits associated with private ownership. An abstract and additional discussion ideas for these and other parts of *The Wealth of Nations* are available in Chapter 6 of our book.

Learning Objectives

After reading and discussing Chapters 1-3 of *The Wealth of Nations*, students should be able to

1. Define 'division of labor' and 'extent of the market'.
2. Give examples of the division of labor.
3. Explain what Smith means by the 'invisible hand'.
4. Understand the connection between private property and the working of the invisible hand.
5. Explain how Smith connects these concepts: self interest, trade, and specialization.

Question Clusters

1. Why, according to Smith, does the division of labor account for 'the greatest improvement in the productive power of labor'?
   a. What does Smith mean by the division of labor?
   b. What, according to Smith, is the connection between private ownership of capital and the division of labor?
2. What does Smith mean when he says: 'It is not from the benevolence of the butcher, the brewer, or the baker, that we expect our dinner, but from their regard to their own interest. We address ourselves, not to their humanity but to their self-love, and never talk to them of our own necessities but of their advantages'?
3. According to Smith, what is the connection between extent of the market and secure private property rights?

Discussion Suggestions

Discussion of Chapters 1-3 of *The Wealth of Nations* provides a framework for discussions of capitalism by Marx and others who are concerned about the implications of specialization and the division of labor on the personal well-being and development of workers as human beings. As we explain in Chapter 6, it is useful to provide students with opportunities to check their understanding of archaic terms like 'corn'. It is also important for students to discuss the connection between private ownership and the workings of Smith's invisible hand.

'THE MANIFESTO OF THE COMMUNIST PARTY', KARL MARX AND FRIEDRICH ENGELS

The Communists Manifesto offered a powerful critique of mid-nineteenth century capitalism. It called on workers to unite to overthrow the existing social conditions, and it concluded with the stirring words: 'Working men of all countries, unite!' Marx and Engels argued that the social conditions they lament were a product of modern capitalism as well as the two classes that evolved from it, the bourgeoisie and the proletariat. The problem is that the modern conditions of production induced by the division of labor give rise to worker exploitation. In addition, the concentration of property ownership which permits the existence of the bourgeoisie leads to productive forces that can no longer be controlled, causing periodic crises that endanger capitalism itself. This system leads in turn to a modern working class, laborers who sell themselves as commodities. In so doing, they become slaves of the bourgeois class whose treatment of them creates their bitterness and antagonism. At the same time, the poorer part of the middle class gradually joins the proletariat because it can no longer compete against newer methods of production. Thus, the exploitation of labor increases.

Because the existence of private property is responsible for producing class antagonisms and exploitation, the *Manifesto* calls for abolishing private property. It offers a 10-point agenda as a means of diminishing the power of the bourgeoisie. Its goals are to narrow differences in income, centralize production, change the conditions of work, provide free education for all, and so on. The authors believe that as class distinctions disappear and production is centralized under government auspices, there will emerge a new political and social order 'in which the free development of each is the condition for the free development of all' (p. 244).

Learning Objectives

After reading and discussing these selections from *The Communist Manifesto*, students are expected to

1. Explain the basis for the *Manifesto*'s critique of capitalism.
2. Describe the consequences that private property ownership and the resulting class antagonisms have on the institution of capitalism.

3. Describe how the *Manifesto*'s description of how capitalism works as a market system compares with Adam Smith's description.
4. Evaluate the power of the language used by Marx and Engels, particularly in contrast to the style of most economists.

Question Clusters

1. Why do Marx and Engels issue their call to action in the electrifying words: 'Workers of all countries, unite!'?
2. What is the meaning of the special terms used in the *Manifesto*: bourgeoisie, proletariat, bourgeois society, classes, class antagonisms, class struggle?
3. How does property play such a crucial role in producing the class-based society of capitalism?
   a. What is the significance of the different kinds of property mentioned in the *Manifesto*?
   b. What mechanisms engendered by the institution of property lead to the emergence of classes and class antagonisms?
4. What do the *Manifesto*'s authors mean when it says 'the proletariat will use its political supremacy to wrest, by degrees, all capital from the bourgeoisie, to centralize all instruments of production in the hands of the state, i.e., of the proletariat organized as the ruling class'?
   a. How will the proletariat acquire 'political supremacy'?
   b. What kinds of measures are likely to be used?
   c. Must these measures entail violence? Why or why not?
5. Why does the *Manifesto* say that once the proletariat wins supremacy it will 'increase the total of productive forces as rapidly as possible'?
   a. How does this statement square with an earlier statement that 'get[ing] over these [periodic] crises' will require the 'enforced destruction of a mass of productive forces'?
   b. In what sense are 'the conquest of new markets, and [by] the more thorough exploitation of the old ones' alternatives to the destruction of productive forces?
6. What is the meaning of the statement, 'These laborers, who must sell themselves piecemeal, are a commodity . . . '?
   a. Why are workers characterized variously as 'soldiers', 'slaves', and 'enslaved'?
   b. How do these characterizations relate to the claim that workers are exploited?
   c. How might Adam Smith have reacted to this statement?

7. What is the meaning and implications of the *Manifesto*'s statement: 'Hence, the cost of production of a workman is restricted, almost entirely, to the means of subsistence that he requires for his maintenance, and for the propagation of his race'?
8. What kind of society would evolve if the *Manifesto*'s scenario came to pass, as described in its statement: 'In place of the old bourgeois society, with its classes and class antagonisms, we shall have an association in which the free development of each is the condition for the free development of all.'?
   a. What is the meaning of the word 'association' above?
   b. How would the *Manifesto*'s ten-point program change the relationship among the social classes and create the kind of association predicted above?
9. What kind of empirical evidence would support the thesis of the *Manifesto* about the changing strength of the two classes, the bourgeoisie and the proletariat?

Discussion Suggestions

This reading selection is designed to acquaint students with *The Communist Manifesto*'s powerful critique of the workings of capitalism as described by Adam Smith in the *Wealth of Nations*. Whereas Smith focuses on market mechanisms, Marx and Engels take a broader look at societal implications of these market mechanisms. What makes this selection so interesting is that it provides a macro analysis of capitalism in contrast to the largely micro analysis presented by Smith. Thus, a discussion of the *Manifesto* can help principles students gain an appreciation for the link between micro and macro analysis.

It should be noted that the reading is a selection from the much longer *Communist Manifesto*. The excluded parts expand on conditions affecting the emergence of modern bourgeois society, and on different forms of socialism existing in the first half of the nineteenth century. While interesting, these other sections are not essential in understanding the central ideas of the *Manifesto*.

'CONCLUDING NOTES ON THE SOCIAL PHILOSOPHY TOWARDS WHICH THE GENERAL THEORY MIGHT LEAD', JOHN MAYNARD KEYNES

In this concluding chapter to *The General Theory,* a book that propelled macro theory into the mainstream of economic thinking, Keynes highlights the implications of his new approach for illuminating contemporary concerns about capitalism and particularly economic inequality. He begins by explaining the impact of direct taxation and of the human propensity to consume upon the distribution of wealth, finding that some degree of inequality is both inevitable and essential. He goes on to examine the role of the rate of interest in explaining both the present and future distribution of wealth. He concludes that as long as capital is scarce, the rentier class will continue to exist, and inequalities in income and wealth will persist. The only way to eliminate the rentier class is not by revolution, as Marx and Engels would insist, but by overcoming the scarcity of capital.

Keynes then explains what can be done to overcome the scarcity of capital, such as taxation, fixing the rate of interest, and other measures. However, he warns that to assure full employment the government may be required to undertake a 'comprehensive socialization of investment'. Doing so is likely to entail additional controls that must be balanced with 'the advantages of decentralization and of the play of self-interest'. What makes this chapter so interesting is that Keynes considers income distribution issues and how best to ameliorate economic inequality. He sees a tradeoff between greater economic efficiency and any effort to redistribute income and wealth.

Keynes concludes by discussing the importance of ideas in affecting economic policy, noting that the power of ideas gradually overcomes the power of vested interests. He ends with perhaps the most widely quoted statement elaborating the power of ideas.

the ideas of economists and political philosophers, both when they are right and when they are wrong, are more powerful than is commonly understood. Indeed, the world is ruled by little else. Practical men, who believe themselves to be quite exempt from any intellectual influences, are usually the slaves of some defunct economist (pp. 383-4).

Learning Objectives

After reading and discussing Keynes' essay student should be able to

1. Explain the impact of direct taxation, the propensity to consume, and the interest rate on both the present and future distribution of wealth.
2. Interpret the relationship between the rentier class, the scarcity of capital, and the distribution of income and wealth.
3. Explain what steps are required to bring about full employment.
4. Spell out the role of ideas and their effects on economic policy.

Question Clusters

1. Why, according to Keynes, does he begin this final chapter of a book that focuses on macroeconomics with a discussion of the distribution of income and wealth?
   a. What, according to Keynes, is the link between macroeconomics and the distribution of income and wealth?
   b. How do direct taxation and the propensity to consume affect the distribution of wealth?
   c. Why does Keynes state that some degree of inequality in the distribution of income and wealth is inevitable?
2. What reasons does Keynes advance for the scarcity of capital and what does he see as the means of overcoming the scarcity of capital?
   a. What is the role of the rentier class in accounting for the scarcity of capital?
   b. What is the role of the rentier class in accounting for disparities in income and wealth?
   c. How does the fate of the rentier class differ in the views of Keynes and Marx?
   d. In what sense is full employment related to the scarcity of capital?
   e. What does Keynes mean by this statement: 'It is better that a man should tyrannize over his bank balance than over his fellow citizens.'?
3. Why does Keynes conclude that a 'somewhat comprehensive socialization of investment will prove to be the only means of securing an approximation to full employment.'?
   a. What is the meaning of a 'comprehensive socialization of investment'?
   b. How can a 'comprehensive socialization of investment' be balanced with 'the advantages of decentralization and of the play of self-interest'?
4. Keynes states, ' It is certain that the world will not much longer tolerate the unemployment which, apart from brief intervals of excitement, is associated – and, in my opinion, inevitably associated – with present-day capitalist individualism'.
   a. Is Keynes suggesting that the capacity of authoritarian states to solve the problem of unemployment at the expense of efficiency and of freedom is greater than capitalist individualism, which not only leads to greater efficiency but also permits greater freedom?
   b. What would Keynes say regarding the fall of communism in Eastern Europe and the former Soviet Union?
5. What do you think leads Keynes to his belief in the power of ideas?
6. What does Keynes see as the natural evolution of the economy and its structure or organization in contrast to the views of Smith and Marx?

a. What, if any, implicit references do you find to the ideas of Marx and Smith in Keynes' work?
b. What does Keynes mean by the statement that in the 'ideal commonwealth men may have been taught or inspired or bred to take no interest in the stakes.'?
c. Would Smith have agreed with this statement? Why or why not?
7. How would you summarize Keynes' views about the 'advantages of decentraliztion and of the play of self-interest'?

Discussion Suggestions

Students reading much of *The General Theory* find Keynes' exposition difficult to follow. The chapter is difficult, perhaps, because it takes a much broader view. Still, the chapter is not easy reading because it requires considerable background knowledge. If students read the chapter after they have been introduced to two key terms from the Keynesian system, namely, the propensity to consume, and the marginal efficiency of capital, they should not have much difficulty with this selection. This selection offers rich possibilities for tying togethcr the earlier selections by Smith and by Marx-Engels. Before discussion of the chapter ends, it is useful to have students voice their reactions to Keynes' closing paragraph on the power of ideas.

'PROLOGUE' AND 'THE MARCH INTO SOCIALISM', JOSEPH A. SCHUMPETER

The thesis of Schumpeter's book, *Capitalism, Socialism, and Democracy*, is best described in his own words:

Can capitalism survive? No, I do not think it can. The thesis I shall endeavor to establish is that the actual and prospective performance of the capitalist system is such as to negative [negate] the idea of its breaking down under the weight of economic failure, but that its very success undermines the social institutions which protect it, and 'inevitably' creates conditions in which it will not be able to live and which strongly point to socialism as the heir apparent (p. 61).

Schumpeter also makes the important point that

[a]nalysis...never yields more than a statement about the tendencies present in an observable pattern. And these never tell us what will

happen to the pattern but only what would happen if they continued to act as they have been acting in the time interval covered by our observation and if no other factors intruded. 'Inevitability' or 'necessity' can never mean more than this. Prognosis does not imply anything about the desirability of the course of events that one predicts (p. 61).

With this as background, in this selection Schumpeter explains his paradoxical and ominous conclusion. He claims that the great success of capitalism will be uncut by destructive forces that are inherent in a capitalistic system. He is particularly concerned here with what he calls 'laborist capitalism' and the possibilities it raises for creating continuing inflationary pressures. He concludes with several recommendations for constraining these forces.

Learning Objectives

After reading and discussing these selections from Schumpeter's *Capitalism, Socialism, and Democracy*, students should be able to

1. Define the economic systems of socialism and capitalism, and identify their key characteristics.
2. Explain what differentiates these terms: laissez faire, free enterprise, and capitalism from 'liberalism' and 'socialism'.
3. Describe the forces that undermine the social institutions underlying capitalism.
4. Explain the various tasks that economists can undertake: advocacy, prognosis, diagnosis, and analysis.

Question Clusters

1. Why, according to Schumpeter, will capitalism fail to survive?
   a. What does Schumpeter mean by capitalism?
   b. In what sense is Schumpeter prognosticating the demise of capitalism?
   c. What does Schumpeter mean by prognosticating, and how is this term related to his discussion of the role of advocacy, prognosis, diagnosis, and analysis?
2. What explains Schumpeter's paradox, i.e., that the very success of capitalism will undermine its future?
   a. What does Schumpeter identify as the key characteristics of 'socialism'?
   b. What does Schumpeter mean by the 'disintegration of capitalist society'?

c. Why, according to Schumpeter, does he conclude that the 'capitalist order tends to destroy itself'?

d. Does Schumpeter believe it inevitable that these forces of disintegration will persist? Explain.

3. What, according to Schumpeter, explains recent factors [as of 1949] that were accelerating the tendency toward the socialist goal?

a. What are these factors?

b. Why should wars play such a role?

c. What is the role of inflation in 'weakening the social framework of society'?

d. What remedies exist for dealing with inflation?

e. How effective are these remedies?

f. What is the role of unionism in the struggle against inflation?

4. If Schumpeter were alive today, how would he describe the position of our economic system along the continuum from 'unfettered capitalism' to 'socialism'?

a. Where do you think most of his contemporary economists in 1949 would have placed the economy along the same continuum?

b. Where do you think most contemporary economists today would place the economy along this continuum?

5. Was Schumpeter correct in his concerns about the impact of inflation?

a. What has been the result of 'the private enterprise system [being] permanently burdened and 'regulated'?

b. Has the economy been 'permanently burdened and 'regulated' beyond its *powers of endurance*'? [Emphasis added]

6. What knowledge of the economy and economic conditions at the time he wrote would help you understand more fully Schumpeter's thesis and the reasoning behind it, particularly the 'march toward socialism'?

Discussion Suggestions

This reading is likely to be difficult for students because of its wide scope. The selection reads as if Schumpeter wanted to be very careful about how his words would be read and interpreted today. This concern accounts for his attempt to differentiate among various descriptions of capitalism as well as between advocacy, prognosis, diagnosis, and analysis. Students should be able to see what factors he takes into account in developing his thesis that capitalism will fail. It would help students to have a clear understanding of the many different words Schumpeter uses to describe capitalism, among them: 'laissez faire', 'free enterprise', 'private enterprise', 'unfettered capitalism', 'liberalism', and 'laborist capitalism'. Based on their reading and understanding, students might be asked whether they see similar tendencies today, and what these tendencies mean for the future of capitalism. In discussing Schumpeter's recommendations, it may be helpful to give students some background about the early post-WWII economy and the then-widespread concern about the growing power of labor to increase wages and, in the process, accelerate inflation.

'THE RELATION BETWEEN ECONOMIC FREEDOM AND POLITICAL FREEDOM', MILTON FRIEDMAN

Friedman begins his classic book, *Capitalism and Freedom*, by addressing the link between economic and political freedom. He refutes the widespread view, prevalent when he wrote this book, that economic freedom and political freedom are unconnected, and that no difficulties arise in combining differing degrees of economic freedom with differing degrees of political freedom. He argues that economic freedom, while a component of freedom more broadly conceived, is an end in itself and at the same time a means toward achieving political freedom.

He asserts that economic freedom in the form of competitive capitalism promotes political freedom by separating economic power from political power, thereby allowing them to offset each other. Yet, as concerns about economic welfare became ever more dominant in the nineteenth and twentieth centuries, centralized control of economic activity increased. Ultimately, collectivist economic planning failed in large part because the loss of personal liberty was so high.

The challenge capitalism faces is the need to coordinate the economic activities of large numbers of people. Friedman believes that the best means of accomplishing this coordination is through informed voluntary cooperation and exchange among individuals, what is called competitive capitalism. Freedom of exchange is essential, as are the 'rules of the game' established through government to facilitate voluntary cooperation and exchange.

For economic freedom to flourish, political freedom must prevail, meaning that coercive forces must be held in check. Concentrations of political power must be eliminated or, where that is impossible, appropriate checks and balances must be established. As long as market activity is separated from political control, the market eliminates coercive power. Friedman goes on to note that while economic power is inevitably decentralized, the decentralization of political power is much more difficult to achieve and maintain.

Finally, Friedman comments on the opportunities available to people in a capitalist society; they benefit from the political freedom to openly advocate and promote the idea of socialism. He contrasts this situation with that of a socialist society where the possibilities of dissent are strictly limited because of the absence of economic freedom.

Learning Objectives

After reading and discussing Friedman's essay, students should be able to

1. Define various kinds of political and economic freedom.
2. Explain the linkages between economic freedom and political freedom.
3. Explain the preconditions for economic freedom and the benefits it produces.
4. Explain how economic freedom depends on political freedom.
5. Through an essay, apply Friedman's analysis to the contemporary world.

Question Clusters

1. What does Friedman mean by this statement: 'Economic arrangements play a dual role in the promotion of a free society. On the one hand, freedom in economic arrangements is itself a component of freedom broadly understood, so economic freedom is an end in itself. In the second place, economic freedom is also an indispensable means toward the achievement of political freedom.'?
   a. What does Friedman mean by saying, 'economic freedom is an end in itself'?
   b. In what sense is 'economic freedom . . . an indispensable means toward the achievement of political freedom'?
   c. What does Friedman mean when he refers to the 'direct' versus the 'indirect importance of economic freedom as a means to political freedom'?
   d. In what sense might political freedom be an 'indispensable means' toward the achievement of economic freedom?
2. What does Friedman believe are the preconditions so that the 'economic activities of large numbers of people' can be effectively coordinated?
   a. How do these preconditions ensure that a free economy will do 'this task so well'?
   b. How do these preconditions become self-reinforcing ways of limiting coercive power?
   c. How do these preconditions 'permit wide diversity'?
3. How does Friedman use economics to explain the mechanisms available in different types of political-economic systems to advocate changing the current economic system?
   a. What kind of analysis does he employ?

   b. Why would it be difficult for individuals in a socialist state to convince other people of the virtues of a capitalist economic system?

   c. What makes it possible for this apparatus to operate in a capitalism system?

   d. What conditions have led to continuing efforts in the US to change our capitalist economics system?

Discussion Suggestions

Friedman's essay is essential reading for help in understanding the distinctive nature of capitalism and the close links between economic and political freedom. Student discussion will be facilitated if they have beforehand some knowledge of the terminology he uses, including such terms as: 'democratic socialism', 'totalitarian socialism', 'competitive capitalism', 'economic totalitarianism', 'political totalitarianism', 'central planning', 'a free private enterprise exchange economy', 'neighborhood effects'. Underlying Friedman's essay were his concerns about the erosion of these freedoms as the scope of government widened in the early post-WWII years. The groundwork for these changes were laid in the New Deal legislation of the 1930s, the economy mobilization during WWII, and signs of the continued growth of the welfare state in the 1950s. Friedman's essay is also useful in understanding the relationship between 'perestroika' and 'glasnost', which are discussed in the readings about the Soviet transition that began under Gorbachev's initiatives in the late 1980s.

'REFLECTIONS: THE TRIUMPH OF CAPITALISM', ROBERT L. HEILBRONER

Well known as the author of *The Worldly Philosophers*, Robert Heilbroner puts into the larger context of economics and politics the rise of capitalism, its competition with socialism and its recent triumph over socialism in this wide-ranging essay written shortly after the collapse of the Soviet Union.

Heilbroner begins by reviewing the pessimistic prospects for capitalism voiced by the great economists: Smith, Mill, Marx, Marshall, Keynes, and Schumpeter. He then goes on to indicate why their prognoses were so wide of the mark, reflecting not only their static conceptions of economic growth, but also a failure to appreciate the dynamism of a capitalistic system.

A key element in his analysis is the interplay between two centers of authority, namely, the economic and the political realms, and the challenge of managing the relationships among these two realms. The boundaries between them have changed and continue to change, from the age of Smith, who saw a limited role for government, to the present when government has extended its reach into the economic realm in ways that Smith could never have anticipated.

Heilbroner sees further encroachment of the political realm into the economic realm as growing international trade steadily increases the interdependence of the world economy. How this situation will evolve remains to be seen. He also touches on the links between democracy and capitalism, arguing that the democratic aspect of capitalism is both a source of strength and weakness, with democracy built on what he calls the 'horizontality of democracy, and capitalism on the 'verticality of wealth'.

Finally, Heilbroner speculates on the future of socialism and the possibility of a convergence between the systems of capitalism and socialism. He argues that to succeed, socialism must incorporate important elements of capitalism. He also wonders to what degree capitalism can embrace the best elements of socialism. The essential question is what will 'work well enough'.

Learning Objectives

After reading and discussing the Heilbroner selection, students should be able to

1. Explain why the great economists were so pessimistic about capitalism's prospects and so wrong in their assessment.
2. Clarify Heilbroner's distinction between capitalism as 'working' and 'working well enough'.
3. Describe the links between the economic and political realms and the shifting boundaries between them.
4. Explain the connections between capitalism and democracy.
5. Explain how the increased internationalization of economic relations is likely to further shift the boundaries between the economic and political realms.

Question Clusters

1. What, according to Heilbroner, accounts for the individual and collective pessimism of the great economists – Smith, Marx, Keynes, and Schumpeter – about the long-run prospects for capitalism?
   a. What were the views of Smith, Marx, Keynes, and Schumpeter?
   b. How and why did the views of these economists differ?
   c. Why, according to Heilbroner, did each of these economists so seriously misjudge the likely course of events?
2. What does Heilbroner mean when he speaks of capitalism as a 'regime'?

    a. What does he mean by the word 'regime'?

    b. Why does he describe 'business' as the universal class in the regime of capitalism?

3. Why does Heilbroner make the distinction between the two centers of authority, the political realm and the economic realm?

    a. What does he mean by 'realms'?

    b. What is the relationship among these two realms in capitalism as it contrasts with a centrally controlled economy?

4. In what sense, according to Heilbroner, has capitalism triumphed?

    a. Has capitalism really triumphed on its own terms? Explain.

    b. In what sense has capitalism 'worked well enough'?

    c. In what sense has socialism failed?

    d. What challenges must be met to make socialism work?

5. What makes Heilbroner's writing so powerful?

    a. What literary devices does he employ to make his prose so vivid?

    b. Find and point out some of his most telling phrases, most engaging sentences, etc.

Discussion Suggestions

This essay is as remarkable for its comprehensiveness as it is for its ability to provoke our thinking about what we describe as different kinds of economic systems. It is impressive in emphasizing the pessimistic views of the great economists about the future of capitalism. It is discerning in pinpointing what gives capitalism its unexpected dynamism. Finally, it is illuminating in showing the implications of the triumph of capitalism over socialism, some version of which Heilbroner seemingly favors. In discussing this selection, attention should be given to Heilbroner's powerful and engaging writing style. His liveliness contrasts sharply with the often dull prose of economists. Heilbroner's use of metaphors is especially striking and powerful. Pointing out some of the special features of Heilbroner's writing style can benefit students who have been subjected to the leaden prose that characterizes most economics textbooks.

OVERVIEW

What makes this chapter so appealing is the final selection by Heilbroner. He views the decline and eventual demise of the Soviet Union and its planned economy as the 'triumph of capitalism'. He does so in the context of recounting what a string of great economists has had to say, among them Smith, Marx and Engels, Keynes, Schumpeter, and Friedman. Moreover,

Heilbroner writes with such verve and style that students are bound to be drawn into his frame of thinking. If there is time for students to read and discuss only one selection in this chapter, we believe they can profit most from the Heilbroner essay. However, many questions remain about the triumph of capitalism captured in these selections.

1. Have the collective fears aroused by Marx and Engels, by Keynes, by Schumpeter, and by Friedman been resolved? What about their individual fears? Exactly what is the nature of each of their fears?
2. Does Heilbroner make a convincing case that capitalism has triumphed? What new problems does Heilbroner see on the horizon?
3. Is there any reason to fear that the continued success of capitalism will be its undoing, as predicted by Schumpeter? Explain what forces may be contributing to the demise of capitalism.
4. How do you think Friedman would respond to the Heilbroner analysis?
5. Based on your observations, what new challenges face capitalism now and into the first part of the twenty-first century?

8. Transition Economics

Perhaps the most fascinating late twentieth century development in international economics was the disintegration of the Soviet command economy and subsequent efforts to construct a new economy that would possess many attributes of Western capitalism. By the early 1980s, the weaknesses of the Soviet economy had become too serious for its leadership to ignore, though much of the West was unaware of these developments because of the Soviet regime's secrecy. Shortly after assuming the Presidency in the mid-1980s, Mikhail Gorbachev began his quest for reform. He wanted to return to the ideals of socialism promoted by Lenin more than half a century earlier.

But events moved more quickly than he or anyone else expected. The Berlin Wall fell, the Soviet Union began breaking up, and pressure for greater reform increased. Soviet economists could see that the old command economy could not be repaired, and realized there was an opportunity to propose radical reforms in the Russian economy, most importantly to restructure it along the lines of Western capitalism.

The readings in this section describe the halting and often misdirected efforts to reshape the Russian economy and the mixed success of these efforts as they evolved through the 1990s. The challenge of moving from a command economy to a market-based economy was formidable. What to do first? How to provide a reasonably smooth transition from the old to something new? How to create the institutions needed so that a new market-based economy could flourish and grow? How to establish incentives to replace the previous command structure? How to create the concept of property rights? How to distribute state-owned property to its now independent citizens? The problems of making this transition were difficult to imagine.

The best we can do is give a series of snapshot views that capture the initial planning and subsequent implementation of economic reform measures. The first selection by Soviet President Gorbachev (1987) describes what had been happening to the Soviet economy over the previous decade and outlines his steps to restore the principles of socialism. His plan calls for more than economic restructuring. It calls for enlisting the support of the Russian people in reinvigorating its economic and political systems.

By 1990, the pace of changes made it clear there could be no return to the ideals of Lenin's socialism. Instead, pressure mounted rapidly to remake the economy along Western lines. A group of top experts was convened to produce a blueprint for change. That group, headed by academician S. S. Shatalin (1990), presented a list of 'fundamental rights' around which a market-based economic system would be built. The scope of these rights was breathtaking; they touched on every aspect of political and economic life.

Another group of economists began devising a transition plan, with a consensus that it should be implemented rapidly. The result was a 500-day plan that presented a detailed timetable showing what had to be done first and what would have to follow (Yavlinsky *et al.*, 1991). Again, the scope of the transition plan was breathtaking in its ambition. It required quickly building the essential economic institutions on which the new market-based economic system would rest, while at the same time minimizing the inevitable disruption this massive transition would cause.

Feige, though not the only American to become involved in transition planning, wrestled with the challenge of dividing the Soviet Union's state-owned assets among individuals and various levels of government The question was how to arrive at an appropriate distribution, one that would be 'fair' to individuals and sufficient to enable governmental units at all levels to continue functioning. The mechanics of distributing these assets are complicated, particularly because the economy had to function throughout this transition.

The difficulties to be overcome were enormous. The politics of economic reform almost guarantees that reform efforts will fail, according to Hewitt, writing in 1989. Moreover, the lessons coming out of economic restructuring in Eastern Europe were neither uniform nor encouraging (Jefferson and Petri, 1990). Thus began the development of a vast literature consisting of 'transition economics'. Reform did not go smoothly. Second-guessing was pervasive.

By the end of the 1990s, experts began to sort through the evidence to find out what could be learned from the Russian experience, what had succeeded, what had failed, and what could be done. One prominent Soviet expert is represented here, Marshall Goldman (2000). He analyzes why privatization failed, why the advice offered by the experts was flawed, and what must be done now to get the program of economic reform back on track.

The story of Russia's transition is not ended. The process will continue. Exactly what form it eventually takes remains to be seen.

'PERESTROIKA: NEW THINKING FOR OUR COUNTRY AND THE WORLD', MIKHAIL GORBACHEV

Mikhail Gorbachev, who became the leader of the Soviet Union in 1985, describes his plan for revitalizing the Soviet economy and Soviet society. The essence of his plan is captured in a single word, *perestroika*. Gorbachev begins by describing the gradual decline through the late 1970s and early 1980s in the economic system, as well as the emergence of behaviors by people – from individuals to bureaucrats and on up to the Central Committee – that were destructive to the ideals of socialism envisioned by Lenin 70 years earlier. This selection is remarkable because it represents the first open indictment of the economic, social, and moral failures of socialism. It analyzes recent developments in the Soviet economy and society that account for the slowing rate of economic growth, an inability to improve the lot of the masses, and a steady erosion of the type of society envisioned under socialism. The reforms that Gorbachev initiated with this statement and those that followed have fundamentally changed not only the character of the Russian economy, but also its political structure.

Learning Objectives

After reading and discussing this selection, students should be able to

1. Explain the meaning of 'perestroika' and 'Lenin's socialism'.
2. Describe the reasons for initiating the process of perestroika.
3. Explain the goals of perestroika.
4. Discuss the relationships between perestroika, socialism, and democracy.

Question Clusters

1. How, according to Gorbachev, can perestroika revitalize the Soviet economy and at the same time return to the ideals of Lenin's socialism?
   a. What is the meaning of perestroika? Of Lenin's socialism?
   b. What is the connection between Gorbachev's perestroika and Lenin's socialism?
   c. What led both Gorbachev and Lenin to offer their views on what must be done to protect or save 'socialism', Gorbachev in 1985, and Lenin in his 'last works'?
   d. What parallels are evident in how the Soviet leaders tried to deal with the problems afflicting socialism in the early 1920s and in the 1980s?
2. Why, in discussing the reasons for implementing perestroika, does Gorbachev refer to the 'braking mechanism'?
   a. What does he mean by the 'braking mechanism'?
   b. What does he mean by 'gross output drive' and how it contributed to the 'braking mechanism'?
   c. What accounts for the 'wage-leveling' Gorbachev describes?

    d. What is the meaning of the 'residual principal' and its relationship to braking?

3. What is the connection between the braking mechanism and the factors leading to 'a gradual erosion of the ideological and moral values of our people'?

    a. What does he mean by the 'gradual erosion'?

    b. What accounts for the pervasiveness of this erosion, permeating as it did the entire society, ranging from the average citizen to the highest levels of Soviet leadership, its Central Committee?

    c. Why did earlier attempts to correct the problems described by Gorbachev fail to succeed?

4. What is the meaning of the policy of 'restructuring', also referred to as 'renovating' society?

    a. What does he mean in saying that restructuring involves 'restoring the principle of socialism'?

    b. What does Gorbachev mean when he states, 'socialism is the living creativity of the masses'?

    c. What is the importance of ensuring that 'we need broad democratization of all aspects of society'?

5. How, according to Gorbachev, will perestroika restore the fundamental principle of socialism: 'From each according to his ability, to each according to his work'?

Discussion Suggestions

This selection and the others in this chapter can be read with profit by students in introductory courses as well as by those in intermediate micro theory courses. The selection gives contemporary students an understanding of what triggered the dramatic changes in the Soviet Union from the mid-1980s well into the early 1990s. Above all, it gives students some sense of how the enthusiasm surrounding the tremendous economic gains of the 1920s and 1930s was gradually diminished, first by the terrible costs of World War II, then by the effort to make up for their war-time losses, and finally by the waning enthusiasm for the ideology of Marxism as the older generation died off and new generations looked increasingly to the West for inspiration and hope.

    Students should be invited to compare the nature and tone of Gorbachev's statement with that of *The Communist Manifesto*. Profitable comparisons can also be made with Heilbroner's essay, 'The Triumph of Capitalism' in which he discusses the two 'realms': the political and the economic.

'MAN, FREEDOM, AND MARKET', S. SHATALIN

This statement describes the kind of political-economic system that leading economists believed the former Soviet Union should strive to achieve through the process of economic reform. Its goal was 'to move toward a market-oriented economy at the expense of the state but not at the expense of the people' (p. xi). Thus, the suggested program is designed to help realize the right of citizens to a better, more decent life.

The plan lists and elaborates eight categories of fundamental rights, including the (1) Right to Property, (2) Right of Citizens to Economic Activity, (3) Right of Citizens to Freedom of the Consumer Market and to Fair Prices, (4) Right of Citizens to Growing Incomes and Social Guarantees, (5) Right of Enterprises to Free Economic Activity, (6) Rights of the Republics to Economic Sovereignty, (7) Economic Rights of the Center, and (8) Right of Society.

Specifying the rights of the various constituent groups in the Russian economy was essential in designing a program of reform leading to a market-based economic system. Interestingly, this statement negated a comparable set of 'restrictions' on rights that made it possible for the former command economy to operate as it did.

Learning Objectives

After reading and discussing this paper, students should be able to

1. Explain the goals of the program outlined by the Shatalin Task Force.
2. Explain how the Rights are linked, particularly to the first right, that of private property.
3. Outline the challenge you see in moving to this new rights-based economic and political system.

Question Clusters

1. What does Shatalin mean by saying that the reform is motivated by 'a fundamentally new economic concept. It plans to move toward a market-oriented economy *at the expenses of the state, but not at the expense of the people*'(emphasis added)
   a. What is the ultimate goal?
   b. What are the expected effects of realizing this goal?
   c. How is this goal to be achieved?
   d. What will be required of citizens to ensure the plan's goal is realized?

2. In what sense is the right of private property central to all rights discussed in this chapter?
   a. What is the meaning of this sentence: 'By giving property back to the people, the social orientation of the economy will manifest itself.'?
   b. What problems will arise in distributing state property?
   c. How will the people's right to property be achieved?
3. What is the meaning of this statement: 'Citizens of a great power have become hostages of empty shops and enslaved by production and distribution monopolies.'?
   a. Why do people have so much money?
   b. What does the report propose as a way of enhancing the consumer market?
   c. What problems will arise in the 'transition to free prices'?
4. What is the meaning of the statement that the need for a structural rearrangement 'is not the fault of the market, but rather is due to its absence'?

Discussion Suggestions

This selection should help students to better understand the complex institutional infrastructure that undergirds our economic system. The selection also provides an interesting contrast to the effort by Milton and Rose Friedman to develop for the United States an Economic Bill of Rights in 'The Tide Is Turning'.

'THE LOGIC AND STAGES OF THE TRANSITION TO A MARKET ECONOMY', G. YAVLINSKY, AND OTHERS

Developing a plan to create an effective market economy is a formidable task and the ultimate challenge for a command economy. Here is the result: a 500 day 'big bang' approach. The complete process of transition is described, starting with a list of the high priority tasks. The Plan then describes in detail what must be done in four successive periods: 'The First 100 Days – A Program of Extraordinary Measures', 'The 100th to 250th Days: Liberalization of Prices with Austere Financial Constraints', 'The 250th to 400th Days: Market Stabilization', and 'The 400th to 500th Days: Beginning of the Upswing'. The actions that must be taken are numerous and are described in considerable detail. The process is complicated by the need to introduce a new market-based system while at the same time destroying the cold war command economy, but yet maintaining certain elements of it during the period of transition. The challenge lies in blending the two systems and ensuring that each operates at a reasonably efficient level.

Learning Objectives

After reading and discussing this selection, students should be able to

1. Explain the rationale for the 500-day plan for transition and reform of the Soviet economy.
2. Reconstruct the rationale for what is to be done in each of the plan's four stages.
3. Describe the rationale for expecting the achievement of certain benchmark goals by the end of each time period.
4. Explain the unstated assumptions behind the 500-day plan.

Question Clusters

1. What is the meaning of the Plan's statement: 'The transition from a command economy to the market economy has its own internal logic, which must be respected for this process to be successful.'?
   a. Why does this logic depend on bringing about 'radical institutional changes' and concurrently 'stabilization, primarily in the monetary and financial fields, and in the sphere of price setting'?
   b. What conflicts are apparent in making this transition?
2. Why does the restructuring program have to be implemented so quickly, as indicated by the statement: 'No time can be lost'?
   a. What reasons are given for the quick 500-day implementation of the plan?
   b. Why is it so important to deal immediately with the monetary system'?
3. How does the quick 500-day implementation schedule square with this statement: 'The proposed outlines of the reform and the sequence of steps to be taken reflect an understanding of the fact that the transition to a market economy . . . is a relatively long process involving radical structural reorganization of the national economy and dramatic changes in the attitudes and behavior of millions of people.'?
   a. How can these two statements be reconciled?
   b. How do these statements indicate which changes should receive highest priority?
4. What rationale is offered for allowing each of the republics to develop their own programs of reform?
   a. What areas of reform are delegated to the republics?
   b. What areas of reform are reserved for the nation as a whole?

   c. What would seem to be likely conflicts between reform at the republic
      level versus the national level?
5. What do you think of the feasibility of successfully implementing this 500-
   day plan? If it can't be fully implemented, what are the alternatives?

Discussion Suggestions

Students should be expected to come away with two major ideas. One is the
fact that the American economy operates as it does based on institutions and
practices that have evolved over long periods of time and that we often take
for granted. The other is the monumental challenge faced by the Soviet people
in creating a whole network of new institutions in a country where there has
been no recognized value for individual effort and creativity.

'A MESSAGE TO GORBACHEV: REDISTRIBUTE THE WEALTH', EDGAR L. FEIGE

Feige's proposal for redistributing the assets of the Soviet Union after its
collapse in the early 1990s indicates the complexity of transferring to the
people the assets and wealth of a centralized, planned economy. Such a
transfer was essential in developing a new economic system that would
approximate capitalism by allowing individuals to make their own decisions
about how best to allocate their share of the formerly publicly-held wealth.
Feige presents a plan for making this transfer equitably and efficiently.

Learning Objectives

After reading and discussing the Feige paper, students should be able to

1. Explain how the plan would help achieve the goals of perestroika.
2. Describe what Feige means by a 'share economy' and what this means for
   how the shares would be divided.
3. Explain what mechanisms are required to facilitate this shift to a 'share
   economy'.
4. Discuss the realism of the Feige plan for effecting this redistribution of
   wealth from the state to its individual citizens.

Question Clusters

1. What, according to Feige, would constitute a fair distribution of Soviet
   wealth from the state to individual members of that state?

   a. What is the meaning of the term 'social privatization' as Feige uses it?

   b. How is the concept of 'social privatization' related to the concepts of perestroika and glasnost?

   c. What advantages does the 'social privatization' approach have for the redistribution process?

2. What does Feige mean by a 'share economy', and how is it related to 'social privatization'?

   a. What do these two terms mean?

   b. What kinds of behavioral effects would be produced by dividing up the state's assets among the different groups of recipients?

3. How would what Feige labels as 'critical obstacles' undercut a successful move toward a share economy?

   a. What is the meaning and significance of the 'ruble overhang'?

   b. What is the meaning and significance of 'budget deficits'?

   c. What is the meaning and significance of 'transitional unemployment'?

   d. What must be done to counter these obstacles?

4. What is the role of 'citizen shares' in Feige's scheme?

   a. What is the meaning of the 'bundling' of these shares?

   b. How would these shares provide a basis for central government revenue needs?

   c. What impact would the existence of these shares have on the 'ruble overhang'?

   d. What other benefits does Feige see emerging from citizen shares?

   e. What obstacles may obstruct the success of the share economy?

5. If Feige's redistribution were accomplished, is there any way to estimate how wealth might be distributed in the Soviet Union?

Discussion Suggestions

What should be apparent to students but may still need to be emphasized is the absence of institutions of the kind already in place in the US that would be needed to facilitate the massive transfer of assets from the Soviet state to its citizens. It would be instructive to ask students to construct a list of these institutions that we take for granted in the US economy. Students should also be asked to think about how successful the redistribution of assets might be if the Feige plan were implemented.

'ECONOMIC REFORM IN THE USSR, EASTERN EUROPE AND CHINA: THE POLITICS OF ECONOMICS', E. A. HEWITT

Writing at the beginning of the process of economic transition in the USSR, Hewitt focuses on the obstacles to successful economic reform in the former Communist state. Reviewing past reform efforts, he finds these efforts have produced little apparent effect. Central to understanding why reforms fail is that politicians, not economists, govern the process. Hewitt outlines three important political reasons why reforms fail. But he also observes that economists are not well equipped to devise strategies for transition. Though they recognize the importance of the various stages in the transition process, economists have not constructed a clear transition strategy. Nor are they able to predict where the process might lead. Until political leaders are willing to compromise on their equity goals, little progress can be achieved. In short, this selection highlights how political forces are likely to shape the reform process. Hewitt's paper is the first of many that raise questions about the likely success of efforts to reform the Soviet economy.

Learning Objectives

After reading and discussing this selection, students should be able to

1. Clarify the links between political leaders and economists in the Russian economy.
2. Describe why economic reform programs have not worked.
3. Explain what is needed for a successful program of economic reform.

Question Clusters

1. What, according to Hewitt, is the effect of ignoring 'some of the most elementary principles of economics' in designing and implementing programs of economic reform?
   a. What are these 'some of these most elementary principles'?
   b. Why are these principles ignored?
   c. Why is it that the 'politicians, not economists, govern the entire process [of economic reform]'?
   d. What differentiates the role of economists and politicians in command economies versus those in market economies in promoting economic reforms?

e. What does Hewitt mean and of what relevance is his statement that in the West 'most economic policy is considered too important to be left solely to economists'?
2. Why must economists also be held responsible for the difficulties of current economic reform efforts?
   a. Why are economists, according to Hewitt, ill-equipped to devise strategies for economic transition?
   b. Why haven't economists developed a method of analyzing issues in economic reform?
   c. What particular problems should their methods of analysis address?
   d. How should the blame for lack of a theory of transition be shared between Eastern and Western economists?
3. What does Hewitt mean when he states, 'Political leaders in centrally planned economies aspire to achieve efficiencies characteristic of capitalism, while remaining true to the equity goals that form the rationale for the party's management of the economy'?
   a. What is the significance of this observation?
   b. Why do these leaders continue to hold this view?

Discussion Suggestions

This paper examines the extent to which economics and politics are intertwined, a fact of life that students need to appreciate earlier rather than later in their studies. Students should be encouraged to consider why economists are better at analyzing pieces of a system rather than the system as a whole. It might be appropriate to introduce the Keynes quote from *The General Theory* about the power of ideas and their eventual triumph over the power of vested interests. Thus, while politicians may control the transition process, it is the triumph of the ideas of economic and political freedom that have forced them to deal with the difficulties of the transition process.

'FROM MARX TO MARKETS', GARY H. JEFFERSON AND PETER A. PETRI

The authors of this collection of short papers describe the restructuring of Easter Europe as 'the great economic experiment of our time'. They hasten to add that 'there is still no successful example of the transformation of a command system into a market economy' (p. 4). Four of the six statements are the focus of attention in this module. Jefferson and Petri set the stage by describing some of the changes in Eastern Europe economics and their efforts at market reform. Paul Mauer, in describing the situation in Hungary, argues that the challenge lies in strengthening markets and private control. In the case of Poland, Stanislaw Wellisz advocates 'shock therapy' to resolve political conflict and economic mismanagement. Lawrence Summers suggests that though the Soviet Union's problems are severe, the new republics may be best equipped to develop their own versions of market reform.

This reading reveals that there is no single path to economic reform, and that the goals of reform and the means of achieving them rest heavily on the specific circumstances of each country. This is aside from disputes among reformers within each country about the most effective means of economic reform. The question clusters focus in part on differences among the three countries, and in part on different dimensions of reform. Taken together, the authors indicate that the experience with recent reform efforts elsewhere needs to be drawn upon in designing a new reform program for Russia.

Learning Objectives

After reading and discussing this selection, students should be able to

1. Describe the big issues that must be resolved in the transition to a market-oriented economy.
2. Outline the appropriate timing of the critical steps in economic reform.
3. Clarify why the transition process differs so substantially from one country to another.
4. Define the meaning of privatization and the questions it poses for reformers.
5. Outline their understanding of the transition process.

Question Clusters

1. Regarding the quest for economic reform, what makes the situations in Poland and Hungary so different from each other and from the Soviet Union?
2. How do the problems of privatization compare in Hungary, Poland, and the Soviet Union?
3. What are the challenges in allowing the price system to reflect supply and demand conditions?
4. What accounts for differences in the views of the authors regarding which reforms must come first and in what sequence the others must follow?
5. To what extent do political conditions influence these analyses of the possibilities for reform, in Hungary, Poland, and the Soviet Union?

Discussion Suggestions

Every effort should be made to allow students to understand the differences among countries in their transition processes and how these differences reflect the particular circumstances surrounding the development and implementation of the reform process. There is no one way.

'REPRIVATIZING RUSSIA', MARSHALL GOLDMAN

Marshall Goldman, a long-time student of the Soviet Union, has closely followed Russia's transition to a market economy. He has argued that many of the reforms urged by Western economists were too simplistic because they failed to recognize the incentives these reforms would create and what effects these incentives would have in shaping a new market economy in Russia. Goldman also argues that privatization failed. It created a new set of problems that undermined the very market economy that privatization sought to create. He concludes by offering recommendations designed to cope with these new problems.

This reading selection provides an assessment of the outcome of Russia's decade-long effort to create a market system. What it makes clear is the important role of economic institutions in providing a structure within which individuals and firms can pursue their own interests. At the same time, these institutions must be powerful enough to counteract the always present incentives on the part of individuals and firms to capture gains that would not be available in a competitive market economy.

Learning Objectives

After reading and discussing the 'privatization' article, students should be able to

1. Describe the meaning of privatization and explain how it was accomplished.
2. Explain why privatization failed in Russia but succeeded in other countries.
3. Explain the new incentives created by privatization and the results it produced.
4. Explain what can be done to offset these incentives and thereby help to realize the goals of privatization.

Question Clusters

1. Why, according to Goldman, did privatization fail?
   a. What assumptions were made by the experts about people's responses to the incentives created by privatization?
   b. In what sense were these assumptions incorrect?
   c. What conditions were required, according to Goldman, for privatization to succeed?
   d. To what extent were these conditions met?
   e. What distinguished the privatization programs of other countries and accounted for their success?
2. How did the economic and political condition of Russia in this period contribute to the failure of privatization?
   a. What role was played by the absence of a market infrastructure?
   b. What role was played by government corruption, and what contributed to that corruption?
3. What, according to Goldman, can be done to remedy the absence of 'a workable market infrastructure' that caused privatization to fail?
   a. How useful would it be to import the laws and regulations that have proved to be successful in other nations?
   b. What 'must be done to redress some of the privatization abuses of the past'?
   c. Why is Goldman optimistic that his proposals will be effective in offsetting the adverse effects of privatization?

Discussion Suggestions

This reading selection helps students see the outcome of Russia's decade-long effort to create a market system. At a minimum, it should be used in conjunction with the Jefferson–Petri selection.

OVERVIEW

These seven snapshots of the economic transition from what was the Soviet Union to what is now Russia offer a dramatic picture of the unprecedented changes that occurred in less than two decades. The big question that for years will occupy the minds of those with an interest in the transition is: Could it have been done better and more smoothly? The answers are ambiguous, as revealed by the following questions:

1. Why did Gorbachev's vision for a return to Lenin's socialism fail? Was the failure rooted in economics, politics, or both?
2. Why was the statement of fundamental rights by the Shatalin group too drastic to initiate all at once?
3. Why was the Yavlinsky 500-day plan hopelessly optimistic? In what sense?
4. Was the Feige plan for redistributing income and wealth also hopelessly optimistic? Why? In what sense?
5. Why wasn't more attention paid by the Russian leaders and by Russian economists to the warnings of Hewitt and to the experience of other countries described by Jefferson and Petri?
6. To what extent does the evolution of the transition reflect the customs and traditions and vested interests that had developed under the former political-economic situation, that is, the combination of a dictatorship and command economy?
7. How can the lessons that emerge thus far from the Russian transition be codified?
8. How does a society make amends for the mistakes of the past as they are revealed by Goldman? For example, can the inequitable distribution of income and wealth that resulted from privatization be rectified?

PART THREE

Discussing Macroeconomics

9. Monetary Policy

Two characteristics that separate those people who have studied economics from those who have not are an understanding of the limits of monetary policy and an appreciation of the importance of good monetary policy. Growing up in the Greenspan era, today's students take low inflation for granted. They have not experienced directly the costs associated with living in high inflation times.

At the same time, the media bombard us with suggestions that we should expect more from monetary policy than we get. Some criticize Federal Reserve decisions to raise interest rates when inflation threatens because they believe it will hamper growth and job creation. Others argue that the Federal Reserve should be more responsive to the electorate.

The business sections of our media are an exception. They anticipate and analyze Federal Reserve policy announcements as if they were the key to future economic performance. But why? Those with a little knowledge know that the Fed has direct influence only on the rate that one bank charges another for the overnight lending of funds.

In this chapter, we offer six works that allow students to explore monetary policy from various vantage points. *Maestro* is Bob Woodward's look at the Federal Reserve from the beginning of the Greenspan years until 2001. *Maestro* looks at monetary policy as the result of a highly complex interplay between politics and economics.

We include three articles that investigate how monetary policy should be conducted. The article by William van Lear provides an overview of the 'rules versus discretion' policy debate. It explains the compromises required in committing to conduct policy according to a verifiable plan while reserving the right to react to individual situations as they demand. The first article by John Taylor examines practical problems faced by a central bank that has decided to follow a policy rule. It argues that policy rules have value even when it does not make sense to follow them verbatim. The article by Laurence Meyer makes the case for a dual mandate for monetary policy when the alternative is exclusive commitment to maintaining a particular inflation level.

The second article by John Taylor outlines the approach to monetary policy that gave rise to the now well-known 'Taylor rule'. Along the way, he explains current thinking about the channels through which changes in monetary policy affect output, inflation, and employment. Finally, we include

Robert Lucas' Nobel lecture on monetary neutrality in which he explains why changes in the growth rate of money have no real effects in the long-run, but in the short-run stimulate economic activity.

MAESTRO: GREENSPAN'S FED AND THE AMERICAN BOOM, BOB WOODWARD

On August 3, 1987, the United States Senate confirmed Alan Greenspan as chairman of the Federal Reserve. As of August 2004, Greenspan had been Fed chair for 17 years and had directed monetary policy under three republican presidents and one democrat. One thread of *Maestro* provides a chronology of the Greenspan Fed that focuses on the financial crises and important changes in monetary policy. Another thread studies Greenspan himself – his leadership style, his approach to his work, his relationships with presidents and co-workers, and the public persona he created for himself. Finally, Woodward explains the politics of monetary policy. He describes the pressures placed by cabinet members and Congresspersons on the policy makers and on Greenspan himself and explains how Greenspan responded to those pressures.

The book begins with the transition period between Paul Volcker and Alan Greenspan. Some in the Reagan administration favored replacing Volcker with Greenspan because they thought he would be a better 'team-player'. After providing some background on Greenspan himself, Woodwards's first chapter focuses on the Black Monday stock-price crash that provided the first real test of Greenspan's leadership. It explains how Greenspan arrived at the decision to make a public statement affirming the Fed's 'readiness to serve as source of liquidity'(p. 40). It also describes the behind-the-scenes lobbying of E. Gerald Corrigan, president of the New York Fed, to exhort institutions to make their scheduled payments and avoid financial gridlock.

Chapters 2 and 3 cover the period of late 1988-1989, when the Fed began raising interest rates to cool the economy and offset threatened inflation. The decision, coming in the final weeks of the presidential campaign, produced an angry response from James Baker, former Treasury Secretary and manager of the Bush campaign. After the election, the Bush budget director, Richard Darman, publicly stated that Fed policy was too tight and intimated that any recession would be the fault of the Fed. Woodward describes Greenspan's explosive reaction and his suggestion that such criticism might force the Fed to raise interest rates in order to prove its independence.

Chapter 4 provides the first insights to Greenspan's views on federal deficits. Greenspan favored the 1990 agreement between Congress and the Bush Administration that would lower the deficit by $500 billion over five years. Woodward explains how Greenspan convinced the Federal Open

Market Committee to approve an 'asymmetric directive' toward lowering interest rates, but to wait until the budget agreement passed to actually lower rates. He did so on October 29. The chapter also explains the roles played by Greenspan and Corrigan during the Latin American debt crisis, which threatened balance sheets of many large US banks.

The foci of Chapter 5 are Fed policy during the recession of 1991 and Bush's decision to reappoint Greenspan as Fed chair. During 1991, Woodward reports that Greenspan actively campaigned for lower rates, much to the consternation of some Fed Bank presidents and members of the Board of Governors who wanted a more cautious approach and more consultation on policy decisions. Woodward reveals that some thought Greenspan had made a deal: lower rates for reappointment. By the end of 1991, it was clear that the easing was warranted. Despite Greenspan's lowering of the fed funds rate from 7 to 4 percent during the year, the economy remained in trouble.

Chapter 6 describes the transition from the Bush to the Clinton presidency. Woodward reports that Greenspan 'hoped Bush would win reelection' (p. 88). But at the F.O.M.C. meeting on October 6, 1992, Greenspan recommended against further rate decreases and managed to gain agreement for the decision by all, including the Bush appointees. After his election, Clinton invited Greenspan to Little Rock. Woodward reports that Greenspan was quite taken with the new president, finding him focused, engaged, and receptive to Greenspan's views on the economic benefits of lower deficits. Woodward reports that Greenspan left the meeting wondering whether Clinton's receptivity had been 'some kind of show' (p. 97). Clinton left the meeting convinced that he could do business with Greenspan.

Chapters 7 through 12 cover the years of the Clinton Administration. Woodward develops several themes. He explains how Greenspan convinced Clinton to undertake deficit reduction and later credited Clinton with making possible the low interest rates of the 1990s. Woodward argues that Greenspan was one of the first economists to identify evidence in the data of new economic forces at work. Greenspan was first puzzled by the simultaneous rise in business profits and fall in official measurements in productivity. He urged government statisticians to investigate disaggregated data and discovered a source of downward bias to productivity statistics. Woodward also describes the 'soft landing' that Greenspan's Fed engineered in the mid-1990s by raising interest rates just enough to head off inflation. Woodward suggests that by timing the rate increases just right, Greenspan's Fed avoided a recession.

Woodward writes extensively about Greenspan's leadership style. Greenspan would talk at length with board members, lobby them hard for his policy positions, and encourage them to support directives that left the timing of policy actions to Greenspan himself. In this way, Greenspan gathered responsibility for policy to himself. Alan Blinder, appointed vice chair of the Fed in 1994, chafed at what he perceived as Greenspan's concentration of power, and did not seek reappointment.

In the remaining chapters, Woodward talks about the response of the Fed to the Asian financial crisis and the transition between the Clinton and Bush administrations. Woodward describes behind-the-scene efforts by William McDonough, president of the New York Fed, to find either a buyer or funding source for Long-Term Capital Management after the hedge fund incurred large losses connected to the Asian crisis. In 2000, Clinton again reappointed Greenspan as chair and suggested that no one would blame Greenspan '...for wanting to go out now on top' (p. 222). Greenspan said 'Oh no, this is the greatest job in the world. It's like eating peanuts. You keep doing it, keep doing it, and you never get tired' (p. 222).

The epilogue of the Touchstone edition to *Maestro* covers the early period of George W. Bush's administration until September 11, 2001. Woodward explains Greenspan's decision to back the first Bush tax cut, a decision that some in government criticized and others thought might be politically motivated. The reader has the sense in the end that Greenspan himself has become an American institution. Presidents come and go – Greenspan remains constant.

Learning Objectives

After reading and discussing *Maestro*, students will be able to

1. Explain why it is sometimes necessary during a crisis for the Federal Reserve to provide liquidity to financial markets.
2. Discuss whether it is appropriate for Fed personnel to pressure financial institutions to make payments during financial crises.
3. Explain what a 'soft landing' is and how Greenspan engineered a soft landing during the mid-1990s.
4. Describe the kinds of political pressure faced by policymakers at the Fed.
5. Decide whether or not Alan Greenspan did a good job of resisting political pressure.
6. Make the case that Alan Greenspan is an effective Federal Reserve chair.
7. Decide whether it has been good or bad for monetary policy that Alan Greenspan has, in large measure, assumed control of policy decisions.
8. Explain why Greenspan thinks it is important for monetary policy makers to keep an eye on stock prices.

Discussion Questions

1. Why does Woodward characterize Greenspan as someone who is 'conducting the orchestra but does not play an instrument'?
   a. Does Woodward believe that Greenspan has no direct way to affect the 'music' of the US economy?
   b. Who are the instrumentalists that Greenspan conducts and why would they follow the lead of 'conductor' Greenspan?
2. According to Woodward, how important a role did the Fed play in avoiding an economic catastrophe:
   a. After the 'Black Monday' fall of stock prices on October 19, 1987?
   b. After the Asian financial crisis in 1997-1998?
   c. According to Woodward, was it appropriate for Gerald Corrigan and William McDonough to maneuver behind the scenes as they did?
3. According to Woodward, is the Fed under Greenspan independent of political pressures?
   a. What are the sources of political pressures that have faced and continue to face the Greenspan Fed?
   b. What is the evidence for and against the proposition that the Fed operates independently of these pressures?
4. According to Woodward, is Greenspan
   a. An astute economist?
   b. An able politician?
   c. A good leader?
5. In your own view, how powerful is Alan Greenspan and how important is he to our economy?

Discussion Suggestions

Students find *Maestro* to be a surprisingly easy read and more interesting than they expected. We typically reserve only a single 75 minute class for discussion of *Maestro* and find that students are able to develop good answers to the above questions with that amount of time. Students find particularly interesting the nexus between monetary policy and politics. Viewed academically, monetary policy may seem a dry subject. However, on the ground, its implementation involves political maneuvering, passionate bargaining, and all the other trappings of a high-stakes game. A good follow-up exercise to discussing Maestro is to consider what has happened since the book's end. We sometimes ask students to search for evidence about Greenspan's current views and his current relationship with the administration. The fact that he did not support the second Bush tax cut but did support the first provides further opportunity for discussion and lots of teachable moments.

'A REVIEW OF THE RULES VERSUS DISCRETION DEBATE IN MONETARY POLICY', WILLIAM VAN LEAR

William van Lear reviews the cases for and against monetary policy rules and concludes that history casts doubt on the efficacy of rules-based monetary policy. He begins by acknowledging a consensus among economists that policy discretion creates instability and a bias towards inflation. Those who favor a rule believe that the Fed cannot stimulate the economy in the long run, and that Fed stimulus leads to the self-fulfilling expectation of higher inflation. Rules proponents also believe that commitment to a rule better protects the Fed against pressure from office holders who want high employment in the period immediately preceding elections.

Those who oppose rules and favor discretion challenge rules on both theoretical and empirical grounds. Rule opponents doubt the existence of a natural rate of unemployment and think that the Fed may face an eventual and inevitable balance of unemployment and inflation. They doubt that the Fed could estimate the natural rate accurately, even if there were one. They challenge the hypothesis made by rules proponents that agents have rational expectations about future inflation. And they believe that the Fed must exercise discretion to offset the many shocks to the money supply that occur within the banking sector.

After reviewing the cases for rules and discretion, van Lear defends his own view that '...heterodox theory and historical experience cast doubt on the efficacy of a rules-based monetary policy'. In defending his conclusion, he challenges the neo-classical view of how inflation is generated.

Learning Objectives

After reading and discussing van Lear's article, students should be able to

1. State and explain the case for monetary policy rules.
2. State and explain the case against monetary policy rules.
3. Connect the case for or against rules with beliefs about the Phillips curve, the mechanisms through which inflation is generated, and other features of macro models.
4. Explain what van Lear means by 'heterodox theory'.
5. Decide whether they favor monetary policy rules or monetary policy discretion.

Question Clusters

1. What, according to van Lear, are the most important points in the case for monetary policy rules?
   a. What does van Lear mean by a monetary policy rule?
   b. What, according to van Lear, is the connection between the shape of the long-run Phillips curve and the case for rules?
   c. Why, according to van Lear, is inflation targeting an example of a monetary policy rule?
   d. How, according to van Lear, does a monetary policy rule insulate a central bank from political pressure?
2. What, according to van Lear, are the most important points in the case for monetary policy discretion?
   a. What does van Lear mean by policy discretion?
   b. How does van Lear connect the shape of the long-run Phillips curve and the case for discretion?
   c. What connection does van Lear make between the need for policy discretion and the fact that money growth depends on private sector credit demand?
3. Why does van Lear think the case for discretion is stronger than the case for rules?
   a. What does van Lear mean by heterodox policy?
   b. Does van Lear's case for discretion amount to more than a case against rules?
   c. How does van Lear's view of how the macroeconomy works compare with the view presented in this course? What are the similarities? The differences?
   d. Should the Fed commit to a monetary policy rule or should it exercise discretion? Why?

Discussion Suggestions

Discussion of the article by van Lear provides students with an opportunity to review the case for commitment to a rule in the context of an article that is comprehensive and not technical. Whatever their own views, all should benefit from dealing with van Lear's challenge to a growing consensus among theoretical economists that rules are superior. Students who favor rules will benefit by arguing against van Lear's position. Students who favor discretion will benefit by investigating which parts of van Lear's argument they find most compelling. The article provides instructors with a valuable opportunity to have students connect their policy prescriptions to their beliefs about how the macroeconomy works.

'THE MONETARY TRANSMISSION MECHANISM: AN EMPIRICAL FRAMEWORK', JOHN B. TAYLOR

In this article, prepared for a symposium on the monetary transmission mechanism, John Taylor outlines the approach which gave rise to the 'Taylor rule'. First, Taylor explains that his approach is distinguished by its focus on financial market prices. Short-term and long-term interest rates and the exchange rate are the key prices through which changes in monetary policy are transmitted to real economic activity and to inflation. A focus on prices is better than a focus on the quantity of money because of apparent instability in money demand functions that have probably resulted due to changes in financial technology and regulations.

Taylor next explains that the distinction between nominal and real interest rates is crucial for understanding the transmission mechanism. Taylor's approach assumes that expectations are rational, but that wages and prices are slow to change so that a rational agent expects slow adjustment of inflation to shocks. Thus, changes in monetary policy can cause changes in real interest rates. Taylor emphasizes that a complete description of the mechanism must include a reaction function that explains how the monetary policy authority reacts to changes in economic conditions.

Taylor believes that exchange rate changes are an important part of the transmission mechanism. An increase in domestic interest rates with no change in foreign interest rates causes an appreciation of the domestic currency and a subsequent decrease in exports and increase in imports as buyers throughout the world respond to the implied changes in the relative prices of domestic and imported goods. Taylor displays a chart that shows that the exchange value of the dollar closely tracked the difference between US and foreign interest rates between 1973 and 1995.

What are the policy implications of the mechanism that Taylor presents? Taylor reasons that flexible exchange rates are better than fixed rates because flexible rates imply lower variability in real output and inflation. He also explains the implications of his earlier research on policy rules: a rule whereby the short-term interest rate responds partly to inflation and partly to real GDP does a good job of stabilizing the economy, as well as a good job of explaining how the Federal Reserve has set short-term interest rates.

Taylor continues his analysis by considering whether the transmission mechanism has changed in recent years. His answer is 'slightly' for Germany and Japan, and 'more so' for the United States. In general, his analysis suggests that real output is now less responsive to a given change in monetary policy than it was in the 1970s. Taylor next lists and rebuts several criticisms that other scholars have made of his views on the transmission mechanism. In particular, he argues that there is a substantial body of evidence that shows that changes in real interest rates cause real economic effects despite the contrary view of some.

Taylor concludes his discussion of the transmission mechanism by comparing current views with those that emerged from Milton Friedman's framework for analyzing monetary policy in 1970. Taylor believes that much progress has been made. The current framework is international in its perspective. It uses rational expectations to implement the distinction between nominal and real interest rates. It incorporates formal models of sticky prices to explain how changes in nominal demand are split between changes in output and inflation. It is essentially empirical and thus invaluable for policy applications. Finally, Taylor acknowledges that while much has been done, much more needs to be done; he briefly suggests how future research might be directed.

Learning Objectives

After reading and discussing the Taylor article on the transmission mechanism, students should be able to

1. Define a transmission mechanism.
2. Explain what Taylor means when he says that the monetary transmission mechanism focuses on financial market prices rather than quantities.
3. Explain what Taylor means when he says that his framework is empirical and not merely theoretical.
4. Explain the connection in Taylor's mechanism between the real rate of interest and rational expectations.
5. Explain the role of exchange rates in Taylor's mechanism.
6. Interpret what Taylor's critics have to say and decide how well Taylor answers them.

Question Clusters

1. What, according to Taylor, is the mechanism by which changes in monetary policy are transmitted to output and inflation?
   a. What is meant by a monetary transmission mechanism?
   b. What does Taylor mean when he says that his monetary transmission mechanism focuses on financial market prices?
   c. Why, according to Taylor, are exchange rates part of the transmission mechanism?
   d. What does Taylor mean when he says, 'The relationship between real interest rates and nominal interest rates is guided by two key

assumptions that underlie most financial market price models: rational expectations and rigidities of wages and goods prices'?

2. What does Taylor mean by a 'reaction function'? Why is a reaction function part of the framework for analyzing the monetary transmission mechanism?

   a. What does Taylor mean by an 'optimal monetary policy rule'?

3. According to Taylor, has the monetary transmission mechanism changed in recent years?

   a. What changes in financial markets might lead one to suspect a change in the mechanism?

   b. How does Taylor use Figure 2 to answer the question?

4. Which of the criticisms of the Taylor transmission mechanism seem most important?

   a. How well does Taylor responds to these criticisms?

   b. Is Taylor's mechanism an improvement on the framework for policy analysis offered by Milton Friedman in 1970?

Discussion Suggestions

Taylor's article describing the monetary transmission mechanism can be profitably read and discussed by principles students. Indeed, Taylor himself has argued (Taylor, 2000) that monetary policy is the proper focus for the macro content of the principles course. Reading and discussing the article would certainly help students better understand discussions of monetary policy and announcements of policy changes that appear in the media. The article also provides a good springboard for consideration of whether the monetary authority should preserve discretion or commit to a rule. Depending on where the article appears in the principles course, the instructor may need to supply students with a glossary of terms such as rational expectations, real interest rates, long-term interest rates, bi-lateral capital flows, and the term structure. However, a student who understands these concepts only at an intuitive level can still obtain the learning objectives listed above.

For an intermediate student, the article provides a very nice supplement to the monetary policy section of the course. Students will benefit from comparing Taylor's views on the monetary transmission mechanism with the explanations from their text. They will also benefit from considering the meaning and importance of the fact that Taylor's framework is empirical. And they will benefit from considering criticisms of the mainstream view and discussing how well Taylor answers them.

'INFLATION TARGETS AND INFLATION TARGETING', LAURENCE H. MEYER

Meyer begins by acknowledging that there is widespread agreement that a low and stable rate of inflation should be an objective of monetary policy. Other issues are less settled. Should monetary policy have other objectives? If so, should the inflation objective take priority? Should policy objectives be explicitly stated? If policy objectives are explicit, what statistics should be used to define them and at what levels should they be set? In this article, Mayer argues for a dual mandate which includes as its primary objective low and stable inflation, and as a secondary objective a reduction of variability of output relative to potential output. He argues for an explicit inflation target of 2 percent expressed in terms of the CPI, and for no explicit target associated with the output stability objective.

Meyer tracks the evolution of policy objectives in the United States and explains differences in stated policy objectives for the US and for inflation-targeting regimes such as New Zealand. He then makes a four-point case for a dual mandate. One plank in his platform is that macro theory shows that monetary policy can only hit an inflation target in the long run but that it can help stabilize output in the short run. A second is that society wants both inflation and output stability. A third is that a hierarchical mandate provides the central bank with needed flexibility in the conduct of monetary policy. Meyer points out that the Taylor rule describing well how the Federal Reserve has set short-run interest rates during recent years reflects the dual mandate because it shows short-run interest rates rising when inflation rises above its target and when the output gap is positive. Finally, Meyer argues that a dual mandate makes for a more credible and transparent monetary policy than the alternative practice of publicly adhering to inflation targeting while privately seeking to stabilize output.

Meyer closes by turning his attention to practical considerations. He explains why he favors a two percent inflation target rather than price level stability. He explains the advantages of making the inflation target explicit and public and states it in terms of a target rate rather than a range. He argues that it would be politically infeasible to state a target for the unemployment rate since the Federal Reserve would then occasionally have to say that unemployment needed to increase. He concludes by suggesting that adopting an explicit inflation target would provide some assurance of continuity when the leadership of the Federal Reserve changes.

Learning Objectives

After reading and discussing Meyer's article, students should be able to

1. Define dual mandate, inflation targeting, policy transparency, policy credibility, loss function, and Taylor rule.
2. Explain why Meyer believes that the US monetary policy should be guided by a dual mandate.
3. Explain why Meyer believes that the US should set an explicit target rate of inflation but not for the unemployment rate.
4. Use the loss function and Taylor rules to illustrate how US monetary policy follows a dual mandate.

Question Clusters

1. What, according to Meyer, are the important components of the case for a dual mandate for monetary policy?
   a. What does Meyer mean by a 'dual mandate'?
   b. How does Meyer use equation (1) to represent a dual mandate?
   c. Why, according to Meyer, is there sometimes a tradeoff between inflation stability and output stability?
   d. How does the Taylor rule provide a useful characterization of a dual mandate?
2. Why does Meyer believe it would be a good idea for the Federal Reserve to set an explicit target for the inflation rate?
   a. Why would such a target improve the 'transparency' of monetary policy?
   b. What does Meyer mean by transparency?
   c. Why does Meyer believe that transparency is a good thing?
   d. Does Meyer believe that setting an explicit inflation target is compatible with a dual mandate?
3. What, according to Meyer, are the most important practical problems associated with setting an explicit inflation target?
4. Are you convinced by Meyer's arguments?
   a. Should the US retain a dual mandate or should it adopt the single mandate of price stability?
   b. Should the Fed set an explicit target for the inflation rate or should it simply commit to the general principle of price stability?

Discussion Suggestions

The Meyer article permits students to discuss policy while considering the point of view and practical issues confronted by a member of the Federal Reserve Board of Governors. Meyer's arguments are clear and not technically demanding, thus both principles- and intermediate-level students can profitably discuss the article. Students find it interesting to explain Meyer's argument for the dual mandate and to consider whether the US would be better off adopting pure inflation targeting.

Instructors should alert students to a pesky typo in the article. On page 7, Meyer says that $a=0$ is the pure inflation targeting case. Clearly, he means that $a=1$ is the pure inflation targeting case.

'DISCRETION VERSUS POLICY RULES IN PRACTICE', JOHN B. TAYLOR

In this now famous paper, John Taylor shows that a simple policy rule accurately explains the shape of time line for the federal funds rate between 1987 and 1992. To follow the Taylor rule, the Fed would increase the interest rate when output or inflation rises above their long-run target values. When inflation rises, the rule requires the Fed to raise the interest rate by more than the increase in inflation so that the inflation-adjusted federal funds rate rises.

After explaining the rule, Taylor discusses the practical problems that policy makers face as they make a transition from discretionary policy to a rule, or from one rule to another. At the start of the transition, people will spend some time watching to determine whether the Fed is committed to the new rule. Economic rigidities such as contracts may slow response to the new rule and lengthen the transition.

Taylor argues that while blindly following a simple rule is not practical, a policy rule has practical value. He suggests that target values for the federal funds rate implied by the Taylor rule along with other input could be considered by the F.O.M.C. He also suggests that policy makers might think of the rule as guiding principles rather than prescriptive ones.

Taylor concludes the article with two case studies. In the first, he explains why mechanically following a Taylor rule would not have been a good response to the oil price shock associated with the first Gulf War. The rule does not distinguish permanent from temporary increases in the price level. Since there was substantial evidence that the oil price shock would have only a temporary effect on prices, it made sense for the Fed to raise the federal funds rate by less than the amount the Taylor rule would call for .

Taylor explains that when long-term interest rates increase, policy makers must decide whether the increases are due to expected inflation or to increases in the real rate. In the first case, the Fed would raise the federal funds rate; in the second, it might not. Such a dilemma occurred in early 1990 when long-term interest rates rose sharply. Since there was evidence that the higher rates were due to expectations of higher capital demand associated with the reunification of Germany, the Fed decided not to raise the federal funds rate.

Learning Objectives

After reading and discussing Taylor's article, students should be able to

1. Explain the difference between commitment to a policy rule and the use of policy discretion.
2. Use the Taylor rule to determine situations in which the Fed should lower the federal funds rate and others in which it should raise the rate.
3. Explain why Taylor believes that the Taylor rule does a good job of explaining actual monetary policy.
4. Question the claim that the Taylor rule provides a useful guide for policy.
5. Explain why the two case studies provide evidence that the Fed should not mechanically follow the Taylor rule.

Question Clusters

1. Why, according to Taylor, does the Taylor rule given in equation (1) provide a useful guide for monetary policy?
   a. What, according to Taylor, are the general benefits of following a policy rule?
   b. Does the Taylor rule make sensible prescriptions for raising and lowering the federal funds rate?
   c. Why, according to Taylor, should policy makers not follow the Taylor rule automatically?
   d. How, according to Taylor, should the F.O.M.C. use the Taylor rule?
2. What, according to Taylor, is the difference between policy discretion and using the Taylor rule as a guide to policy?
   a. What does Taylor mean by discretion?
   b. How does discretion differ from a rule?
   c. Why does Taylor believe that policy makers should not follow a rule in a mechanical way?
   d. Are the policy decisions described in the two case studies examples of discretion or flexible use of a rule? Why?
3. Is Taylor correct or incorrect in arguing that there is a role for policy rules '...in a world where simple algebraic formulations of such rules cannot and should not be mechanically followed by policymakers.'? Why?

Discussion Suggestions

The article provides an excellent opportunity for students to discuss how often abstract academic research can affect economic practice. In our view, the line between discretion and flexible use of policy rules is not at all clear. Discussing this article should be instructive for students and teachers alike.

'NOBEL LECTURE: MONETARY NEUTRALITY', ROBERT E. LUCAS, JR.

Robert Lucas describes the progress that he and other economists have made in explaining two principles of monetary theory described by David Hume. The first is that money is neutral within quantity theory; that is, given one equilibrium, there is a second where the money supply and the price level are both doubled and real variables are unchanged. The second is that an increase in the supply of money at first 'quickens the diligence of every individual before it encrease the price of labour' (Hume, 1970, p. 38).

Lucas points out that the evidence for the first principle is strong. Cross-country comparisons show that long-period-average inflation rates and long-period-average money growth rates are very highly correlated, while average money growth rates and average output growth rates are, in general, not correlated. The evidence for the second principle is less common. Some data sets show positive correlation between money growth and output as Hume suggests. Others do not.

Accounting for the two principles with the same model has proved to be a challenge that is difficult and not yet fully met. The right way to approach this challenge, according to Lucas, is with a microeconomic framework that promotes equilibrium and rational expectations, in which agents hold money as part of an optimal strategy.

One general equilibrium approach that can explain why money is held is Samuelson's consumption loan model. In the model, overlapping generations exist. The young work, but they do not consume. The old would like to consume, but they do not work. One way to have the young willingly transfer some of their product to the old is to endow the old with money. There is an equilibrium for the model in which the young exchange goods for money because they rationally expect to reverse the transaction when they are old.

While the Samuelson model exhibits quantity-theory neutrality, the short-run effects of increasing the money supply depend on how money is introduced. In some versions, an increase in money growth works through an inflation tax and lowers real activity. In others, the increase in money growth stimulates the economy because some agents interpret resulting price increases as temporary advantageous opportunities to supply their particular good. While others have explained a short-run positive effect of money growth with sticky wages or prices, all these models rely on specific assumptions about agent strategies; none obtains the desired result from assumptions about tastes and technology alone.

Lucas concludes that the important distinction between 'anticipated' and 'unanticipated' changes in money growth resulted from attempts by many researchers to build explicit models that could explain Hume's two principles. While he laments that empirical findings show that the effects of unanticipated money appear not to be transmitted through price surprises, he expects continued progress to result from the creation of explicit theories that fit the facts.

Learning Objectives

After reading and discussing Lucas' Nobel Lecture, students should be able to

1. Recount the two principles of modern monetary theory that Lucas attributes to Hume.
2. Explain the sense in which evidence for long-run monetary neutrality is stronger than the evidence for a short-run positive effect of money growth on real economic activity.
3. Explain what Lucas means by a general equilibrium rational expectations model, and why Lucas believes that explaining the short-run positive effect of money growth must be done in the context of such a model.
4. Explain how agents will respond when the primary effect of an increase in money growth is an inflation tax.
5. Explain how Lucas' models tend to account for a monetary stimulus to real activity.
6. Use the ideas in the Nobel lecture to discuss what objections Lucas would make to the standard textbook IS–LM model.

Question Clusters

1. Why, according to Lucas, should economists use a general equilibrium rational expectations model to explain the two principles of monetary theory described by David Hume?
   a. What are the two principles described by Hume?
   b. According to Lucas, are Hume's two principles in agreement with the data?
   c. What does Lucas mean by a general equilibrium rational expectations model?
   d. Why does Lucas believe that economists must use a general equilibrium rational expectations model to explain Hume's principles?

2. How, in his own work, has Lucas explained the positive stimulus to real economic activity that results from an increase in money growth?
   a. What does Lucas mean when he says that an agent may treat an increase in money growth as '...a real shift in his favor and respond by producing more'?
   b. What is the $\varphi(x)$ function that Lucas introduces, and how does he use it to explain the stimulative effect of money growth?
   c. Why does Lucas believe that the task of explaining the stimulating effect of money growth is only partially completed? What, according to Lucas, remains to be done?
   d. How different is Lucas' approach to explaining the positive effect of an increase in money growth to the approach used in macro theory courses?

Discussion Suggestions

Lucas' Nobel lecture is suitable for discussion in an honors section of an intermediate theory course, in an advanced macroeconomics course that focuses on policy, or in a capstone course for seniors. By discussing the article, students will gain a better understanding of what an economic model is. Such discussion will provide an opportunity for students to critically appraise the macroeconomic models and macro policy analyses they have encountered as undergraduates. It is exciting for students to view the frontiers of a discipline and to realize that they can understand and appreciate at least some of the issues dealt with by trailblazers such as Lucas.

OVERVIEW

It is unlikely that any instructor would assign all six of the articles on monetary policy in a single course. So we conclude this chapter with several suggestions for groupings of articles and questions that instructors could use to help students gain an overview.

The first grouping we consider are the articles by van Lear, Meyer, and the Taylor article on discretion and rules in practice. All three articles suggest that mechanical commitment to rules is unwise. But Taylor and Meyer both suggest that rules are, nevertheless, valuable. We suggest the following questions:

1. If William van Lear, Laurence Meyer, and John Taylor were all members of the Federal Reserve Board of Governors, would they agree on the proper role of policy rules in the conduct of monetary policy?

2. Meyer, van Lear, and Taylor all object generally to the mechanical implementation of policy rules. Do any of them have more fundamental objections to the use of rules? If so, what are they?

The second grouping includes the article by Taylor on the monetary transmission mechanism and Lucas' Nobel lecture. Both Lucas and Taylor believe that changes in the quantity of money have no real economic effects in the long run. Both explain why changes in the quantity of money do have short-run real effects, however the ways in which they approach the question are quite different. To encourage students to compare the ideas of Lucas and Taylor, we suggest the following questions:

1. While both Lucas and Taylor believe that an increase in the supply of money can stimulate economic activity in the short run, they explain those changes in very different ways. How similar are the Lucas and Taylor transmission mechanisms? Are there fundamental differences?
2. Would Lucas agree with Taylor that the distinction between nominal and real interest rates is crucial for understanding the transmission mechanism?

Bob Woodward emphasizes the importance that Alan Greenspan placed on balancing the federal budget during the Clinton Administration. He also makes clear that members of the Board of Governors faced strong political pressure to vote for monetary policy favored by the Administration and other interest groups. To provide students with an opportunity to connect these issues, instructors could ask the following questions:

1. As Woodward tells it, Alan Greenspan encouraged the Clinton Administration to balance the federal budget. Would John Taylor have agreed that balancing the budget was important for monetary policy?
2. Bob Woodward documents that Alan Greenspan and other members of the Board of Governors were under constant pressure from the Administration and Congress to provide the kind of monetary policy these groups favored. What impact does this well-documented political pressure have on the debate between those who favor monetary policy by rules and those who advocate monetary policy by discretion? Does van Lear think that putting political pressure on the Fed is a good or a bad thing? What about Meyer? Taylor?

10. Unemployment and Inflation

In 1752, David Hume suggested that the effect of a monetary expansion on economic activity depended on how the expansion occurred. In the long run, Hume argued that an increase in the quantity of money would do nothing more than cause a proportionate increase in prices. In the short run, Hume suggested that an increase in the supply of money '...must first quicken the diligence of every individual before it encrease the price of labour' (Hume, 1970, p. 38). Since Hume, economists have worked to understand when a monetary expansion has real effects and when it does not.

In 1958, W. H. Phillips observed a negative relationship between the unemployment rate and the rate of wage growth in the United Kingdom. Today, economists use the term 'Phillips Curve' to refer to a graph that shows an inverse relationship between unemployment and price inflation. In 1960, Paul Samuelson and Robert Solow suggested that the Phillips Curve should be viewed as a menu of inflation–unemployment options, and that the Fed should use monetary policy to put the economy at the point on the Phillips Curve that maximized social welfare. Edmund Phelps and Milton Friedman disagreed. They argued that in the long run, real wages adjust to equate the supply of demand for labor and that the unemployment rate equals the level associated with this equilibrium. They called this the natural rate of unemployment. In the long run, they argued, the Phillips Curve was not a curve, but vertical; no tradeoff existed.

In this chapter, we make suggestions for discussing several articles that deal with unemployment, inflation, or the connection between them. The first is Milton Friedman's Nobel lecture in which he describes progress toward a theory of unemployment and inflation as evidence that economics is a positive science. Friedman explains that economists responded to Phillips' hypothesis by looking for a negative relationship between unemployment and inflation in other data sets. They found that the rate of inflation associated with full employment appeared to be different in different economies and at different times. They responded with a theory that differentiated between anticipated and unanticipated inflation and used the distinction to modify the Phillips Curve.

The second article is 'The Ends of Four Big Inflations', in which Thomas Sargent studies the ends of hyperinflations in Austria, Hungary, Poland and Germany. The standard view is that reducing inflation entails huge economic costs that come in the form of higher unemployment and reduced output growth as the hyperinflated economy adjusts to lower money growth. Sargent disputes the standard view, and shows that the unemployment costs associated with ending these four hyperinflations were much lower than predicted by standard theory. The key, explains Sargent, is that the hyperinflations ended with a credible change in regime. Given regime change, expectations adjusted quickly and relatively little unemployment occurred.

In 'Reaganomics and Credibility', Thomas Sargent studies questions concerning whether government budget deficits cause inflation. Inflation, he argues, may be thought of as a dynamic game played by the central bank, the fiscal authority, and the public. The years of the Reagan presidency are particularly interesting because, Sargent argues, the strategies of the monetary and fiscal authorities were sharply in conflict. Under Paul Volcker, the Fed appeared committed to a tight policy that would lower inflation. At the same time, the fiscal authority passed tax cuts and ran budget deficits. Unlike cases of the hyperinflations that Sargent describes in the previous article, the public was not presented with clear evidence of a change in regime. Instead they watched a game of chicken unfold between the fiscal authority and the Fed. Given the lack of credible regime change, the unemployment costs of reducing inflation were large.

In 'Past and Prospective Causes of High Unemployment', Paul Krugman asks why the unemployment rate in Europe is higher than the unemployment rate in the United States. Krugman is not talking about business-cycle unemployment or movements along Phillips Curves. Rather, he documents that the natural rate of unemployment is higher in Europe than in the United States and attempts to explain why. Krugman argues that unemployment has risen in Europe for the same reason that wage inequality has risen in the United States – a shock to global labor markets that favors workers with the skills to operate effectively in the information age. He shows how such a shock interacts with a generous welfare system in Europe to support high unemployment and with a weaker safety net in the US to produce high inequality.

'NOBEL LECTURE: INFLATION AND UNEMPLOYMENT', MILTON FRIEDMAN

In 1968, the Bank of Sweden established its prize for economic science in memory of Alfred Nobel. As Friedman reports, many doubted that economics should be viewed as equal to exact empirical sciences such as physics, chemistry, and medicine. In the first part of his lecture, Friedman argues that the natural sciences are no more scientific than the social sciences. In both, there are hypotheses, but no certain knowledge. In both, the body of positive knowledge grows with the failure, patching up, and replacement of hypotheses. In both, experiments may or may not be possible, but are never completely controlled. In both, it is impossible to avoid interaction between the observer and what is observed.

In the second part of his lecture, Friedman illustrates the positive scientific character of economics by discussing the evolution of hypotheses on the Phillips Curve – the relationship between inflation and unemployment. The first stage of analysis was the widely believed hypothesis of a negative relationship between inflation and unemployment that was causal and offered a 'stable tradeoff to policymakers' (p. 454). As economists undertook empirical studies of the Phillips Curve, they uncovered evidence that did not support the hypothesis. The rate of inflation associated with full employment appeared to shift over time and to differ in different countries.

Friedman argues that there is no need to assume a stable relationship between unemployment and inflation in order to explain why acceleration of inflation lowers unemployment. The key is to distinguish between anticipated and unanticipated changes in nominal demand in the presence of long-term labor and capital commitments. An increase in inflation initially raises demand and lowers unemployment. When the surprise wears off, the stimulative effect disappears and unemployment returns to its equilibrium rate whatever the rate of inflation.

The second stage of Phillips Curve analysis was the development of the natural rate hypothesis which distinguished between the short-run and long-run effects of unanticipated changes in nominal demand and proposed no tradeoff in the long run. Producers initially interpret an unanticipated increase in aggregate demand as an unexpectedly favorable demand for their particular products, and increase production. Workers interpret an increase in nominal wages as an increase in the real wage. As perceptions adjust, the effect wears off and producers and workers return to prior levels of output and labor supply.

Even as work on the natural rate hypothesis continued, economists began work on a third stage of Phillips Curve analysis when they observed that higher inflation rates have often been accompanied in the long run with higher unemployment rates. The possibility that higher inflation might cause higher unemployment led to great concern on the part of policy makers in the mid-1970s. This would have been inconceivable twenty years earlier. Friedman reviews empirical evidence for a positive relationship, and concludes that the relationship appears to have changed from negative to positive in the postwar period.

Friedman conjectures that a small change to the natural rate hypothesis is sufficient to account for the positive relationship. During the period of transition from a low inflation rate to a high one, inflation is unlikely to be steady. High variability in the inflation rate may raise the natural rate of unemployment in two ways. First, inflation variability will shorten contracts and increase the use of indexation. Second, high variability may make it more difficult for the price system to coordinate economic activity. Both effects of inflation variability lower economic efficiency and might account for an increased natural rate of unemployment.

Friedman concludes with the observation that his lecture amounts to a standard story about the revision of scientific theory that nevertheless has far-reaching implications. The substantial changes that have occurred in the mainstream view of the relationship between unemployment and inflation have not occurred as the result of ideological warfare, but rather as the result of the failure of one hypothesis to account for the data. The changes in the mainstream view have led governments everywhere to a more conservative view of the benefits of stimulative policy. It is important for humanity, says Friedman, to have a correct understanding of the positive nature of economic science.

Learning Objectives

After reading and discussing Friedman's Nobel lecture, students should be able to

1. Understand Friedman's case that economics and physics are more similar than dissimilar.
2. Explain how and why views on the relationship between unemployment and inflation have evolved during the postwar period.
3. Use Figure 2 to explain the Friedman–Phelps natural rate hypothesis.
4. Explain why the data presented in Table 1 and Figures 3 and 4 support Friedman's view that the long-run Phillips Curve may have a positive slope.
5. Explain why Friedman believes, along with Pierre du Pont, that '[b]ad logicians have committed more involuntary crimes than bad men have done intentionally'.

Question Clusters

1. Why, according to Friedman, is economics properly thought of as a science more similar than dissimilar to physics and chemistry?
    a. How, according to Friedman, does economics make up for the lack of laboratory experiments?

b. Why, according to Friedman, is it important to separate value judgments from scientific judgments? How does economic science make the needed separation?

c. What does Friedman mean when he says, along with Pierre du Pont, that '[b]ad logicians have committed more involuntary crimes than bad men have done intentionally'?

2. Why, according to Friedman, does the evolution of the economic explanation of the relationship between unemployment and inflation demonstrate that economics is a positive science?

a. What does Friedman mean by the Phillips Curve?

b. How has the economic explanation of the Phillips Curve evolved?

c. What does Friedman mean by the 'natural rate' hypothesis?

d. Why, according to Friedman, may the natural rate hypothesis not be the last word on the Phillips Curve?

e. What, according to Friedman, are the implications for economic policy of the evolution in the positive theory of the relationship between unemployment and inflation?

3. Why, according to Friedman, may the Phillips Curve be positively sloped?

a. What does Friedman mean by the 'variability of inflation'?

b. Why, according to Friedman, may increases in inflation variability reduce economic efficiency?

c. How do Friedman's observations on inflation variability explain a positive slope to the Phillips Curve?

d. Why do Table 1, Figure 3, and Figure 4 provide evidence for a positively sloped Phillips Curve?

e. Does Friedman's explanation for the positive relationship between unemployment and inflation make good sense?

Discussion Suggestions

Friedman's Nobel lecture may be profitably discussed by students in both principles and intermediate macro courses. In the principles course, instructors may want to place more emphasis on Friedman's defense of economics as a positive science. In the intermediate macro course, instructors may want to emphasize the evolution of theories on the Phillips Curve. The article provides a good opportunity to ask students to interpret information from tables and graphs and explain how it is used in support of argument. A good follow-up activity would be to have students do research to determine what has happened since 1977 to Friedman's hypotheses about a positively sloped Phillips Curve.

'THE ENDS OF HOUR BIG INFLATIONS', THOMAS SARGENT

In this article, Thomas Sargent counters the standard view that lowering the inflation rate is very costly. The cost of lowering inflation is often measured with the sacrifice ratio: the percentage of one year's real GDP that must be forgone to reduce inflation by one percentage point. A typical estimate of the US sacrifice ratio is 5, which implies that reducing inflation by 1 percent costs 5 percent of real GDP or, using Okun's law, 2.5 percent unemployment. The standard view implies that lowering inflation from the late 1970s rate of 9 percent to the late 1980s rate of 4 percent cost over a trillion 1996 dollars of real GDP.

Sargent disagrees with the standard view. According to Sargent, history shows that inflation can be ended quickly and with much lower output and unemployment costs provided that there is a credible change in the policy regime that produced the inflation. Sargent studies post World War I hyperinflation in Austria, Hungary, Poland, and Germany. In each case, he argues that governments ran substantial fiscal deficits and financed them by increasing the money supply. In each case, hyperinflation resulted. In each case, the inflation ended quickly after a credible regime change. The regime change always included restrictions on the amount the central bank could lend to the treasury. In each case, Sargent shows that the nominal stock of money continued to grow after the inflation ended and that unemployment was not worse after the regime change than before.

Sargent concludes with a description of the policy regime in Czechoslovakia. Although faced with many of the same external pressures faced by the hyperinflation countries, Czechoslovakia ran only modest deficits after 1920, did not engage in inflationary finance, and did not experience hyperinflation.

Learning Objectives

After reading and discussing 'The Ends of Four Big Inflations', students should be able to

1. Define a policy regime and a policy regime change.
2. Explain why Sargent believes that a change in policy regime can lower inflation without high unemployment cost.
3. Construct an argument in support of Sargent, using evidence from the tables.
4. Use the data to characterize the common elements of the hyperinflation episodes in Austria, Hungary, Poland, and Germany.

5. Explain whether the data for Czechoslovakia supports or contradicts Sargent's hypothesis.

Question Clusters

1. Why, according to Sargent, do data describing hyperinflation in Austria, Hungary, Poland, and Germany support the conclusion that a change in policy regime can lower inflation at low cost?
   a. What does Sargent mean by a change in policy regime?
   b. What evidence does Sargent provide that a change in policy regime occurred in each of the hyperinflation countries?
   c. What evidence does Sargent provide that the change in policy regime caused the end of each hyperinflation?
2. What does Sargent mean when he says that '...it was not simply the increasing quantity of central bank notes that caused the hyperinflation....'?
   a. Why, according to Sargent, did note circulation continue to grow rapidly after each hyperinflation ended?
   b. According to Sargent, can a government end a hyperinflation with a 'currency reform' that replaces an old currency with a new one?
3. Why, according to Sargent, does the case of Czechoslovakia support the view that hyperinflation is caused by a particular kind of policy regime?
   a. What sort of policy regime produces hyperinflation?
   b. What evidence does Sargent offer that the policy regime in Czechoslovakia was not hyperinflationary?
   c. What features of the data for Czechoslovakia provide evidence that the Czech policy regime was different from those in Austria, Hungary, Poland and Germany?
4. What does Sargent mean by 'flight' from the crown, krone, and mark?
   a. What evidence does Sargent provide that hyperinflation causes a flight from the domestic currency?
   b. Why, according to Sargent, does such a flight occur?
   c. Is there evidence, according to Sargent, that the flight is reversed at the end of the hyperinflation?
   d. How does the flight from the domestic currency affect the ability of the government to levy an inflation tax on its citizens?
5. Is Sargent's argument correct?
   a. Has Sargent argued persuasively that hyperinflation is caused by a particular kind of policy regime and ends with a change in the policy regime?
   b. Has Sargent argued persuasively that currency reform alone cannot end hyperinflation?

   c. Has Sargent argued persuasively that inflation can be lowered at a cost smaller than implied by a sacrifice ratio of 5?

   d. How would Sargent explain the long and deep recession that followed after Paul Volcker introduced his anti-inflation policy at the end of 1979?

Discussion Suggestions

'The Ends of Four Big Inflations' is one of few case studies of macro policy. Discussing it would be an appropriate assignment in an honors section of a principles course, in intermediate macroeconomics, economics history, or financial markets. Reading and discussing the article provides students with an opportunity to use data to support arguments. Through discussion, we want students to show they understand what Sargent is saying about the connection between policy regimes and hyperinflation. We also want students to describe features of the data that support Sargent's argument and to recognize any features of the data that would contradict his argument.

'REAGANOMICS AND CREDIBILITY', THOMAS J. SARGENT

Thomas Sargent characterizes the interaction between monetary and fiscal policy makers as a dynamic game that requires time to complete. To achieve their objectives, players devise strategies which may be thought of as contingency plans that explain how each will respond to the actions of others.

The relative power of players is important for Sargent. In Nash games, each player takes the strategies of others as given and beyond influence. In Stackelberg games, the dominant player takes into account how others will respond to his strategy, while followers take the dominant players' strategy as given.

Sargent uses a game with three players – the public, the fiscal authority, and the central bank – to analyze the inflationary consequences of government deficits. The public's strategy is to reduce its demand for real money balances as inflation rises and to set an upper limit to its real holdings of government bonds. The fiscal authority sets current and future values of the government budget deficit. The central bank chooses current and future values of the money supply deciding, in effect, how much of the deficit will be financed by money creation and how much will be financed by direct borrowing from the public. Decisions of the fiscal authority and monetary authority must jointly satisfy a dynamic budget constraint.

Sargent uses the game to determine whether government deficits cause inflation. If the central bank is a dominant player and chooses a constant path for the money supply, deficits will not be inflationary because the budget constraint requires that the fiscal authority offset current deficits with future surpluses. If the monetary authority is a follower and finances whatever deficit the fiscal authority chooses, deficits will be inflationary because they cause the money supply to increase now and in the future. Intermediate cases are possible.

Sargent finally asks what sort of dynamic game characterizes the policies of the first term of the Reagan presidency. The anti-inflation monetary policy of Fed Chair Paul Volcker looks like the constant money policy of a dominant central bank. The large structural deficits chosen by Congress and the Administration look like the policy of a dominant fiscal authority. Sargent describes the conflict between these two policies as a game of chicken in which neither authority will concede dominance to the other. He discusses the implications of this failure of the Reagan administration to coordinate policy for the economy.

Learning Objectives

After reading and discussing 'Reaganomics and Credibility', students should be able to

1. Define a dynamic game.
2. Explain the difference between a game with a dominant player and a game without one.
3. Define 'equilibrium' for a dynamic game.
4. Explain, verbally, the meaning of the equation for the price level that is derived from the forward-looking money demand equation.
5. Explain, verbally, the meaning of the government's dynamic budget constraint.
6. Explain why government deficits do not cause inflation when a dominant central bank keeps the money supply constant.
7. Explain why government deficits cause inflation when a dominant fiscal authority runs structural deficits for an indefinite period.
8. Explain what Sargent means when he says that Reaganomics was not credible.

Question Clusters

1. Why, according to Sargent, is it useful to think of monetary and fiscal policy as a dynamic game?

    a. Who are the players in the game?

    b. What are the strategies of the players in the game?

    c. Why does it makes sense to think of a money demand equation as the strategy of the public?

    d. What does it mean for the strategies of the monetary and fiscal players to be coordinated?

    e. What insights are gained when monetary and fiscal policy are thought of as a dynamic game?

2. When, according to Sargent, are government budget deficits inflationary?

    a. How does Sargent use the public's strategy and the government budget constraint to reach conclusions about the inflationary effects of deficits?

    b. Why, according to Sargent, are deficits not inflationary when the Fed is the dominant player?

    c. Why, according to Sargent, are deficits inflationary when the Fed follows a dominant fiscal authority?

    d. According to Sargent, were the Reagan deficits inflationary?

3. What, according to Sargent, were the implications of a lack of coordination between monetary and fiscal policy during the Reagan administration?

    a. What does Sargent mean by policy coordination?

    b. Why does Sargent believe that policy was not coordinated during the first term of the Reagan presidency?

    c. According to Sargent, what insights are gained by thinking of the President and Congress as separate players in the game?

    d. What, according to Sargent, is the connection between policy coordination and policy credibility?

4. Has Sargent done a good job of characterizing the game played by the public, the fiscal authority, and the Federal Reserve?

    a. Is it reasonable to describe the public's strategy as Sargent does?

    b. What were the policy objectives of the Federal Reserve and the fiscal authority during the Reagan years?

    c. How important is the distinction between nominal and real government bonds that Sargent discusses toward the end of the article?

    d. Should the Administration and the Congress be viewed as different players in the game?

    e. What insights can be gained by regarding fiscal and monetary policy as a dynamic game that might be missed by other characterizations?

    f. Do you agree with Sargent that Reaganomics was not credible?.

    g. Would Sargent believe that monetary and fiscal policy are well coordinated today?

Discussion Suggestions

In 'Reaganomics and Credibility', Sargent addresses less technically many of the same questions that he addresses in 'Some Unpleasant Monetarist Arithmetic'. The article provides a good case study for macro instructors who want their students to learn what it means for policy to be time consistent and credible. It also provides an excellent opportunity for macro students to study the implications of the deficits initiated by the fiscal authority during the first term of George W. Bush's Presidency.

Instructors will have to decide whether they want their students to understand the derivation of equation (2.3) or are content to have students understand what (2.3) says about the relationship between prices, inflation, and future values of the stock of money. If students are to understand the derivation of (2.3), we recommend covering that derivation and other technical points before discussion of the article. Otherwise, the instructor may find it necessary to depart from the role of discussion leader and take up the role of expert.

It is important to have students discuss the distinction between nominal and real government bonds. Initially, Sargent keeps the analysis simple by assuming that government bonds are indexed for inflation. Later, he acknowledges that the fact that bonds are not generally inflation indexed provides the government an option of defaulting on the bonds by causing inflation. Instructors can ask how the public's strategy is likely to change when government debt consists of nominal rather than real bonds.

'PAST AND PROSPECTIVE CAUSES OF HIGH UNEMPLOYMENT', PAUL KRUGMAN

In this paper, Krugman addresses what he calls the 'big questions' about European unemployment – why did it rise from low levels relative to the United States in 1973 to double digit levels in the early 1990s, and what, if anything, can be done to reverse the trend. Along the way, Krugman debunks the popular view that high levels of European unemployment are due to increased globalization and rising European exposure to cheaply produced Chinese manufactures. He also provides evidence that rising unemployment in Europe and rising wage inequality in the United States have a common cause.

Krugman first explains the difference between cyclical and structural unemployment and argues that Europe has experienced increases in its natural rate of unemployment. He next suggests that rising European unemployment was not caused by long-lasting effects of prior recessions or on central bank policies that place too much weight on controlling inflation.

Krugman next sets out the model through which he connects unemployment and wage inequality, summarized by Figures 1 and 2. The idea is that an economy's wage distribution is described by a graph that maps percentiles (from 1 to 100) into the wage, expressed as a fraction of the average wage earned by workers in that percentile. An economy that has high wage equality has a flat schedule; one with high wage inequality has a steep schedule. Unemployment benefits are represented by a reservation wage, a horizontal line that divides workers into two groups – those who would earn less than that provided by the dole choose unemployment, and those who would earn more work. A more generous social safety net implies more equality and higher unemployment.

Krugman quickly points out that differences in the generosity of unemployment benefits in Europe and the United States can explain higher European unemployment but not growing European unemployment. He argues then that wage distributions in both Europe and the US have experienced a shock. While the specific nature of the shock is less than fully clear, Krugman suggests that it is related to the introduction of the computer. What is clear, suggests Krugman, is that the shock has disrupted wage distributions in the direction of higher inequality. In Europe, the disruption has led more low-skill workers to choose unemployment. In the US, where unemployment benefits and reservations are low, the disruption has caused more inequality.

Krugman concedes that standard trade theory could explain the growing premium on high-skill labor in Europe and the US as due to increased trade with countries, like China, that are abundant in low-skill workers and increasingly open to trade. Krugman shows that empirical evidence leads to a rejection of the trade-based alternative explanation. Krugman concludes the article with suggestions about what the future may hold and what, if anything, governments might due to lessen the effect of the increased relative demand for high-skill labor.

Learning Objectives

After reading and discussing Krugman's article, students should be able to

1. Explain the difference between structural and cyclical unemployment.
2. Use the data from the article to explain why the growth in European unemployment has been growth in structural unemployment rather than cyclical unemployment.

3. Explain how Krugman uses Figures 1 and 2 to explain the connection between rising unemployment in Europe and rising inequality in the United States.
4. Use Krugman's model and graphs to predict the effects of decreased unemployment benefits in Europe.
5. Explain how Krugman rules out trade with low wage nations as a cause for growing unemployment in Europe and growing inequality in the US.
6. Make reasonable judgments about potential remedies and prospects for the future.

Question Clusters

1. How does Krugman reach the conclusion that there has been a rise in structural unemployment in Europe but not in the United States?
   a. What is structural unemployment? What is the difference between structural and cyclical unemployment? What is the connection between structural unemployment and the natural rate of unemployment?
   b. What evidence does Krugman offer to support the conclusions he reaches about structural unemployment in Europe and the US?
   c. Why is a rise in structural unemployment in Europe but not in the United States an important conclusion?
2. What economic forces according to Krugman explain why the natural rate of unemployment has risen in Europe but not in the US?
   a. How does Krugman use Figures 1 and 2 to explain rising unemployment?
      i. How does one compute the unemployment rate from these figures?
      ii. What forces affect the position of the reservation wage?
      iii. Why does the TT line lie below the PP line?
   b. What does Krugman mean when he says that '...a likely explanation for this rise is the collision between welfare state policies that attempt to equalize economic outcomes and market forces that are pushing toward greater inequality'?
   c. Why does Krugman believe that there is a connection between rising inequality in the US and rising unemployment in Europe? What does he mean by inequality?
   d. Why, according to Krugman, is competition from newly industrializing nations in the third world not the cause of either rising unemployment or rising inequality in the US?
   e. What are the market forces that are pushing toward greater inequality?
   f. How, according to Krugman, can technological change work against unskilled workers?

3. What, if anything, can be done about the problem of rising US inequality and rising European unemployment?

Discussion Suggestions

The article is an excellent companion to the section of an intermediate macro course that deals with unemployment. By discussing the article, students have an opportunity to see an important practical implication of the difference between structural and cyclical unemployment and to think in a disciplined way about compromises that occur when a nation subsidizes the income of the unemployed. The article also provides students with an opportunity to think about macro issues in an open economy setting. They can judge for themselves whether Krugman has done a good job of ruling out 'globalization' as the likely cause for high European unemployment and high US wage inequality.

As a follow-up exercise, instructors can take advantage of the fact that the article was written in 1994 by asking students to determine whether Krugman's arguments are still valid. A first step is for students to check recent unemployment data. In our experience, students approach this task with high enthusiasm. They are genuinely curious to know whether Krugman's phenomenon persists and excited to search for relevant data and evidence.

OVERVIEW

While they pose what appears at first to be very different questions, the four articles in this chapter have a lot in common. The following questions would help students to explore how concepts introduced in one article can be used to understand others.

The first theme to be explored is what Friedman, Sargent, and Krugman have to say about the natural rate of unemployment. We suggest these questions:

1. How would Milton Friedman use the concept of the natural rate of unemployment to explain the ends of the four big inflations described by Thomas Sargent? Would Friedman agree with Sargent that a transition from hyperinflation to low inflation can be accomplished at low economic cost?
2. How would Milton Friedman use the concept of the natural rate of unemployment to explain the systematic difference between the European and US unemployment rate? Does Friedman's view of the natural rate allow that it might be different in different economies?

A second theme is Sargent's idea that the cost of reducing inflation depends on the credibility of the change from high-inflation regime to low-inflation regime. We suggest these questions:

1. Why, according to Sargent, was it more expensive to reduce inflation during the early years of the Reagan administration than it was to reduce inflation in several hyperinflation episodes? What is the connection between the regime changes that Sargent describes in the hyperinflation episodes and the 'game of chicken' between fiscal and monetary policy makers that he describes in the Reagan years?
2. Sargent says that monetary policy can be described as a game with three players: the monetary authority, the fiscal authority, and the public. How and why, according to Sargent, was behavior of the public different in the hyperinflations and in the Reagan years?

A third theme present in the readings is that economics is properly thought of as a science. We suggest these questions:

1. Would Milton Friedman describe the research on inflation presented by Thomas Sargent as evidence that economists are scientists? How does Sargent's research resemble a scientific process?
2. Would Milton Friedman describe Paul Krugman's study of unemployment in Europe and the US as scientific? Why or why not?

11. Economic Growth

In his 1985 Marshall lectures, Robert Lucas suggested, 'When you start thinking about economic growth, it is hard to think about anything else'. Renewed interest in growth has spilled over from research agendas to the classroom. Many intermediate macro texts now include sections on growth and extremely long-run equilibrium that often appear before short-run models designed to explain cycles. Texts that cover growth invariably cover the Solow model and often go on to describe the origins of endogenous growth theory.

In this chapter, we make suggestions for discussing four articles that treat economic growth. The first, by Robert Lucas, builds a variant of the Solow model in which nations begin to grow at different dates. In the model, nations that begin growing later grow more rapidly due to third party effects created by early growers. The model implies that all nations will eventually converge to the same rate of growth. Before that happens, however, it predicts a wide range of national growth rates. Lucas uses the model to explain the apparent failure of national growth rates to converge and to predict convergence in the next century.

A different perspective on the convergence controversy is offered by Mankiw, Romer, and Weil, who argue that the Solow model does a good job of accounting for national differences in growth rates. The article begins by presenting the textbook Solow model and the relationship it implies between output per worker, the rate of saving, and the population growth rate. The authors then take this relationship to data describing growth in 98 countries and argue that it does a good, but not a perfect, job of explaining cross-country differences in output per worker.

The authors modify the textbook model by including human capital as a productive input. They then derive the predictions of the modified model for steady state output per worker and for national growth rates. They emphasize that the proper approach to convergence allows for national differences in saving, population growth, and human capital. They also show that the modified Solow model fits the data well and that estimates of the modified model imply that 'conditional' convergence of growth rates is underway.

The article by Harris and Steindel uses a model of economic growth to describe the costs to a nation when its saving rate declines. The authors begin by documenting the dramatic decline in the saving rate that occurred in the US in the 1980s. They then use a calibrated version of their model to predict the implications of the lower saving rate for the time path of the capital stock, output, and consumption. What was the opportunity cost of the consumption binge in the 1980s? A dramatic decline in consumption relative to levels the nation would have enjoyed if it had maintained its earlier high saving rate. Harris and Steindel conclude by recommending policies to restore higher saving and by simulating the effects of a saving recovery.

Roy Webb disagrees that the decline in national saving that occurred in the 1980s is a matter for concern. Webb argues that the declining saving rate was an optimal response to the increase in wealth that households experienced as asset prices increased during the decade. He suggests that a better measure of the economic health of the household sector is the ratio of its net financial wealth to disposable personal income. Tracking that measure, Webb concludes that there was no fall of savings in the 1980s in the US and that US households remain the wealthiest in the world.

Webb bases part of his argument on the implication of the Solow model that the long-run growth rate depends on the rate of technology growth and not on the rate of saving. Webb charts output per capita between 1869 and 1989 and argues that the chart shows no evidence that US growth has fallen below its long-run path.

The articles that we describe in this chapter provide excellent opportunities for students to put the Solow model through its paces, to assess how well the model explains growth of the nations in the world, and to bring the model to bear on questions of policy.

'SOME MACROECONOMICS FOR THE 21ˢᵗ CENTURY', ROBERT E. LUCAS

In this essay, part of a special issue of the *Journal of Economic Perspectives* devoted to economics at the turn of the millennium, Lucas sets out a version of the Solow growth model designed to capture the essential facts of growth since 1800. Solow's model describes growth of a single country. Lucas' model describes a growing world. However, the countries in the Lucas model did not begin growing at the same time.

In 1800, all the countries in Lucas' model are lined up like horses behind the starting gates. But the gates do not open at the same time. In 1800, only England's gate opens and England begins to grow. Each year, a random mechanism decides which gate will open. Initially this is a highly unequal world where early starters in the income race leave other nations behind.

Lucas introduces two mechanisms that eventually lead to equality. Late starters benefit from technology and infrastructure transfers and grow more rapidly until they catch up with the leaders. Also, the probability that a non-growing nation starts to grow increases as average world income grows.

Lucas calibrates his model to match the level of per capita income in 1800, the level of per capita income in leading nations in 1990, and the fact that growth diffused slowly in the nineteenth century and rapidly in the twentieth. The calibrated model predicts that average world growth and income inequality increase until the end of the twentieth century and then fall thereafter until all the nations of the world grow at their steady Solow growth rates. Solow points out that a researcher studying world income data generated by his model for 1960-1990 might erroneously conclude that income growth convergence was not possible and that inequality of income was permanent.

Learning Objectives

After reading and discussing Lucas' article students should be able to

1. Correctly describe the features of Lucas' model, especially those that Lucas describes as spillovers from growth leaders to late-growing nations.
2. Explain why Lucas' model implies that average growth rates will be very high in the late twentieth century and then fall in the twenty-first.
3. Explain why Lucas' model produces inequality that rises for a long time before eventually falling.
4. Explain how Lucas' model is similar to Solow's growth model and how it is different.
5. Interpret what Lucas means when he says that his model is 'undeniably an economic model'.

Question Clusters

1. What, according to Lucas, accounts for the extraordinarily high rate of growth that occurred in the world between 1960 and 1990?
   a. What in Lucas' model accounts for changes in the world growth rate over time?
   b. What role does Figure 1 play in accounting for changes in the world growth rate? Figure 2?
   c. How is Lucas' model similar to the Solow model that we have studied in class? How is it different?
   d. What does Lucas mean when he says that his model is a 'model of spillovers'?
2. Why, according to Lucas, are growth rates of nations highly unequal in each year in the 1960 through 1990 period?

    a. How does Lucas measure 'inequality' of national growth rates?
    b. What accounts for inequality of growth rates in the Lucas model?
3. Why, according to Lucas, will growth fall and inequality decrease in the twenty-first century?
4. Do you agree with Lucas when he describes his model as an 'economic' model?
    a. What features of the model agree with your view of how growth occurs and diffuses across nations?
    b. What features of the model would you like to see changed?
    c. Are your own predictions for growth in the twenty-first century very different from those of Lucas? How so and why?

Discussion Suggestions

This Lucas essay is an excellent choice for discussion in any intermediate macro class that covers the Solow growth model. Students find it exciting to compare the model they learn about in their text with one that a Nobel Prize winner is willing to use to describe the world today. Our students have had many interesting ideas about the diffusion process that lies behind catch-up growth and rising probabilities for growth starts among non-growing nations.

It is not necessary and may well be undesirable to ask students to figure out the appendix to the paper. Lucas does an excellent job of explaining how his model works. We find that students understand the mechanisms without figuring out how to write them as equations.

'A CONTRIBUTION TO THE EMPIRICS OF ECONOMIC GROWTH', N. GREGORY MANKIW AND DAVID N. WEIL

The authors take Robert Solow seriously by reporting estimates of two equations derived from versions of his model to cross-country data describing economic growth between 1960 and 1985. The first version is the textbook Solow model in which production inputs include capital and labor and technological growth occurs exogenously. The second version augments the first by including human capital as a separate productive input and assuming that human capital is produced with the same process through which other output is produced.

The authors reach several interesting conclusions. First, the data confirm the prediction of the textbook model that output per labor unit varies directly with saving and inversely with the labor growth rate, although the size of responses are larger than the model would allow. Second, differences in saving and population growth account for a lot of the observed cross-country variation in output per worker. Third, when a measure of human capital is added to the model, the fit of the regression model improves, the coefficient on human capital has the expected sign and size, and the size of the coefficient on saving drops to a level consistent with theory. Fourth, growth convergence across nations appears to hold provided that the predicted effects of saving, population, and human capital on output growth are allowed for. Fifth, the augmented Solow model predicts slower convergence than the textbook model.

In the first section, the authors present the textbook Solow model and derive the relationship between output per worker, the saving rate, and the population growth rate that the model predicts will occur across countries at a point in time. They describe the data they use in estimation – a sample of 98 countries and two sub-samples: the 75 countries with higher-quality data and the 22 developed (OECD) countries. They then explain what happens when they take the textbook model to these data. Output per labor-unit varies directly with saving and inversely with the labor growth rate. Coefficient sizes are larger than theory allows. Cross-country differences in saving and population growth account for a large fraction of cross-country variation in output per worker.

In section two, the authors modify the Solow model by allowing human capital to be a third productive input. Unlike endogenous growth models, the authors assume that human capital is produced with the same technology that produces other output. The authors derive a revised regression equation that shows how output per worker varies with the saving rate, population growth rate, and the level of human capital. Using the percentage of the working-aged population that is enrolled in secondary school as a proxy measure of national human capital, the authors refit the Solow regressions. They find that the model now accounts for an even larger share of observed cross-country variation in output per worker, the coefficient on human capital has the expected sign and size, and the size of the coefficient on saving drops to a level consistent with theory. The authors conclude that adding human capital to the Solow model improves its performance.

In section 3, the authors take up the issue of convergence. If saving and population growth rates are the same across nations, the Solow model predicts that the growth rate in output per worker should be inversely related to the level of output per worker. Put another way, the Solow model predicts that nations below their steady state output per worker levels should grow more rapidly. The authors point out that if saving and population growth rates are not the same across nations, then the Solow model predicts conditional convergence – a negative partial relationship between the growth of output and the level of output in an equation that allows for the effects of saving and population on growth. The authors demonstrate that unconditional convergence does not hold for their data, but that conditional convergence does hold. They display a three-part figure that shows how adding saving rates, population growth rates, and human capital to the output growth regression induces the convergence result.

In the fourth section of the paper, the authors discuss whether the Solow model can explain cross-country differences in rates of return and capital flows. Given observed differences in population growth rates and saving rates, the Solow model predicts large cross-country differences in the marginal product of capital. Some authors have argued that the Solow model is contradicted by two facts. First, international differences in real interest rates are not as large as the predicted differences in the marginal product of capital. Second, high-saving countries have high rates of investment. The Solow model would predict that a high-saving country should channel its investment to a low capital country where funds earn a higher rate of return.

The authors offer two rebuttals. Capital markets in poor countries may be far from perfect, so that market interest rates are not equal to the marginal product of capital. Furthermore, funds may not flow to high marginal product countries because agents fear that the receiving country will expropriate them. They conclude that it is premature to reject the Solow model on the grounds that there is too much cross-country variation in the marginal product of capital.

Learning Objectives

After reading and discussing the 'Empirics' article, students should be able to

1. Explain what the textbook Solow model has to say about cross-country differences in output per worker.
2. Describe how the statistics reported in Table I support the authors' conclusions that the textbook Solow model can account for much of the variation in cross-country labor productivity, but is not entirely successful.
3. Explain how the authors introduce human capital into the Solow model.
4. Compare equation (11) with equation (7) in a way that shows how adding human capital to the Solow model alters its predictions about the relationship between labor productivity, saving, and population growth.
5. Describe how the statistics reported in Table II support the authors' conclusion that the data strongly support the augmented Solow model.
6. Define convergence and conditional convergence and explain the difference between them.
7. Make the authors' case that allowing for the role of human capital in the Solow model leads to the conclusion that there is conditional convergence among national growth rates.

8. Explain how the authors use the statistics reported in Tables III and IV to make the case for conditional convergence.

Question Clusters

1. Why, according to the authors, does the Solow model give '...the right answers to the questions it is designed to address.'?
   a. What questions do the authors believe the Solow model can answer?
   b. What do the authors mean by the right answers to those questions?
   c. What evidence do the authors offer that the Solow model gives right answers to the questions?
2. Why, according to the authors, is it important to allow for human capital when testing whether the Solow model is in good agreement with the data?
   a. How do the authors add human capital to the Solow model?
   b. How does the addition of human capital alter the predictions of the Solow model concerning labor productivity?
   c. How do the authors go about testing whether the predictions of the Solow model for labor productivity are in good agreement with data?
      i. How do the authors measure human capital?
      ii. How does the addition of human capital to the equation explaining output per unit labor alter the regression results?
   d. Why do the authors believe that the results in Table II strongly support the augmented Solow model?
3. How do the authors reach the conclusion that national growth rates are converging?
   a. What, according to the authors, is the difference between convergence and conditional convergence?
   b. Why, according to the authors, is it appropriate to test for conditional convergence rather than convergence?
   c. How do the authors test for conditional convergence?
   d. How do the statistics reported in Tables IV through VI support the conclusion that there is conditional convergence among national growth rates?
      i. Why, according to the authors, is it important to allow for human capital when testing for conditional convergence?
      ii. What features of Figure 1 support conditional convergence?

Discussion Suggestions

This article provides an excellent opportunity for students to learn how an economist takes a model to the data. The fact that the authors start with a bare bones version of the Solow model makes the article a good choice for intermediate macro courses. Some instructors will want students to derive the equations of the paper. Others will not. In either case, the resulting equations for output per worker have intuitive explanations so that all students should be able to relate the results to the mechanisms in the Solow model.

The econometrics used by the authors is straightforward so that the paper provides an opportunity to link statistics from the regressions with conclusions about the model. The authors do an excellent job of documenting that allowing for human capital improves the empirical performance of the Solow model. Students can see these differences clearly by comparing the output per worker results in Tables I and II and the growth rate results in Tables III, IV, and V.

'THE DECLINE IN US SAVING AND ITS IMPLICATIONS FOR ECONOMIC GROWTH', ETHAN S. HARRIS AND CHARLES STEINDEL

When it was published in 1991, this article by Harris and Steindel raised an important policy issue: should the United States take public policy steps to restore the saving rate to its previous postwar level? The article still plays a valuable role in the undergraduate economics curriculum as a case study or as an opportunity to compare past predictions with current reality.

The article has two parts. In the first, the authors carefully consider whether the National Income and Product Accounts present an overly gloomy picture of national saving behavior. By NIPA accounting, net national saving, which averaged 7.5 per cent during 1950-1979, fell to 3 percent for the 1980s and 2.2 percent for 1985-89.

Harris and Steindel acknowledge that the NIPA saving rate provides an imperfect measure of the nation's growth in productive capital. They consider alternative measures based on Flow of Funds data. They also make several adjustments to the data to allow for capital gains and foreign savings flows. The basic conclusion that saving in the United States has fallen survives all corrections and re-calculations except one. If one believes, and Harris and Steindel do not, that all stock market price increases in the 1980s were due to increased productivity of the capital stock, then one would conclude that the growth of productive capital was not lower in the 1980s than earlier.

In the second part of the article, Harris and Steindel accept that the net saving rate did fall to about 2.0 by 1990 and investigate the consequences. They use a version of the Solow growth model to predict the future paths of the capital stock, GNP, and consumption relative to the levels that would have occurred if the saving rate had remained at 7.5 percent. The simulations show a 'consumption binge' in the 1980s followed by persistent declines in the relative values of capital, GNP, and consumption thereafter. By 2010, the simulations show consumption falling to 95 percent of what it would have been with the higher saving rate. When they consider a production function with a 'learning-by-doing' technology, Harris and Steindel show that the decline in the saving rate has even more dramatic effects that result because new innovations are introduced more slowly. With learning-by-doing, GNP in 2010 is about 83 percent of the level it would have been with the higher saving rate.

Finally, Harris and Steindel review the prospect for a recovery from the low saving of the 1980s. They show that a gradual increase in the saving rate to traditional levels that begins in 1990 would return the economy to its original trajectory over a period of about 25 years. By 2010, GNP and consumption would have recovered to about 98 percent of their higher-savings-rate levels. They conclude the article by reviewing their chief findings and suggesting policy options.

Learning Objectives

After reading and discussing the Harris and Steindel article, students should be able to

1. Explain how the NIPA saving rate should be corrected to provide a measure of the rate of growth of productive capital.
2. Use the data in Tables 1-6 to demonstrate the veracity of the conclusion that the national saving rate fell between 1980 and 1990.
3. Explain why using equity market valuation and reproduction cost valuation for equities yield very different estimates of the national saving rate.
4. Explain the mechanism through which foreign sources augment domestic saving.
5. Interpret the simulations reported in Charts 1 and 2 and explain how they show the economic cost of the decline in the national saving rate.
6. Explain what Harris and Steindel mean by a 'recovery' and why the capital stock, GNP, and consumption behave as shown in Charts 3-7 after a recovery.

Question Clusters

1. Harris and Steindel consider three concepts of saving: unspent income, increases in wealth, and the supply of capital. Which, according to the authors, should economists use to study the consequences of the decline in saving that occurred after 1980?
   a. What do the three measures have in common?

    b. How do the three measures differ?

    c. How do Harris and Steindel use equation (4) to differentiate among the measures?

2. According to Harris and Steindel, does the conclusion that the saving rate fell substantially after 1980 stand up to careful scrutiny?

    a. How do Harris and Steindel examine the question?

    b. Why, according to Harris and Steindel, should an economist consider as a potential source of saving only the increase in household wealth that exceeds general price inflation?

    c. Why, according to Harris and Steindel, does it make a difference if capital gains are measured with the corporate net worth rather than the corporate equity method? Why do they think the former method is better?

    d. Do you agree with Harris and Steindel when they conclude that in the 1980s...net national saving f(e)ll to its lowest rate of the postwar period'? Why or why not?

3. What, according to Harris and Steindel, are the economic costs of low saving in the 1980s?

    a. How do Harris and Steindel measure the cost of low saving? How is Chart 1 generated and why does it provide a measure of these costs?

    b. What, according to Harris and Steindel, is the connection between low saving in the 1980s and low consumption in the twenty-first century?

    c. What is the difference between traditional, vintage, and learning-by-doing models? Why does it make sense that the cost of low saving is estimated to be higher with a learning-by-doing than with a traditional model?

4. Why, according to Harris and Steindel, will a recovery of past saving behavior eventually raise consumption?

    a. How do Harris and Steindel use Charts 3-7 to show what happens during a recovery of past saving behavior?

    b. Why does the international capital position of the United States change during the recovery?

5. Is low saving in the United States sufficiently important to be a focus of public policy? Why or why not?

    a. What are the strengths and weaknesses of Harris and Steindel's arguments?

    b. Has our economic experience since 1991 tended to confirm or contradict the predictions and warnings of Harris and Steindel?

Discussion Suggestions

Harris and Steindel can be used in several ways in the undergraduate curriculum. The first part of the article permits students to study the connection between saving and investment in the context of an important phenomenon – the decline in the US saving rate. In intermediate or advanced macroeconomics, students can compare the model presented in the appendix with the bare bones Solow model. Even if students have not studied the Solow model, they can detect and explain the mechanisms that underlie the simulations and charts. In our experience, students who have studied intermediate macro do understand why there is a tradeoff between consumption today and tomorrow.

There are many opportunities for exercises following discussion of Harris and Steindel. Students can discuss the Webb article (presented later in this volume) and go on to contrast the two views. Students can also be asked to gather data on the saving rate since 1990 to decide whether low savings is still a concern. In an advanced macro course, students could be asked to write an Excel program that implements the Harris and Steindel growth model.

'PERSONAL SAVING BEHAVIOR AND REAL ECONOMIC ACTIVITY', ROY H. WEBB

In 1992, as the United States economy was struggling to throw off the effects of a recent recession, many analysts blamed sluggish growth on low savings rates experienced during the 1980s. Webb argues that the idea that low savings rates cause sluggish growth is not supported by standard economic theory and not consistent with data on household wealth. In the first part of the article, Webb offers an alternative theory for low saving rates. In the second, he acknowledges that long-run growth may be linked to savings rates, but only if they are redefined to include expenditures that raise human capital.

Because National Income and Product Account (NIPA) measures of income and saving are not derived from mainstream economic theory, Webb cautions drawing conclusions solely upon it. Wealth, he argues, provides a better measure of the economic well-being of a household. The life cycle hypothesis implies that people in households will save during some parts of their lives and not save in others even when income and wealth are sufficient to maintain a constant level of consumption throughout.

Webb points out that the ratio of household net financial assets to disposable personal income rose throughout the 1980s, and that by this measure, households in the United States are wealthier than those in Japan, Germany, France, the UK, and Canada. He acknowledges that the ratio of household debt to income also rose during the 1980s, but attributes the rise to rational responses by households to improved opportunities to borrow provided by increasing efficiency of financial intermediaries. Webb concedes that it is difficult to measure wealth accurately, but concludes that data on wealth contradict the gloomy picture painted by those who rely solely on saving data.

In the second part of the article, Webb reviews the connection between savings rates and long-run growth. He first points out that except for the Great Depression and World War II, the growth path in the United States has been stable for the past 120 years. Webb interprets the decline in the growth rate from 2.1 percent between 1950 and 1973 to 1.6 percent between 1973 and 1989 as a return to the long-run growth rate of 1.7 percent. He points out that the Solow model implies that the saving rate affects the steady state level but not the growth rate of output per person. Of course, there are many growth anomalies that the Solow model does not explain.

Webb next suggests that endogenous growth theory does provide a theoretical connection between saving rates and long-run growth rates. If human capital is an input to the production process and if productivity depends both on an individual's human capital and the average level of human capital in the economy, then there is a positive externality associated with human capital accumulation that explains why higher saving rates imply higher long-run growth rates. But saving rates must be measured properly to detect the connection. Expenditures on human capital development, such as schooling, must be counted as saving.

Webb concludes that saving rates alone tell us little about the short-run health of the economy. He agrees that saving rates can help explain long-run growth provided that they are measured correctly. Unlike the NIPA measure, a proper measure of saving would include expenditures on human capital development.

Learning Objectives

After reading and discussing the Webb article, students should be able to

1. Explain why Webb believes that wealth is a better measure of household well-being than saving.
2. Explain how Webb uses the life cycle hypothesis to support his conclusion that there is no theoretical connection between saving rates and short-run growth.
3. Explain how the data on household wealth contained in Figures 3 and 4 support Webb's argument.

4. Analyze Webb's explanation for the rise in household and corporate debt to income ratios. Explain how the argument works and identify strengths and weaknesses of the argument.
5. Explain what Webb means by endogenous growth theory.
6. Analyze the connection that Webb sets out between saving rates and long-run growth rates. Explain why the Solow model cannot provide a connection but endogenous growth theory can.
7. Compare and contrast Webb's arguments with those of Harris and Steindel. Explain where the two papers agree and where they differ.

Question Clusters

1. According to Webb, is the decline in the personal saving rate that occurred in the 1980s a matter for serious concern?
   a. Why does Webb believe that data on household wealth must be considered in answering this question?
   b. How does Webb use the life cycle model to make his point about the connection among wealth, saving, and household well-being?
   c. How does Webb use Figure 4 to advance his argument?
   d. Does Webb believe that the ratio of household debt to income is rising too rapidly? Why or why not?
2. Does Webb agree or disagree that the low personal saving rate implies a low long-run rate of growth for the US?
   a. How does Webb use Figure 6 to answer this question?
   b. How does Webb use the Solow Growth model to support his view that low saving may be compatible with continued growth of output per capita?
   c. How does Webb use equation (2) to make his point about the Solow model?
   d. What does Webb mean by endogenous growth?
   e. How does endogenous growth fit into a discussion of the long-run effects of a low saving rate?
3. What are the key parts of Webb's argument that '[c]urrent saving data reveal little about prospective consumer spending'?
   a. Why does Webb believe that 'A focus on conventionally measured saving may well divert attention from ... important fundamentals'?
   b. What, according to Webb are the important fundamentals?
4. Whose argument do you find more convincing – that of Webb or that of Harris and Steindel?
   a. Does the nation need new public policy to address the problem of low saving?
   b. What sort of policy do you favor?

Discussion Suggestions

The article by Webb can be profitably discussed by students in several courses. In intermediate macroeconomics, discussing the article provides students opportunities to apply the life cycle and Solow models and to use data to support arguments. In a financial markets course, discussing the article provides students the opportunity to study connections among saving, investment, and growth. It also provides students with an opportunity to think about the impact of increasing financial institutional efficiency on economic well-being.

Depending on whether their students' backgrounds include multiple regression, instructors may either include or skip the subsection of the paper that deals with the correlation of national saving and investment. Webb makes a subtle point here about the lack of causal connection between saving and investment. Skipping the subsection does not leave an important gap between the question Webb asks and his answer.

OVERVIEW

There are several themes that run through the growth articles that we describe. First is the question of whether or not the Solow model can explain the large variation in national growth rates that has been observed since World War II. Some authors have concluded that a fundamental overhaul of growth models is required to explain the apparent lack of convergence. Others, like Lucas and Mankiw–Romer–Weil, argue that only modest amendments to the Solow model are necessary to account for the variation. We suggest these questions:

1. Lucas and Mankiw–Romer–Weil agree that national growth rates will eventually converge. How would you compare the ways in which they reach this conclusion?
2. How different are the variants of Solow proposed by Lucas and Mankiw–Romer–Weil?
3. Through what economic mechanisms does each model explain the large observed differences in national growth rates? Are these mechanisms very different or essentially the same?

The authors of all four articles say that their ideas about growth derive from those embodied in Solow's model. Instructors might ask their students to identify the similarities between the growth process modeled by Solow and those modeled in the other articles. We suggest these questions:

1. What essential components of the Solow model appear to be present in the growth model that Harris and Steindel set out in their appendix?
2. Mankiw–Romer–Weil's equation for output per worker (6, p. 410) and Webb's equation for output per worker (2, p. 86) appear to be essentially the same. Which implications of the equation are most interesting to Webb? To Mankiw–Romer–Weil?
3. Both Harris–Steindel and Webb analyze the implications of low saving using a growth model. What elements of the Solow model are present in the models of Harris–Steindel and Webb? How do you account for the fact that Harris–Steindel and Webb reach very different conclusions using the Solow model?

We have had excellent results when we assign both Webb and the article by Harris and Steindel. The two papers ask the same question and reach different conclusions on the importance of the decline in NIPA saving rates. After discussing the two articles, we ask students to contrast the arguments presented in each and to decide which is stronger. We sometimes give a writing assignment that asks students whether the low rate of household saving that occurred during the 1980s should be remedied by public policy and requires them to support their answer with specific evidence from Harris and Steindel and Webb. The same comparison makes a good examination essay question.

12. Deficits

For most of the twentieth century, budget deficits in the United States were cyclical phenomena. During a recession, the Federal budget moved toward deficit as automatic stabilizers kicked in. The Reagan Administration tax cuts ushered in an era of structural deficits – deficits at full employment. The Reagan tax cuts also caused discussion of government deficits and debt to spill from the halls of the academy into public forums and the halls of Congress. 'Does the deficit matter?' became a question of general interest.

In this chapter, we introduce four articles that help students decide whether or not deficits matter. Discussing these articles can help students learn a lot of economics. As the articles show, analysis of deficits mixes ideas from macroeconomics, microeconomics, game theory, public finance, and monetary theory.

The article by Ball and Mankiw provides a neo-classical perspective on the economic costs of deficits. Ball and Mankiw treat deficits as a decline in national saving and trace that decline through higher real interest rates to lower investment and capital growth, an appreciating exchange rate, and movement of the trade account toward deficit. Ball and Mankiw conclude that economic costs associated with having a lower capital stock are moderate for a national debt equal in size to one-half of national output. What is serious, they argue, is the risk of a hard landing that might occur if many other countries lose confidence in the US assets that they hold.

The Ball and Mankiw article is particularly valuable for students because it is accompanied by thoughtful comments by Robert Johnson and Allan Meltzer. Both Johnson and Meltzer argue that Ball and Mankiw apply the wrong thought experiment to estimate the economic costs of deficits. Both emphasize that reversing deficits must be done through tax and spending decisions that alter incentives, and thus have economic consequences that might dwarf the 'pure' consequences estimated by Ball and Mankiw. Both, however, agree that the risk of a hard landing is a serious cost, and they reflect on why a hard landing might occur.

In the second article, Benjamin Friedman provides a detailed analysis of the impact of the Reagan Administration deficits. While Friedman's analysis is also neo-classical, it is far more detailed. Friedman offers evidence on the validity of each link in the neo-classical chain connecting deficits, interest rates, investment, real exchange rates and the current account. Friedman also discusses both the economic and the political implications of moving from a state of being a net creditor to a net debtor in the world.

In 'Reagonomics and Credibility', Thomas Sargent looks at the Reagan deficits from the prospective of policy coordination. He characterizes the anti-inflation monetary policy of the Federal Reserve and the structural deficits of the fiscal authorities as seriously in conflict. Sargent suggests that the Fed and the Administration behaved as if each expected the other to accommodate their policy. He discusses the consequences for the economy of this failure to coordinate.

Finally, Laurence Kotlikoff enters the deficit debate from a very specific vantage point. Economists have argued forcefully that the day of reckoning concerning the effects of budget deficits and debt will occur when the baby-boom generation begins to retire in numbers. Retirement of the baby boomers will place great pressure on the financial position of the government because Social Security has been a 'pay as you go' plan that largely finances current payments to retirees out of current social security worker taxes. When the baby boomers begin to retire, the ratio of retirees to workers will grow to unprecedented levels.

Some economists and policy makers have advocated privatization of Social Security. They argue that allowing workers to redirect some retirement contributions toward portfolios that include common stocks will increase returns and ease the nation toward a privatized national pension program. Kotlikoff has long concerned himself with issues of inter-generational equity. He studies plans for privatizing Social Security with a dynamic life cycle model and finds that privatizing Social Security can lead to sufficient gains in economic efficiency so that the winners (younger generations) could sufficiently compensate the losers (older generations) to make them as well off as they were in the current pay-as-you-go program.

'WHAT DO BUDGET DEFICITS DO?', LAURENCE BALL AND N. GREGORY MANKIW WITH COMMENTS BY ROBERT A. JOHNSON AND ALAN MELTZER

The article and formal comments were presented at the 1995 Federal Reserve Symposium entitled 'Budget Deficits and Debt: Issues and Options' sponsored by the Federal Reserve Bank of Kansas City. In the paper, Ball and Mankiw clearly and effectively present the neo-classical open economy story. They next give rough estimates of the costs of a national debt that had reached about one-half of GDP in 1995. Finally, they suggest that the largest cost of large deficits may be the increased risk of what they term 'a hard landing.'

Ball and Mankiw begin by presenting the neo-classical theory of deficits. The effects of deficits are first transmitted to the economy in the form of lower national saving. Given US accounting definitions, lower national saving must result in some combination of lower investment and a lower trade balance. To the extent that it causes a lower trade balance, a budget deficit creates a flow of assets abroad as the US receives more goods now in exchange for promises of more goods later. Two mechanisms link decreased national saving to its outcomes. The first is a rise in the real rate of interest that tends to decrease domestic investment and attract foreign saving. The second is an appreciation in the exchange value of the domestic currency that results as foreign savers increase demand for higher yielding domestic assets. The appreciation of the dollar drives the trade account toward deficit. The prediction of neo-classical economic theory is that budget deficits lower national investment, but not on a one-to-one basis. For example, Ball and Mankiw estimate that between 1982 and 1994, US national saving fell by 2.9 percent while domestic investment fell by only 0.8 percent.

Ball and Mankiw next turn their attention to the long-run effects of deficits. First, persistent deficits slow the growth rate of the capital stock, leaving the nation with less capital than it would have had. Second, persistent deficits create foreign ownership of domestic assets, thereby lowering national income as foreigners receive more of the return on assets located in the US. Third, persistent deficits change factor prices – lowering real wages and raising real returns to capital. Fourth, budget deficits may cause future tax increases. The government will not have to raise taxes if the rate of growth of output is higher than the real rate of interest, this is because the government can roll over its debt while economic growth reduces the ratio of debt to GDP. If the growth rate is lower than the real rate of interest, the government must raise taxes or risk the consequences of a debt–GDP ratio that grows ever larger.

Ball and Mankiw provide very rough estimates of the costs of US debt. Suppose, they suggest, a 'debt fairy' suddenly converted the entire stock of the national debt into capital. What would be the impact of this magic intervention on US output, wages, and capital rental rates? Ball and Mankiw estimate that the intervention would eliminate a debt service equal to about 1 percent of GDP, create sufficient capital to raise GDP by 6 percent, raise real wages by 6 percent and lower the return to capital by just under 2 percent. If the economy were closed and there was no offset to private saving from the debt fairy's action, Ball and Mankiw believe their estimate would be about right. Because the economy is open and private saving is likely to fall somewhat, they guess that the effect on GDP might be half as large.

Are these significant effects? In 1995, 6 percent of GDP was about $400 billion, a substantial amount. However, the amount is small relative to the amount that has been lost by nations that have experienced slow growth over the period starting in the mid-1970s.

Ball and Mankiw next turn to the normative question of whether deficits are undesirable. While deficits eventually lower output, they need not lower economic well-being because deficits create both winners and losers. The winners are current taxpayers and future owners of capital. The losers are future taxpayers and future workers. Ball and Mankiw argue that the key normative issue is whether we approve the direction of these redistributions.

In the final section, Ball and Mankiw argue that there is a reason to bring deficits under control. Deficits increase the risk of a 'hard landing'. As its population ages and Social Security and Medicare payments increase, the debt to income ratio of the US is likely to rise. At some point, a rising debt–income ratio may lead to a sharp decrease in demand for US assets by the rest of the world. A hard landing occurs when the US can no longer borrow from nations abroad.

A hard landing could be very hard. Ball and Mankiw reason that loss in confidence in US assets would cause a sudden and sharp drop in their prices that would harm the economy in many ways. Higher yields and loss of confidence would lower investment and exacerbate the decline in real wages caused by deficits. Higher yields would also accelerate the growth of debt as the US faced larger debt service payments.

A hard landing would make it very unlikely that the US could grow out of its debt, and would necessitate an abrupt change to budget surpluses and trade surpluses. Consumption would fall sharply. The large and potentially sudden shift from production of non-tradeables to tradeables would disrupt labor markets and potentially cause high unemployment. The hard landing could also lead to inflation as the price of imports rose and as the Federal Reserve found itself under increasing pressure to buy government debt. In the worst case, a hard landing could trigger a general financial crisis as declining asset prices lead to bankruptcies of firms and financial institutions. Ball and Mankiw conclude that while the effects of a hard landing are speculative, the risk of a hard landing may be the most important reason for seeking to reduce budget deficits.

In his comments, Robert Johnson suggests that the linkage between budget deficits and future productivity and living standards may be weaker than Ball and Mankiw suggest. The problem is that businesses' fixed investment may not be very sensitive to changes in the rate of interest. Government deficits crowd out interest-sensitive spending, but that spending may be on consumer durables and housing rather than capital.

Johnson also points out that the debt fairy parable begs the question of how deficits are to be eliminated. Taxes create distortions. Obviously, raising taxes on capital to eliminate budget deficits would discourage rather than encourage capital formation. Raising other taxes in periods of slack aggregate demand might also discourage investment. Lowering government spending might also reduce investment. For example, government spending on roads or on research and development may be a complement to private investment in capital.

Johnson is more impressed by the risk of a hard landing. He argues that nations that run high deficits are 'hanging out in a bad neighborhood'. If one such nation suffers a collapse in confidence, others are likely to suffer the effects as asset owners reassess asset riskiness and re-balance their portfolios.

Finally, Johnson argues that Ball and Mankiw ignore an important question. What sort of conditions in capitalist democracies lead to rising fiscal imbalance? Is there something about the democratic process and the way campaigns are financed that leads to irresponsible financial decisions? Johnson argues that economists must do a better job of analyzing why governments create deficits in the first place.

In his comments, Alan Meltzer argues that it is important to analyze not only the pure effects of deficits – Ball and Mankiw's debt fairy analysis – but also the way in which budget deficits are eliminated. Meltzer also argues that Ball and Mankiw answer the wrong question. The issue is not whether to eliminate government debt but whether or not to balance the budget. If the deficit, and not the debt, were eliminated, Ball and Mankiw's own calculations imply that the impact on GDP would be only about one-half of 1 percent.

Meltzer argues that the effects of budget deficits on interest rates and exchange rates are small because the rest of the world considers US bonds to be close substitutes for their own. Meltzer provides two charts that compare the deficit to the trade-weighted exchange rate of the United States. The charts reveal no persistent pattern between deficits and real exchange rates between 1960 and 1994.

Meltzer argues that Ball and Mankiw ignore important economic effects of deficit reduction programs. Reductions in government spending change resource use. Government spending and tax rates have incentive and resource allocation effects that may dwarf the debt financing effects that Ball and Mankiw consider.

Meltzer agrees that there is cause for concern about financing of the US deficit. He argues that private investors willingly accumulated additional dollar assets in the 1980s, but that foreign central banks financed a larger share of new foreign borrowing by the US in the early 1990s. If the US generates new debt faster than central banks are willing to absorb it, central banks may substitute stronger currencies in their portfolios. Such changes would have real effects.

Learning Objectives

After reading and discussing 'What Do Budget Deficits Do?', students should be able to

1. Explain the chain of events that links increased fiscal deficits with lower investment and higher trade deficits.
2. Assess whether or not the objections to the Ball and Mankiw analysis presented by Johnson and Meltzer are important.
3. Define what Ball and Mankiw mean by a 'hard landing'.
4. Decide whether or not Johnson and Meltzer agree that a hard landing is a serious risk and a good reason to balance the budget.
5. Explain why eliminating the deficit creates changes in resource use.
6. Explain why the welfare effects of budget deficits are not clear.
7. Evaluate for themselves whether the US should make it a priority to balance the budget.

Question Clusters

1. What, according to Ball and Mankiw, do budget deficits do?
    a. Some economists argue that fiscal deficits and trade deficits are twins. Would Ball and Mankiw agree?
    b. Why, according to Ball and Mankiw, do deficits have long-run effects on the economy?
    c. What do Ball and Mankiw mean by a 'hard landing'?
2. According to Ball and Mankiw, are the likely economic consequences of US budget deficits of large or small importance?
    a. What is the 'debt fairy parable' and how do Ball and Mankiw use it to estimate the economic effects of national debt?
    b. How do Ball and Mankiw conclude that the cost of US national debt is as much as 6 percent of national output?
    c. Why, according to Ball and Mankiw, is it not clear that running budget deficits lowers economic welfare?
    d. Why, according to Ball and Mankiw, is the risk of a hard landing an important reason for reducing budget deficits?
3. Do Robert Johnson and Allan Meltzer agree with Ball and Mankiw's assessment of the economic costs of budget deficits?
    a. What are the most important criticisms that Johnson and Meltzer level at Ball and Mankiw?
    b. What does Johnson mean when he says that having a high national debt is like hanging out in a bad neighborhood?

    c. Why do both Johnson and Meltzer object to the debt fairy thought experiment?

    d. With which conclusions of Ball and Mankiw would Johnson and Meltzer agree?

4. How important is it for the United States to balance its fiscal budget?

    a. Which of the reasons for balancing the budget given by the authors do you find most compelling? Why?

    b. Do you believe that balancing the budget would raise social welfare in the United States? Why or why not?

Discussion Suggestions

The Ball and Mankiw article combined with the published comments by Johnson and Meltzer provide the best overview of the costs and consequences of deficits and debts that we were able to find for this volume. The articles are clearly written and accessible to students of intermediate macroeconomics courses. The article and comments make a lively discussion possible because Johnson and Meltzer raise interesting objections to the neo-classical story told by Ball and Mankiw, and to the 'debt fairy' parable that Ball and Mankiw use to estimate the economic costs of US debt. There are tradeoffs involved in discussing Ball and Mankiw instead of Friedman (next article). Ball and Mankiw provide a broader assessment of the impact of deficits, complete with criticism. Friedman provides a far more detailed study of the Reagan deficits with many references to data. Instructors who are interested in additional writings on the deficit should take a look at the other articles from the 1995 Kansas City Fed Symposium, available on the Bank's web site.

'US FISCAL POLICY IN THE 1980s: CONSEQUENCES OF LARGE BUDGET DEFICITS AT FULL EMPLOYMENT', BENJAMIN FRIEDMAN

Benjamin Friedman argues that the high-deficit fiscal policy initiated by the Reagan tax cuts in 1982 was a costly failure. The resulting deficits forced government borrowing that absorbed about three-quarters of national saving, and led to higher real interest rates, lower capital accumulation, slower productivity and wage growth, and higher foreign debt. Friedman provides empirical evidence for each link in the chain connecting growing deficits to falling wages and increasing foreign debt.

After explaining the implications of large structural fiscal deficits, Friedman asks why they were allowed to occur. He argues that government economists overestimated the stimulative effects of tax cuts by '...a whole new order of magnitude...' and incorrectly assumed that lower tax rates would raise national saving.   Some believed that savers would respond strongly to incentives created by higher after-tax real interest rates. Others thought that households would save more in order to spare their descendants from the burden of future tax increases. These arguments proved wrong. In fact, household saving fell.

Friedman next asks what can be done. He argues that the deficits will not go away by themselves and are likely to have both domestic and international consequences. The domestic consequences include slower growth that results from under-investment. The international consequences include diminished international status that results from being a debtor in the world. Friedman concludes that a remedy will require that hard choices be made and reviews the prospects for government spending cuts and tax increases.

Learning Objectives

After reading and discussing Friedman's article, students should be able to

1. Explain the connections between government budget deficits, real interest rates, investment, productivity, and wage growth.
2. Explain why higher fiscal deficits can lead to higher international debt.
3. Explain how Friedman uses data to support his claims about the effects of high deficits.
4. Discuss the remedies that Friedman proposes and decide which is best.
5. Transfer Friedman's arguments to the current US budget situation.

Question Clusters

1. 'In 1983, the average US worker earned $281 per week. By year-end of 1989, the average weekly paycheck, stated in 1983 dollars, was just $271. To continue on with the current policy of high deficits at full employment probably means more of the same'. What, according to Friedman, is the connection between the high budget deficits of the 1980s and the decline in weekly paychecks that occurred during this same period?
   a. What evidence does Friedman offer to show that the government fiscal deficit was unusually high during the 1980s?
   b. What, according to Friedman, is the role of interest rates and investment in accounting for the slow rise in wages?
   c. What evidence does Friedman present that interest rates were unusually high during the 1980s? Why does Friedman think that interest rates were high?

2. Would Friedman agree that the current US deficit is a twin of the US fiscal budget deficit of the 1980s? Why?
   a. What exactly is the current US deficit?
   b. According to Friedman, what mechanism connects the current deficit to the fiscal budget deficit?
   c. What evidence does Friedman present to support his view that the two deficits are twins?
3. Why, according to Friedman, is the current deficit a matter for public policy concern?
   a. What, according to Friedman, are the economic consequences of the fact that the US became a debtor nation in 1985?
   b. What, according to Friedman, are the hard choices that we face as a result of the twin deficits? Which choice should we take?
4. How would Benjamin Friedman apply his arguments to the current budget situation in the United States?

Discussion Suggestions

We began assigning the Friedman article when 'The Twin Deficits' was considered a current policy issue. We continued to assign it throughout the 1990s because it is an excellent example of a policy case study. In recent years, we follow up discussion of the article by asking students whether Friedman's arguments apply to the current fiscal situation in the US. There are lots of possibilities here, including asking students to replicate Friedman's charts and graphs using more current data. The article provides an excellent opportunity for students to transfer economic principles to a new situation.

One of the real strengths of the article is the way in which Friedman uses data to support his argument. Through discussion, students can better understand how economists use empirical evidence to test and support their theories. It is a good strategy to ask students separate questions about the mechanism that connects, for example, deficits and interest rates and the evidence that the mechanism is operative.

Finally, the article provides an excellent opportunity for instructors to re-enforce student understanding of the open economy IS–LM model. The mechanisms that Friedman emphasizes are precisely those that would be at work when the open economy IS–LM model is faced with a domestic tax cut.

'REAGANOMICS AND CREDIBILITY', THOMAS SARGENT

Sargent uses a dynamic game to describe the interaction between monetary and fiscal policy. To achieve their objectives, players choose strategies that may be thought of as contingency plans that explain how each will respond to the actions of others. Sargent characterizes both the anti-inflation policy of Paul Volcker and the deficit-producing fiscal policies of Congress and the Reagan administration as dominant-player strategies. He describes the conflict between those policies as a game of chicken and discusses the economic implications of the failure to coordinate policy. For a more complete description of this article, see 'Unemployment and Inflation', Chapter 10.

Learning Objectives

After reading and discussing 'Reaganomics and Credibility', students should be able to

1. Explain, verbally, the meaning of the government's dynamic budget constraint.
2. Explain why government deficits do not cause inflation when a dominant central bank keeps the money supply constant.
3. Explain why government deficits cause inflation when a dominant fiscal authority runs structural deficits for an indefinite period.
4. Explain what Sargent means when he says that Reaganomics was not credible.

Question Cluster

What, according to Sargent, are the implications of a lack of coordination between monetary and fiscal policy during the Reagan administration?
   a. What does Sargent mean by policy coordination?
   b. Why does Sargent believe that policy was not coordinated during the first term of the Reagan presidency?
   c. According to Sargent, what insights are gained by thinking of the President and Congress as separate players in the game?
   d. What, according to Sargent, is the connection between policy coordination and policy credibility?

Discussion Suggestions

In 'Reaganomics and Credibility', Sargent addresses in a less technical way many of the same questions that he addresses in 'Some Unpleasant Monetarist Arithmetic'. The article provides a good case study for macro instructors who want their students to learn what it means for policy to be time consistent and credible. It also provides an excellent opportunity for macro students to study the implications of the deficits initiated by the fiscal authority during the first term of George W. Bush's Presidency.

It is important to have students discuss the distinction between nominal and real government bonds. Initially, Sargent keeps the analysis simple by assuming that government bonds are indexed for inflation. Later, he acknowledges that the fact that bonds are not generally inflation indexed provides the government an option of defaulting on the bonds by causing inflation. Instructors can ask how the public's strategy is likely to change when government debt consists of nominal rather than real bonds.

'PRIVATIZING US SOCIAL SECURITY: SOME POSSIBLE EFFECTS ON INTER-GENERATIONAL EQUITY AND THE ECONOMY', LAURENCE KOTLIKOFF

Kotlikoff simulates the effects of privatizing the Social Security system using the Auerbach–Kotlikoff Dynamic Life Cycle Model. The model includes government, household, and firm sectors. Households supply labor, earn wages, and use the proceeds to consume and save in such a way as to maximize lifetime utility. Each household belongs to one of 12 income classes. During the household's life, all income classes experience growth in real wages but none changes classes. Firms maximize profits using a Cobb Douglas technology that combines labor and capital to produce output. Firms are price takers. Government consists of a treasury that collects funds from the private sector and a 'pay-as-you-go' Social Security system that uses current payroll taxes to pay current benefits. Model parameters have been chosen to match essential features of the US economy.

The transition to a private social security system entails three elements. Workers contribute to private retirement accounts. Social Security benefits are awarded to workers and retirees during a transition period. The transition benefits are funded with a consumption tax. Kotlikoff explains that other funding schemes for the transition performed less well.

The chief question addressed by the article is whether privatization will enhance or undermine inter-generational equity. Privatizing Social Security leads to efficiency gains because households respond to the lower taxes on income by supplying more labor and using some of the proceeds to save and increase the capital stock. In the long run, once the transition is complete, all income classes benefit from privatization. Lower classes benefit more, relatively speaking, because they escape the regressive FICA tax. In the short run, older generations are made worse off by privatization because they pay the transition consumption tax. Kotlikoff shows that privatization is Pareto improving in the sense that the winners from privatization could compensate the losers and still be better off.

Kotlikoff concludes that his simulations show that privatization of Social Security can have positive effects both on economic performance and welfare provided that the transition benefits are financed with a consumption tax.

Learning Objectives

After reading and discussing Kotlikoff's article, students should be able to

1. Explain what Pareto improving means and how Kotlikoff demonstrates that his privatization scheme is Pareto improving.
2. Interpret the figures that show the effects on the economy of privatization.
3. Explain why economic agents supply more labor under privatization than under Social Security.
4. Explain why the consumption tax used to finance the transition hurts older generations more than younger generations.
5. Use the two panels of Figure 2 to explain the difference between the welfare effects of compensated and uncompensated privatization schemes.
6. Explain why Kotlikoff is entitled to his conclusion.

Question Clusters

1. According to Kotlikoff, will privatization enhance or undermine generational equity of the Social Security system?
   a. What does Kotlikoff mean by 'generational equity'?
   b. How does Kotlikoff use Table 2 and Figure 2 to support his conclusion?
   c. Why, according to Kotlikoff, are the effects of privatization progressive? What does he mean by 'progressive'?
   d. According to Kotlikoff, who are the losers and who are the winners from a privatization of Social Security? Why do the winners win? Why do the losers lose?
   e. How does Kotlikoff use the concept of a Pareto improvement to answer the question of generational equity?
2. Why, according to Kotlikoff, will privatizing Social Security increase economic efficiency?

a. What are the economic reasons why privatizing Social Security increases efficiency?
b. How does Kotlikoff use Table 1 and Figure 1 to argue that the efficiency gains are substantial?
c. How does Kotlikoff compute the data reported in Table 1 and Figure 1?
3. How does Kotlikoff use the A-K model to study the impact of privatizing Social Security?
   a. What does Kotlikoff mean when he says: 'In the A-K model, privatization requires simply eliminating the Social Security payroll tax'?
   b. How, in the model, do agents respond to the privatization of Social Security?
   c. Why does Kotlikoff assume that Social Security benefits paid during the transition period to complete privatization are financed by a proportional consumption tax? What does he mean by a 'consumption tax'?
4. Are you convinced by Kotlikoff's analysis? Why or why not?

Discussion Suggestions

We have had good results assigning this article near the end of the intermediate macro course. By then, students are used to thinking about the dynamic effects of policy shocks, have used the Solow model to explain changes in capital over time, and have studied labor supply decisions. It is easy to motivate interest in the article because students frequently encounter media reports that suggest that the Social Security program is insolvent and some intervention will be required. Of course, privatization is one intervention that has been frequently suggested.

OVERVIEW

How might instructors help students gain an overview of the articles in this section? We suggest three strategies:

First, instructors might have students discuss Benjamin Friedman and Ball and Mankiw in turn and then ask students to compare the analyses of the economic effects of deficits from these two readings. For overarching questions, we suggest these:

1. How would you compare the economic effects of budget deficits described by Ball and Mankiw with those described by Benjamin Friedman?
2. Do Ball and Mankiw believe that the fiscal deficit and the current account deficit are twins?

3. Would Johnson and Meltzer offer the same criticisms to Benjamin Friedman that they offered to Ball and Mankiw?
4. Does Benjamin Friedman appear to be concerned about the risk of a hard landing?

Second, instructors might ask students to discuss either Benjamin Friedman or Ball and Mankiw followed by Thomas Sargent and then ask them how these two analyses fit together. We suggest these questions:

1. Would Benjamin Friedman agree with Thomas Sargent that monetary and fiscal policy were not coordinated during the Reagan Administration?
2. Is there any connection between the risks of a 'hard landing' as described by Ball and Mankiw and the 'game of chicken' between monetary and fiscal policy authorities described by Sargent?
3. Would Sargent agree with Johnson that the fiscal authority during the Reagan Administration was 'hanging out in a bad neighborhood'?

Third, instructors might have students discuss either Ball and Mankiw followed by Kotlikoff, and then have them investigate connections between the two analyses. We suggest these questions:

1. What, if any, is the connection between the increased economic efficiency that Kotlikoff says will occur if Social Security is privatized with the economic changes that Ball and Mankiw say would occur as a result of intervention by the debt fairy? Would privatization of Social Security work like a debt fairy intervention?
2. How does Kotlikoff's welfare analysis compare with that of Ball and Mankiw? Are the winners the same in each case? The losers?
3. Based on what they say in their comments about Ball and Mankiw, would Robert Johnson and Alan Meltzer be likely to support the privatization of Social Security as described by Laurence Kotlikoff?

PART FOUR

Discussing Microeconomics

13. Thinking About Markets

A major objective of economics instruction is to help students appreciate the power of economic forces in everyday life. Economics has a lot to say about how people coordinate activity. It builds on the principle that individuals respond to incentives, and that both people and policy makers should be aware of unintended consequences of their decisions. Economics also has something to say about conditions under which markets work well and other conditions under which they do not.

This chapter presents several readings that students in the principles course can read and discuss and thereby better appreciate how markets work, why economic forces are powerful, and how incentives shape decisions. Even an elemental grasp of economics requires understanding markets – how they work and how they evolve. The textbook examples frequently fail to do the job because they rely on abstractions rather than the nuts and bolts of how markets work. The purpose of these selections is to help students see the essentials of markets using the simplest examples and to be aware of the tensions between the market and social goals realized through the political process.

The first selection is Adam Smith's Chapter 7, Book I, 'On the natural and market Price of Commodities'. Smith proceeds on a step by step basis to describe markets in what is the now-familiar language of supply and demand. This selection not only displays Smith's keen observational skills, but also the power of his clear prose in describing how prices are determined by the interplay of market forces.

R. A. Radford's classic essay, 'The Economic Organisation of a P.O.W. Camp', shows how markets can develop in what might appear to be the most unlikely circumstances. Radford too displays his keen observational skills in recording how the P.O.W. market developed and evolved. In addition, he does a masterful job of relating the goings-on in the P.O.W. camp market to an array of key economic concepts that were widely familiar at the time to anyone who had studied economics.

F. A. Hayek's essay, 'The Use of Knowledge in Society', explains how markets generate information that guides buyers and sellers in their actions. He argues that to operate effectively within a market there is no need for complete knowledge of the economy or any particular market within it. Rather, participants need only to know the effect of changes which are communicated by prices and changes in prices. Hayek's essay can be viewed as describing the working of the P.O.W. camp market where information was communicated with great speed throughout the camp, and camp inmates responded quickly to prices, which signaled the relative abundance or shortage of goods and services available in the P.O.W. camp.

Robert Heilbroner, in 'Reflections: After Communism', illuminates the role of markets by describing the results of the Soviet Union's command-style economy. There, central planners set prices and output levels and then communicated that information to producers and consumers, all without regard for individual preferences or productive capabilities. The inevitable result was a serious mismatch between what people wanted and what was made available to them. Ironically, illegal markets developed and proved to be essential in correcting the failures of central planning. Heilbroner goes on to discuss socialism and its problems. Finally, he discusses capitalism's challenge in dealing with what he sees as serious ecological problems.

The selection by Milton and Rose Friedman, 'The Tide is Turning', offers a prescription to reverse what they describe as the ever-expanding role of government and its inevitable interference in markets. They believe that public opinion is turning in favor of markets, but lament the inroads already made by government into what they believe should be matters of individual concern. To reverse the tide of ever-expanding government, they advocate a comprehensive set of constitutional amendments that would restrict further expansion and actually produce some contraction in the scope of government policies and programs.

The two essays by Okun approach the issue of capitalism and its reliance on the market in quite different ways. The first essay, 'Rights and Dollars', focuses on the conflict within a democracy between the individual rights conferred by the political system and the unequal distribution of dollars that reign as the currency of the market. He worries that the market may transgress too far into the political sphere, and argues that efforts must be made to insulate the political sphere from the economic sphere. Okun's second essay, 'The Case for the Market', offers a sharp contrast. It extols the virtues of capitalism and the market for their economic efficiency. At the same time, he laments the resulting inequality of income. After debating the pros and cons, he comes down firmly on the side of the market, arguing that the market must be preserved while it is strengthened.

'OF THE NATURAL AND MARKET PRICE OF COMMODITIES', ADAM SMITH

In one of his best known chapters in *The Wealth of Nations*, Smith offers an illuminating and detailed description of how markets work. He does so by focusing on the determinants of what he calls natural prices and the market prices. He goes on to describe what happens in response to disparities between these two prices. Market prices gravitate to the natural price because self-interested owners of stock, land, and labor will commit more resources to production of the commodity whose market price exceeds natural price. Similarly, they will remove resources from production of a commodity whose price falls below the natural price. He argues that fluctuations in the market price tend to affect either wages or profits, depending on whether the market tends to be 'over-stocked or under-stocked with commodities or with labour, with work done or with work to be done' (p. 67). He goes on to discuss the forces that slow and in some cases prevent convergence between actual price and natural price, as well as what happens to actual prices under conditions of 'perfect liberty'.

What makes this selection so interesting is that more than 200 years ago Smith describes the essentials of modern supply and demand analysis, as well as the determinants of the distribution of income. He expresses all of this in clear prose rather than what modern textbooks typically present in graphic displays and less frequently in mathematical formulations. The example he uses to illustrate what happens is arresting. The effect of a public mourning increases the demand for black cloth, raises its price, and leads in turn to higher profits for merchants who have ample stocks of black cloth, and to higher wages for tailors who make mourning garments. Weavers of black cloth do not benefit, however, because the black cloth is needed immediately.

Smith's discussion of the forces that prevent the market price from gravitating back to the natural price also has a modern ring when he talks about the effect of monopoly, trade secrets, regulations, and wage controls.

What is central to this reading selection is the role of self interest that motivates individuals, whether consumers or producers. People respond to the signals from the marketplace, signals that are conveyed through changes in prices. They do so out of self interest, and in the process promote economic efficiency. In short, this selection illustrates well the operation of Smith's 'invisible hand'.

Learning Objectives

After reading and discussing Chapter 7 of *The Wealth of Nations*, students should be able to

1. Explain the difference between the 'natural' and the 'market' price of commodities.
2. Describe how changes in supply and/or demand affect these two types of prices.

3. Explain why some prices vary more than other prices.
4. Explain the factors that inhibit the convergence of market price and natural price.

Question Clusters

1. Why, according to Smith, does the market price of a commodity gravitate toward the natural price of that commodity?
   a. What does Smith mean by natural price? By market price?
   b. What does Smith mean by the phrase 'tending toward it'? Does this mean that differences between market price and natural price will always be small and always get smaller?
   c. What factors, according to Smith, lead to fluctuations in prices?
   d. Why do fluctuations in market price 'fall chiefly upon those parts of its price which resolve themselves into wages and profits'?
   e. What forces explain whether wages or profits are most affected by the fluctuations?
2. What does Smith mean when he says that the quantity of every commodity naturally suits itself to effectual demand?
   a. According to Smith, if the market price exceeds or falls short of natural price, does this mean that supply is not equal to effectual demand?
   b. What does Smith mean when he says 'the quantity of every commodity brought to market naturally suits itself to the effectual demand'?
3. What, according to Smith, accounts for differences between the natural and the real price of a commodity?
   a. Under what conditions, according to Smith, will the market price exceed the natural price?
   b. If market price remains above the natural price, either permanently or for a long period of time, does this mean that supply is not meeting effectual demand?
   c. What factors does Smith say might permanently prevent the equating of market and natural price?
4. What does Smith mean by the term 'perfect liberty'?
5. How does Smith's example of the effect of a public mourning illuminate the workings of the market?

Discussion Suggestions

This chapter is an excellent complement to supply and demand analysis in principles textbooks. Once students get beyond the shock of the archaic language used by Smith, they instantly grasp what he is saying. For students accustomed to literary rather than graphic presentations, this reading selection helps them gain a practical understanding of the workings of markets and the price system.

'THE ECONOMIC ORGANISATION OF A P.O.W. CAMP', R. A. RADFORD

No volume treating discussion in economic literature would be complete without this classic article. In the autumn of 1943, prisoner R. A. Radford arrived at Stalag VIIA in Moosberg, Bavaria, from a transit camp in Italy. He explains how an exchange economy developed and flourished in the camps until early in 1945, when the Allied push into Germany disrupted the supply of Red Cross parcels.

Radford explains that economic activity was an important feature of camp life, and that many of the same forces that produce predictable economic outcomes in the outside world were at work in the camp. Markets took time to organize. In transit camps, where prisoners had little incentive to learn about their surroundings, barter prices for goods varied widely and opportunities for arbitrage were present. In permanent camps, economic activity was more organized, prices converged and were well known. Cigarettes functioned as money, held and accepted by smokers and non-smokers alike. Individuals who spoke Urdu profited from trade with Indian prisoners. Others who could not sought to regulate those who could.

Radford explains why the intrinsic usefulness of cigarettes was a disadvantage to their use as money. Smokers persistently lowered the stock of money. When delivery of Red Cross packages was interrupted and the stock of cigarettes not replaced, prices tended to fall. Right after delivery of parcels, prices would rise. Camp members had to contend with inflation and deflation that made holding inventories and timing purchases risky. Radford points out that a fall in the supply of cigarettes not only lowered prices generally, but also changed the price structure. When parcels were quite scarce, basic foodstuffs such a bread rose in value relative to less essential items.

Radford reports on several attempts made by prisoners to regulate the working of market forces. In response to the high spirits that accompanied D-Day, the camp entertainment committee organized a store that bought and sold foodstuffs at market prices and used them to produce snacks and meals sold at a companion restaurant. The store used its power as a large buyer to attempt to keep prices steady. It also issued a paper currency, called the 'Bully Mark' that was backed by food rather than cigarettes. As long as parcels were delivered regularly, the restaurant and store flourished and camp prices remained stable. When parcel delivery was disrupted, the shop suffered from a change of relative prices and became glutted with the goods that prisoners valued less in hard times. The shop, restaurant, and Bully Mark ultimately failed.

According to Radford, most prisoners believed that there was a just price for each good and resented those who offered them less. Prisoners also resented middlemen, although they traded with them and depended upon them for advances of goods and cigarettes. 'Prices moved', says Radford, 'with the supply of cigarettes, and refused to stay fixed in accordance with a theory of ethics' (p. 200).

Learning Objectives

After reading and discussing the Radford paper, students should be able to

1. Explain why a system of exchange developed among the prisoners.
2. Spell out what factors determined the complexity of the prison market system.
3. Describe how external events affected the prison market system.
4. Explain the parallels between the prison economy and an economy outside the prison camp.

Question Clusters

1. What, according to Radford, accounts for the development of an exchange system within the P.O.W. camp?
   a. To what extent does the evolution of this system depend on the equality (or lack of it) in the distribution of supplies? Differences in individual preferences? Both?
   b. How equally were the supplies distributed initially? Why were prisoners unhappy with their particular allotment of supplies?
   c. Could the supplies have been repackaged so that the initial distribution would have left everyone happier? How? Would such a distribution have been viewed as equitable by prison authorities? By the Red Cross? By the prisoners?
2. How effectively did this exchange system operate?
   a. What led to the evolution of a barter system?
   b. Why did a 'currency' emerge? What was this currency? What were the merits of using this particular item as currency rather than some other commodity?
   c. To what extent could the exchange system adjust to unforeseen events? And, how did these unforeseen events lead to different kinds of adjustments?

    d. Who gained and who lost as a result of these adjustments? How did prisoners work to offset the results of these unforeseen events?
3. Why, according to Radford, did prices fluctuate in the camp, and by how much did they fluctuate?
    a. What could be done to reduce the amount of fluctuation?
    b. What interest was there in reducing the amount of price fluctuation?
4. What led over time to a system of fixed prices?
    a. What were the real and the stated reasons for fixing prices?
    b. What groups gained the most and the least from the system of fixed prices? Did the system of fixed prices prove to be viable? Explain.
5. What do you think Radford meant by the last sentence of his paper: 'On the 12th of April, with the arrival of elements of the 30th US Infantry Division, the ushering in of an age of plenty demonstrated the hypothesis that with infinite means economic organization and activity would be redundant, as every want could be satisfied without effort'?

Discussion Suggestions

The question clusters will help clarify the nature of markets and how they spring up even in the most unlikely situations. As noted above, Smith's description of the price of mourning cloth is most illuminating, and one that students can understand. The real benefits come from asking students to relate this reading to other reading selections. The most obvious comparison is with Adam Smith's, 'On the natural and market price of commodities'. Students should be encouraged to identify the similarities and differences in the situations described by the authors. A quite different comparison is with Hayek's paper on 'The Uses of Knowledge'. Students should be challenged to show how Hayek's paper can illuminate what happened in the P.O.W. camp, and how what happened in the P.O.W. camp can illuminate Hayek's analysis. Students should be encouraged to identify links to other reading selections. It may be important for students to review the other selections if they have not read them recently.

'THE USE OF KNOWLEDGE IN SOCIETY', F. A. HAYEK

Designing an efficient economic system – a rational economic order – hinges on finding some way of bringing together the often partial and contradictory knowledge that is widely dispersed among individuals. The economic problem that needs to be solved is not that of allocating scarce resources, taking knowledge as a given, but rather how to secure the best use of resources known to some members of society for ends whose relative importance only these individuals know.

Hayek argues that economic planning does not work because it must be done centrally, based on the limited knowledge available to the planners. The alternative, competition, decentralizes planning by bringing together many separate individuals whose knowledge differs. The economic system that will be most efficient makes the fullest use of all existing knowledge, not just that possessed by expert planners. Hayek contends that neither agreed-upon scientific knowledge nor statistical aggregates used to measure economic performance provide this kind of knowledge.

The knowledge needed for a capitalistic system to operate effectively is far less than the complete knowledge assumption taken as given in most economic analysis. As Hayek points out, decision makers do not need to know everything about a market but only how changes affect it. This information is reflected in prices, which serve to coordinate the activities of individuals and lead to responses by other individuals who have no knowledge of what factors triggered earlier change in, say, prices. In short, the price mechanism communicates information, offering a process by which knowledge is constantly communicated, acquired, and used by individuals to make decisions.

Learning Objectives

After reading and discussing this selection, students should be able to

1. Describe the various types of knowledge discussed by Hayek.
2. Explain why the knowledge possessed by both economic planners and individuals is less than complete.
3. Explain the coordinating function served by prices.
4. Elaborate why individuals in a capitalistic system can operate effectively with so little information.

Question Clusters

1. Why is Hayek so critical of the common assumptions in economic analysis about possession of all relevant information, a given set of preferences, and complete knowledge of available means?
   a. What does Hayek mean by each of these terms?
   b. Why does he speak about 'data', and what is the nature of these 'data'?
   c. What does he mean by 'knowledge of particular circumstances of time and place'?
2. Why is economic planning destined to fail?

3. Why, according to Hayek, is so little information needed to operate effectively in a complex market economy?
   a. What is the minimum information needed by economic planners and individuals?
   b. Does the minimum differ for planners and for individuals? How? Why?
   c. What happens when some individuals possess more information than other individuals?
4. Why does Hayek comment on the importance of the division of labor and the 'rapid adaptation of changes in the particular circumstances of time and place'?
5. Why does Hayek use the term 'marvel' in his discussion of the economy of knowledge?
6. What is the significance of the quotation from Alfred Whitehead in advancing Hayek's argument?

Discussion Suggestions

Students can profit from reading this essay in conjunction with the famous article by R. A. Radford, 'The Prisoner of War Camp'. While Hayek discusses the importance of knowledge at the conceptual level, Radford demonstrates the importance of knowledge about 'the particular circumstances of time and place' to understanding why and how the prison camp economy developed as it did. Just as students may have difficulty with the conceptual approach taken by Hayek, they may also have difficulty – but of a different kind – with the 'time and place' focus of the Radford article. Although economists typically lead with theory and follow with application, we suggest in this case starting with the application in the Radford article and then moving to the Hayek essay, which focuses on the conceptual framework. Students will quickly see the principles enunciated by Hayek after having read and discussed the Radford article. In addition, they will be less surprised by the seeming novelty of Hayek's approach. In discussing the Radford article, students should be asked to draw any parallels they can find with Adam's discussion of prices in his Chapter 7 of Book 1.

'REFLECTION: AFTER COMMUNISM', ROBERT L. HEILBRONER

Robert Heilbroner here describes what he calls the tragedy of socialism. He focuses on the demise of Soviet Communism in the late 1980s, and the failure of central economic planning, along with the impossibility of coordinating the activities of millions of producers and consumers. The root of the problem lies in the command system (which is why the Soviet Union was described in economic textbooks as a 'command economy'). Assembling, interpreting, and then acting on the vast amounts of information required for centralized economic planning is an impossible task. Even if a realistic plan could be developed and implemented, these plans are too rigid to accommodate fluctuations in supply and demand, natural calamities, and technical progress. Nor is there any guarantee the bureaucracy in charge of the planning system can make good decisions.

The problems of maintaining a planned economy began to emerge in the 1960s with a long, steady erosion in the quality of life in the Soviet Union. This change led to President Gorbachev's 'perestroika', which called for reforming the Soviet economy by freeing it up from the restrictions under which it labored. In other words, the plan was to introduce a modified form of capitalism. Doing so created two realms of power, the realm of economic power dealing with economic activity and a political realm dealing with the traditional functions of government. The existence of two separate centers of power generated conflict, with each realm seeking to intrude on the other.

Heilbroner believes that the prospects for socialism are bleak in view of what has happened. Though socialism may have some appeal in suggesting the kind of world in which our grandchildren would like to live, the only hope might be a socialistic capitalism. But even this possibility seems remote, unless the world's growing ecological problems force dramatic changes on capitalism. What will emerge in such a circumstance is left for the reader to ponder.

Learning Objectives

After reading and discussing this selection, students should be able to

1. Explain why the Soviet planning system faltered and then collapsed.
2. Explain the inherent shortcomings in 'command' economics.
3. Explain the concept of perestroika and its implications.
4. Explain the challenge of achieving some of the key goals of socialism while an economy is in transition to some form of capitalism.

Question Clusters

1. What does Heilbroner mean when he says, 'The economic side of the Russian collapse...came as a shock'?
2. Why does Heilbroner point to 'the economic system itself' as the villain in the deterioration of the Soviet economy?

a. What accounts for the conflicting views of economists about the virtues of economic planning?
b. What makes national economic planning so inherently difficult?
c. What is the importance of 'success indicators' in achieving the goals of economic planning?
d. How were the problems of central planning 'fixed'?
3. What forces were unleashed by 'perestroika' and 'glasnost'?
a. What is the meaning of these two terms?
b. What obstacles have slowed the transition to a market-based economy?
4. What does Heilbroner mean by the phrase, 'Not Socialism'?
a. Does he believe the Soviet collapse will mean a move toward some modified version of capitalism?
b. What are the virtues and defects of capitalism as viewed by Heilbroner?
c. In what sense does Heilbroner see 'market socialism' as a kind of middle way?
5. What do you think of the importance Heilbroner places on ecological problems in moderating capitalism to produce what he calls a 'social order capitalism'?
6. What are your reactions to Heilbroner's writing style and his extensive use of metaphors?

Discussion Suggestions

This selection should be read in conjunction with the other Heilbroner selection, 'Reflections: The Triumph of Capitalism'. It is probably best read before 'Triumph' as a way of establishing that the Soviet system had indeed collapsed and why it collapsed. With this as background, 'Triumph' may make more sense to contemporary college students, who were small children at the time of the Soviet collapse. While discussing the selection, students should be encouraged to identify and comment on Heilbroner's skillful and lively use of language.

'THE TIDE IS TURNING', MILTON AND ROSE FRIEDMAN

This selection comes from the popular, 1979 best-selling book, *Free to Choose*, coauthored by Milton Friedman and his wife, Rose. The book is both a restatement and an extension of Milton Friedman's 1962 book, *Capitalism and Freedom*.

In this concluding chapter, the Friedmans suggest that the movement away from ever-growing government may be reversing itself, citing a number of indicators of change. But, after reviewing unrelenting pressure to expand the functions performed by government, particularly the federal government, they believe the only way to curb continued growth is through constitutional means. In practice, this means creating and adopting what they call an Economic Bill of Rights. When fully developed, and they admit to the preliminary nature of their proposal, this Economic Bill of Rights would parallel the Constitutional or political Bill of Rights enacted shortly after the US Constitution was ratified in 1789. The larger purpose of this Bill of Rights would be to preserve economic liberty and ensure a better balance between human freedom and economic freedom.

Learning Objectives

After reading and discussing this selection, students should be able to

1. Explain the major forces that account for the ever-growing and widening scope of government activity.
2. Explain what an Economic Bill of Rights would accomplish and how it would operate.
3. Explain how an Economic Bill of Rights would be effective in ensuring continuation of the Friedmans' conclusion that '[t]he two ideas of human freedom and economic freedom working together came to their greatest fruition in the United States'.
4. Explain how to develop the Economic Bill of Rights so that it would parallel the Bill of Rights reflected in the first ten amendments to the US Constitution.

Question Clusters

1. What do the Friedmans mean by their title, 'The Tide is Turning'?
   a. What do they mean by the word 'tide'?
   b. What do they mean by the word 'turning'?
   c. What do the authors mean by 'climate of opinion'?
   d. What factors shape the 'climate of opinion'?
   e. What are the links between opinion and behavior?
2. What do the authors mean when they speak of an 'invisible hand' in politics?
   a. How does this 'invisible hand' contrast with the 'invisible hand' of Adam Smith?
   b. Why do these two kinds of 'invisible hands' operate so differently?
   c. How are conflicts resolved between general and special interests?
3. What do the authors mean by an 'Economic Bill of Rights'?

    a. Why is there a need for this kind of Bill of Rights?
    b. What are the likely effects of passing such a Bill of Rights?
    c. What form would such a Bill of Rights have to take?
4. Why do the authors give central importance to limitations on taxing and spending?
5. What would appear to be the obstacles to enacting an Economic Bill of Rights?

Discussion Suggestions

This is a provocative and challenging reading selection, provocative because it connects economics and politics more intimately than any other selections except the Friedman selection and the first two Okun selections. In ideal circumstances, students would have read the Friedman selection because it establishes the link between economic and political freedom. In conjunction with the Okun selections, this Friedman selection should help sharpen the discussion about the role of government. It involves not the balancing of efficiency versus equity, or rights versus dollars, in the words of Okun, but rather balancing, or regaining equilibrium between economic and political freedoms.

'RIGHTS AND DOLLARS', ARTHUR OKUN

In Chapter 1, Okun sets the stage for his thesis by describing the conflict between economic efficiency and equality, and the compromises society must make in attempting to balance these two seemingly conflicting goals. While in a democracy political and social rights are distributed equally, the unequal distribution of income and wealth makes it possible for some to transgress the usual limits of these political and social rights.

Okun contends that the market needs a place and the market needs to be kept in its place. This recurrent dual theme of the book distinguishes Okun both from radical thinkers who would abolish or seriously limit market capitalism and from exponents of laissez-faire capitalism, who would strengthen the role of market forces. Okun values the market as a decentralized and efficient system for spurring and channeling productive effort and for promoting experiment and innovation; he also sees it as a protector of individual freedom of expression. But he insists that other values must be protected from the potential tyranny of the dollar's influence, and that many rights and powers should not be able to be bought for money. The importance of these and other values, and the problems of protecting them from trespass by the market are the subjects of this chapter.

Learning Objectives

After reading and discussing this chapter, students should be able to

1. Explain the nature of the conflict between the political and economic systems.
2. Explain the meaning of dollars and rights, and the compromise between them.
3. Explain how the concept of balanced dollars and rights is related to the concepts of economic efficiency and equality.

Question Clusters

1. What does Okun mean by the terms equality and efficiency?
2. Why does Okun make a distinction between rights and dollars?
   a. What does he mean by rights and dollars? Universal entitlement rights? Positive rights? Negative rights?
   b. What are the main features or characteristics of rights?
   c. In what sense does the distribution of rights come at the expense of equity and freedom?
3. In what sense can dollars transgress upon rights?
   a. What are some examples of these transgressions?
   b. What can be done to limit the effect of these transgressions?
4. What does Okun mean when he says 'The domain of rights is full of infringements on the calculus of economic efficiency'?
   a. What features of rights lead to this conclusion?
   b. Why does the distribution of rights stress equality even at the expense of equity and freedom?
5. What reasons does Okun give for establishing what can be called 'inefficient' rights?
6. Where does Okun suggest drawing the line between the domain of rights and that of the marketplace?
7. In what sense could this chapter have been written by a political scientist?

Discussion Suggestions

Every effort must be made to ensure that students have a firm grasp of this first chapter of Okun's book. A clear understanding of it will greatly facilitate their comprehension of the succeeding chapters. For many of them, the contrast between the equality of political rights and the inequality of individuals to engage in market activities will give them new insights. Working through the question clusters will help them grasp the essential concepts and theme of the book. To assist in this effort, students need to begin with an understanding of such terms as 'liberty', 'pluralism', 'libertarianism', and 'externalities'.

'THE CASE FOR THE MARKET', ARTHUR OKUN

In Chapter 2, Okun lays out the case for capitalism, with its emphasis on rights and freedoms in the marketplace. He begins by considering the ethics of the reward system and identifies the two principal sources of the inequalities in income and wealth, namely, private ownership of property and market-determined wages and salaries. He explains why he rejects rewards for contribution as an ethical principle, but feels forced to accept it, within limits, as a pragmatic necessity. He then compares the degree of efficiency, equality, and freedom provided by our current mixed system of capitalism with that obtainable from full-fledged socialism. In so doing, he conveys his strong skepticism about the merits of socialist proposals. He concludes that we must stick with capitalism because a collectivized society would cost too much in economic efficiency to warrant the gains that might be produced by reducing disparities in income and wealth.

Learning Objectives

After reading and discussing this chapter, students should be able to

1. Explain the rights and freedoms of the marketplace.
2. Describe the tensions between the rights and freedoms of the marketplace and the distribution of rewards from the marketplace.
3. Elaborate how Okun tries to balance the benefits of efficiency with the gains from greater equality in income.

Question Clusters

1. What does Okun mean by the rights and freedoms of the marketplace?
   a. What links does he makes between property rights and freedom?
   b. In what ways do property rights enhance personal freedom?
   c. Can 'collectivized ownership' enhance personal freedom?
   d. How do bureaucracies 'transgress' on the rights and freedoms of the marketplace?
2. Why is the 'tolerance . . . for economic inequality so puzzling'?
   a. Why are the non-affluent so charitable toward the rich majority?
   b. What are the views of radicals about economic inequality?

   c. In what sense can inequalities of opportunity as well as discrimination be viewed as 'flaws rather than fundamental defects of the system'?

3. What ethical issues are raised by the system of rewards under capitalism?
   a. What factors explain differences in economic rewards?
   b. What advantages and disadvantages does Okun see in moving toward a collectivized economy?

4. How does Okun justify his preference for greater equality in the distribution of income and in the distribution of rights?
   a. What worries does he discuss and what is the basis for these worries?
   b. What is his view of self-interest and of competition?

5. On what grounds does Okun conclude that though 'the ethical case for capitalism is totally unpersuasive, the efficiency case is thoroughly compelling to me'.

Discussion Suggestions

Here, students get the other side of Okun's story. Thus, it is important to have students discuss Chapter 2 as soon as possible after discussing Chapter 1. A useful question to help them focus on what they value and how their values might have been influenced by the combination of these two readings might take this form: How would people you know place themselves on the efficiency versus equity issue? Why would they do so? What is your position?

OVERVIEW

The selections presented here are designed to provoke students to think about what markets can and do accomplish, to give students differing perspectives on markets, and to reveal the tensions between markets and the political environment within which they operate.

Several themes emerge. The first is what might be called the spontaneity of markets. They seem to arise out of some innate propensity among individuals, in the words of Adam Smith, to 'truck and barter', and the fact that markets generate the information needed for individuals to participate effectively in markets. The power of these forces becomes apparent in the descriptions by Smith and Radford of two quite different situations in which markets developed, and in Hayek's elaboration of the knowledge-generating function of markets. The need for markets is also described by Heilbroner, who details how illicit markets emerged even within a centrally planned economy to compensate for the absence of official markets, which, if they had existed, would have conveyed the information required by the centrally-planned economy to operate efficiently.

The second is the conflict regarding the scope of markets and the inevitable pressures to restrict their activity. Okun offers an insightful discussion of the conflict between rights in the political sphere and dollars in the economic sphere, and how each sphere intrudes on the other. He concludes with a strong defense of markets, though he recognizes the need for some restraints on markets. The Friedmans, by contrast, believe the growth of government is interfering seriously with markets, thereby compromising economic freedom. To at least counter, if not reverse this trend, the Friedmans propose a Bill of Economic Rights that would prevent further government intrusion into the market system.

Taken together, these selections generate several questions:

1. Is there some natural propensity among people to want to enter into exchanges that are in time regularized as markets, as suggested by Smith, Radford, Hayek, and Heilbroner?
2. Is there some similar, perhaps natural, tendency among people to want to regulate exchanges carried out in markets? What do the above four authors have to say on this matter in their reading selections? Elsewhere?
3. What accounts for Okun's attempt to find a balance between individual rights and the market? Is he rejecting the positions taken by Smith, Radford, Hayek, and Heilbroner? Does Okun seem to succeed in his effort to find such a balance?
4. What would Okun say to the Friedmans, and what would the Friedmans say to Okun after examining each other's position?
5. In what sense is there a need for a Bill of Economic Rights comparable our political Bill of Rights? Would a Bill of Economic Rights allow, in the words of Okun, too much intrusion by the market into the domain of individual rights? If so, might there be a way to impose some limits on economic freedom so as not to further compromise individual rights?

14. Incentives and Markets

Markets appear in a variety of forms. Some work well; others work less well because of what are called market failures. Similarly, attempts to correct for market failures often lead to what are called non-market failures. Both market failure and non-market failures create incentives that individuals and groups quickly seek to exploit. This chapter's selections explore some of these issues.

The first selection is Akerlof's famous lemons article, 'The Market for "Lemons": Quality Uncertainty and the Market Mechanism'. Akerlof explains how markets may fail when information is asymmetrically available to agents. Car sellers know whether their car is a lemon or not. Car buyers do not. A buyer offers a price that is lower than the value of a good used car because the buyer knows that car could turn out to be a lemon. As a result, owners of good cars leave the market. Akerlof uses asymmetric information to explain why older people find it difficult to buy health insurance and why minority workers have difficulty finding employment.

The second article by Barnett and Kaserman, 'The "Rush to Transplant" and the Organ Shortages', discusses medical transplantation of organs. The authors argue that the ban on the sale of cadaveric organs has created perverse incentives that have resulted in large increases in the number of medical centers conducting transplants, an increase in the cost of transplant services, and a decline in the quality of those services. They argue that these unintended consequences have arisen as medical centers attempt to obtain the economic rents that result from harvesting cadaveric organs.

The third selection is a classic article, 'Reflections on Price Control', by Galbraith, which deals with price controls in World War II. He seeks to explain why economists were generally wrong in their pre-war assumptions that price controls would not work in war-time. Galbraith discusses what made it possible for controls to work as well as they did. In addition to the importance of the structure of price and other kinds of control (e.g. rationing, raw material allocations, etc.), he emphasizes the importance of 'stigma' in keeping people in line. Interestingly, he finds the presence of imperfect markets, principally oligopolistic industries, contributed to the success of the price control program.

The next selection is another chapter from the *Wealth of Nations*, 'On the Expense of the Institutions for the Education of Youth'. It explores the implications of who pays for education, on how attentive faculty members are to their teaching duties, and to a lesser degree, on how attentive students are to their own reasons for attending college: namely, to learn. Much depends on how the costs are shared. To the degree costs are borne by the state, the incentives for faculty to excel are weak. To the degree that the costs are borne by students, professors will perform in ways that will attract more students who are interested in learning. This is vintage Smith: many concrete examples describing what happens, and experiences to draw upon elsewhere that help illustrate the points he makes.

The next selection is from a book, *Choices and Consequence*, by Schelling, who tries to understand why there has been so little economic analysis of criminal activity and what he terms 'the criminal industry'. To promote work on the economics of crime, he develops parallels between different sectors of the criminal industry and more traditional industries. He seems to be saying that we can learn much by applying to 'underworld' activities what we have learned about 'legitimate' activities.

The next selection, by Wolf, breaks new ground in his attempt to develop a classification of non-market failures that parallels the traditional discussion of market failure. Wolf calls non-market failures government actions that seek to remedy market failures but generate incentives that undercut their own effectiveness. Though the costs of non-market failure are difficult to isolate and measure, he argues that these costs should be considered more carefully in addressing market failures.

The final selection, from 'The Perfect Demographic Storm: Entitlements Imperil America's Future' by Kotlikof and Burns, examines what might be called the political market for the reform of two major entitlement programs, Social Security and Medicare. The authors apply the technique of generational accounting to analyze the looming problem of paying the costs of this country's rapidly-growing entitlement programs. They also propose solutions, none of which is likely to be popular.

'THE MARKET FOR "LEMONS": QUALITY UNCERTAINTY AND THE MARKET MECHANISM', GEORGE A. AKERLOF

In this, the original 'Lemons' paper, George Akerlof connects asymmetric information and market failure. Akerlof illustrates the connection by describing new and used markets for automobiles, and then shows how asymmetric information affects markets for health insurance, labor, and credit. In the final section, he discusses institutions that can counteract the problems created by asymmetric information.

Akerlof envisions a world with two kinds of automobiles – lemons and good cars. Car buyers know that the probability that a car is good is less than 1. The purchaser of a new car will, with experience, revise the probability that his car is good and have better information about the quality of the car than others. Since prospective buyers cannot tell the difference between a good car and a lemon, the two must fetch the same price in the used car market. Also, the used car price must be lower than the new car price, even if the car is only weeks old, because otherwise the owners of lemons would simply trade them in for another draw from the new car distribution. A market failure results because lemons drive the good cars from the used car market and the owner of a good car cannot realize its true value by selling it.

Akerlof uses market failures that result from asymmetric information to explain why older people have more trouble obtaining health insurance – at any price. An individual will know more about her health than will be revealed by an insurance check up. As the price of insurance rises, healthy old folks prefer to self-insure, and the average medical condition of insurance applicants deteriorates. Medicare may be wise policy. Everyone may be willing to pay the expected cost of Medicare, and yet no private company would offer insurance at that price because of the inevitable adverse selection.

Akerlof investigates the problems of hiring minority workers and lending funds in developing countries through the lens of asymmetric information. He argues that employers may take ethnicity into consideration because they cannot, at reasonable cost, tell the difference between more capable and less capable individuals. He points out that firms in India develop relationships with managerial and family groups: in the first case to establish a reputation for honest dealing, in the second to have access to non-market enforcement mechanisms.

Akerlof concludes by noting that many institutions arise to counteract problems associated with asymmetric information. He suggests that guarantees, warranties, brands, and chains all exist at least in part to minimize the lemons problem.

Learning Objectives

After reading and discussing the 'lemons' article, students should be able to

1. Explain what is meant by asymmetric information and provide examples of markets and products where information asymmetry exists.
2. Explain what is meant by adverse selection.
3. Reconstruct Akerlof's argument that asymmetric information leads to adverse selection.
4. Explain why adverse selection creates market failure.

5. Explain how asymmetric information and adverse selection lead firms to join managing agencies in India.
6. Use the concepts of asymmetric information and adverse selection to explain the great difference in interest rates caused by banks and local moneylenders in developing countries.

Question Clusters

1. What does Akerlof mean by 'asymmetric information'?
   a. How does the example of the used car market illustrate asymmetric information?
   b. The example of health care for the elderly?
   c. The example of minority hiring?
   d. The example of credit markets in developing countries?
2. Why, according to Akerlof, can asymmetric information about product quality lead to market failure?
   a. What does Akerlof mean by 'adverse selection'?
   b. What is the connection between adverse selection and market failure?
   c. What, according to Akerlof, is the market failure in the used car market? The medical insurance market? The developing country credit market?
   d. How does Akerlof use asymmetric information and adverse selection to explain the unwillingness of some employers to hire minority applicants?
   e. What did George Stigler mean when he said, 'in a regime of ignorance Enrico Fermi would have been a gardener'?
   f. Why, according to Akerlof, are the costs of dishonesty greater than the amount by which people are cheated?
3. What, according to Akerlof, are remedies for the 'lemons' problem?
   a. How does joining an association like a 'managing agency' provide a remedy for firms?
   b. In what sense is borrowing from family members a remedy?
   c. Why is Medicare a remedy?
   d. How would you use Akerlof's ideas to explain the business plan of the 'CarMax' company (www.carmax.com)?
4. In your view, is adverse selection an important economic problem?
   a. Is adverse selection a powerful economic concept?
   b. Should consideration of adverse selection guide economic policy?
   c. What kinds of policy should pay particular attention to the problems of asymmetric information and adverse selection?

5. How does the utility-based example given by Akerlof in section II illustrate a market failure resulting from asymmetric information and adverse selection?
   a. How is asymmetric information built into the example in section II. B.?
   b. How does Akerlof derive the demand for automobiles?
   c. Why is it true that no trade will take place between group one and two no matter the price of an automobile? Why is that result important?
   d. Why is the example of section II. C. an example of symmetric information?
   e. How does comparison of the examples of sections II. B. and II. C. support the conclusion that asymmetric information is the source of market failure?

Discussion Suggestions

Many students can profitably read and discuss Akerlof's article because the main ideas of the article may be comprehended without following the utility theory example presented in Section II. Principles instructors may wish to focus attention on the definitions of asymmetric information and adverse selection, how they help explain economic puzzles, and how they can guide economic policy. Intermediate micro instructors may wish to focus attention on the welfare results, and require their students to complete the derivations in section II. Question cluster 5 is meant to be used in a course where students are expected to work through Akerlof's utility theory analysis.

'THE "RUSH TO TRANSPLANT" AND ORGAN SHORTAGES', A. H. BARNETT AND DAVID L. KASERMAN

Normally, entry of firms into an industry lowers profit, cost, and prices paid by consumers. Entry of hospitals into the transplant industry, however, has raised costs and generally led to a lower quality of care for transplant recipients, and, hence, a higher quality-adjusted price for transplants. But why?

Barnett and Kaserman trace these perverse effects of hospitals' entry into the transplant industry to a root cause – public policy that prohibits purchases and sales of cadaveric organs. By keeping the price of organs at zero, public policy has kept the quantity of transplantable organs from growing with demand. At the same time, the number of hospitals offering transplants has increased dramatically. For example, heart transplant centers in the US increased from 12 in 1983 to 148 in 1989. Growth in the number of transplant centers and no growth in the number of available organs have combined to lower the average number of transplants conducted by any center, to raise the costs of those transplants by raising average fixed costs and increasing demand for transplant surgeons, and to lower improvements in quality associated with learning-by-doing on the part of transplant teams.

But why the growth in transplant centers? Barnett and Kaserman explain that the prohibition on sales of cadaveric organs has created rents and that the increase in transplant centers is an attempt to capture those rents. While federal regulations require hospitals to list them on a united organ sharing network, they permit the harvesting hospital to transplant them in many cases. The way for a hospital to capture rents is to harvest and transplant as many organs as possible.

Perversely, the increase in transplant centers raises costs and lowers the average quality of care for the transplant patient. The addition of each new transplant center lowers the average number of transplants performed at each one, and raises average fixed costs associated with maintaining surgical and treatment teams and specialized operating theaters. In equilibrium, the economic profit of entry must be zero, but the cost of a transplant will be high.

Learning Objectives

After reading and discussing this article, students should be able to

1. Explain why the prohibition on the sale of cadaveric organs creates economic rents.
2. Reconstruct Barnett and Kaserman's explanation of the connection between the shortage of organs and the growth in transplant centers.
3. Interpret Figure 1 and explain how the authors use it to support their explanation of the effects of an increase in transplant centers.
4. Describe and explain the economic consequences of prohibiting the sale of cadaveric organs.
5. Judge whether or not they favor permitting a market in cadaveric organs.

Question Clusters

1. Why, according to Barnett and Kaserman, has there been a large increase in the number of transplant hospitals even though there has been no increase in the number of transplant organs?
   a. Why, according to the authors, has the number of transplants not grown with improvements in transplant technology?
   b. Why, according to the authors, do hospital administrators have an incentive to open a transplant center?

   c. What, according to the authors, have been the economic consequences
      of the growth in transplant centers?
2. Why, according to Barnett and Kaserman, do laws prohibiting the sale of
   cadaveric organs raise the price and lower the quality of transplants?
   a. Why, according to the authors, do the laws raise the cost of a transplant?
   b. Why, according to the authors, do the laws lower the quality of
      transplant patient care?
   c. How do Barnett and Kaserman use Figure 1 to explain their reasoning?
3. Should we repeal the laws that make it illegal to buy and sell cadaveric
   organs?
   a. What would be the economic consequences of such a repeal?
   b. What, in your opinion, are other consequences of the repeal?
   c. Are you in favor or opposed to a repeal? Why?

Discussion Suggestions

The Barnett and Kaserman article provides an excellent opportunity for both
principles students and intermediate microeconomic students to discuss the
public policy implications of a particular price regulation. For principles
students, the article provides an excellent opportunity to practice thinking like
an economist by examining the incentives created by a price regulation and
the unintended consequences of imposing it. For intermediate microeconomic
students, the article provides an opportunity to apply what they know about
entry, rents, economic profits, and declining cost industries.

'REFLECTIONS ON PRICE CONTROL', J. K. GALBRAITH

Fighting World War II required a full-scale mobilization of the US economy.
As production of military supplies and equipment expanded rapidly after the
Pearl Harbor attack in December 1941, the supplies of many finished goods
and services began to contract as raw materials of all kinds were diverted from
civilian to military uses. To head off expected sharp increases in prices, early
efforts were made to introduce price and wage controls, to ration civilian
goods in short supply, and to allocate raw material resources to meet military
priorities. New agencies were created to handle these duties, and many of the
nation's economists were hired to administer these new programs.

    Among them was John Kenneth Galbraith, who later served as a professor
of economics at Harvard and is widely known for his writing about economics,
which include *The Great Crash*, *The Affluent Society*, and *The New Industrial
State*. Shortly after the war ended, Galbraith, in this particular reading

selection, describes his understanding of how price controls operated and the effects they produced.

Galbraith begins by wondering why economists before the war undervalued the likely efficiency of price controls. He goes on to explain the benefits of overall price controls introduced in Spring 1942. He maintains that the reason why prices for rationed consumer goods and allocated producers goods remained stable was not mysterious. The answer lay in the industrial structure and the extent to which buyers could and did identify with sellers. This identification was facilitated by monopoly and oligopoly. Price enforcers found it much easier to communicate with the small numbers of sellers in these markets. Moreover, during the war these large firms continued using the same approach to setting prices as they had before the war, thereby lending an additional element of stability to prices.

Galbraith concludes that price controls would have been impossible to administer in an economy with pure or perfect competition. What made it possible for price control to succeed was the nation's 'sympathetic price structure', meaning the size and concentration of major industries involved in wartime production.

Learning Objectives

After reading and discussing this selection, students should be able to

1. Explain why economists were skeptical about the effectiveness of price control as an emergency policy measure.
2. Describe how informal rationing and enforcement helped to prevent price increases.
3. Explain how market structure operated to restrain price level increases.
4. Clarify how the passage of time affected price level increases.

Question Clusters

1. Why, according to Galbraith, 'did economists before the war generally undervalue the efficiency of price control as an instrument of emergency policy'?
   a. What does Galbraith mean in using the term 'undervalue'?
   b. What does Galbraith mean by the 'efficiency of price control'?
2. How effective was the G.M.P.R. (General Maximum Price Regulation) in holding down prices?
   a. What was the G.M.P.R.?
   b. What does Galbraith claim were the advantages of the G.M.P.R.? How did it work? How effective was it?

c. What is the meaning of the statement: 'Without [adequate taxation, savings, and wage stabilization] the ceiling would in the long-run become *administratively unenforceable and socially harmful*'?

d. What is the meaning of the term 'inflationary gap' in the context of the G.M.P.R.?

3. What does Galbraith mean by a 'disequilibrium at legislated prices'?

4. What does Galbraith mean in referring to a 'sympathetic market structure' as an aid in preventing price increases?

a. What does Galbraith mean by this term, and why does he use it?

b. What are the advantages to price control enforcement that result from the prevalence of monopolies and oligopolies?

c. Why is custom so important to price stability?

d. What is the importance to price stability of excess capacity in these kinds of firms?

5. What does Galbraith have to say about the impact on costs (and hence prices) of increasing costs?

a. What is the Defense Plan Corporation (D.P.C.)?

b. Why can Galbraith say that, because the government provided plant and equipment to private firms, the 'existing supply of fixed plant ceased to be a factor shaping the supply curve'?

c. What is the link Galbraith sees between decreasing costs and market imperfections in affecting price level increases?

6. What does Galbraith mean by his final sentence: 'Yet one could say of overall price control that, while it proved itself a rugged instrument of war-time economic policy, it also proved that, if initiated *de nouveau*, it is administratively all but impossible'.

Discussion Suggestions

Students are likely to gain the most from reading and discussing this selection in intermediate theory courses and industrial organization courses. By then they will have a good understanding of the meaning and significance of price controls, rationing, and market structure.

'OF THE EXPENSE OF THE INSTITUTIONS FOR THE EDUCATION OF YOUTH', ADAM SMITH

Smith describes different approaches to paying the expenses of education, what we would commonly call the 'costs' of education. He states that because education benefits the whole society, the expenses may be defrayed by the general contribution of the whole society, i.e., through public revenues. At the other extreme, he argues that it might be advantageous to have these expenses paid by the immediate beneficiaries of education, namely students, perhaps with the assistance of their parents. Still another possibility is to pay these costs by voluntary contributions from individual members of society. Within this framework of possibilities, Smith explores the implications of who pays for the costs of the effectiveness of the teaching.

Learning Objectives

After reading and discussing the Smith selection, students should be able to

1. Explain the different methods that are and could be used to finance the education of the young.
2. Describe the effects of different methods of payment on the incentives of teachers that affect the quantity and quality of their work effort.
3. Explain why the work effort of teachers differs among individual teachers.
4. Explain how the quantity and quality of work effort expended by students may be affected by the incentives they recognize.
5. Outline how Smith's analysis can be applied to current questions about the financing of education, both elementary-secondary education and higher education.

Question Clusters

1. What does Smith mean when he says that 'exertion ...is always in proportion to the necessity they are under of making that exertion'?
   a. What is the meaning of 'rivalship and emulation render excellency...an object of ambition, and frequently occasion the very greatest exertions.'?
   b. What is the effect of being 'born to easy fortunes' on being eminent in that profession [law]?
2. What is the effect of student fees on work effort by teachers?
   a. What happens when fees constitute part of the emoluments of the teacher?
   b. What happens when teachers are prohibited from accepting fees?
   c. What does Smith mean by the statement, '[i]t is the interest of every man to live as much at his ease as he can.'?
3. How does 'the authority to which he is subject' affect the performance of teachers?
4. What is the impact on students of different kinds of regulations concerning attendance?

a. Analyze this statement: 'The discipline of colleges and universities is in general contrived, not for the benefit of the students, but for the interest, or more properly speaking, for the ease of the masters'.
   b. Why are students 'generally inclined to pardon a great deal of incorrectness in the performance of his [the teacher's] duties'?
5. What advantages does Smith see in private schools?
6. How does Smith describe what might be called the societal benefits of higher education?
7. Do you agree with Smith's view that where the masters 'really perform their duty, there are no examples, I believe, that the greater part of students ever neglect theirs'?

Discussion Suggestions

This selection appeals to students because Smith discusses what accounts for the quality of teaching, something about which most students are acutely aware. Smith's presentation is quite straightforward, and students should have little difficulty understanding it. What they may fail to see is that Smith's analysis applies equally to students, inasmuch as most students, except for some who attend private colleges and universities, rarely pay the full costs of their schooling. They are financed (subsidized) by taxpayers through below-cost tuition, by merit and/or need-based grants, by subsidized loans, and often by their parents. Turning Smith's analysis around to focus on students will assuredly provoke lively discussion and make apparent to students how incentives affect both their behavior and the behavior of their instructors. This selection can also serve as a base for discussing the effects of vouchers in elementary and high school grades, and financial aid for students attending colleges and universities.

'ECONOMICS AND CRIMINAL ENTERPRISE', THOMAS SCHELLING

In this reading selection, taken from his 1984 book, *Choice and Consequence*, Schelling asks why economists have devoted so little attention to the economics of crime. As he sees it, crime is another form of economic activity, illegal though it may be. Such 'underworld' activity needs to be examined, and this can be done by using the conventional tools economists apply to the 'overworld' of legitimate economic activity.

The author notes that criminal activity varies widely in how it is organized and carried out, from the highly organized and secretive Mafia to small-time crimes committed by individuals, most of which involve theft of what can be called consumer goods. Racketeering operates on a different scale, by either destroying competition through criminal monopoly or by taking the gains of somebody's economic activity through extortion. Other forms of criminal activity of interest to Schelling include what he calls 'black-market monopolies', cartels, and organized criminal services.

Schelling argues that large scale criminal organizations can be analyzed to good effect by taking an industrial organization approach. Any such analysis will be complex because the nature of activities carried out in support of criminal activity are so different from those in support of the conventional production of goods and services. He moves on to discuss market structure, but notes that the essential ingredient for analyzing the economics of crime requires 'analysis of market adjustments' to change. Performing such an analysis is not easy because evidence of who benefits and who loses is often hidden from view. There are also what he calls 'institutional practices' that determine the profitability of criminal activity, involving the various ways that criminals extract revenue to finance criminal activity.

After raising questions about the benefits and costs from a policy perspective, Schelling concludes by suggesting that eliminating all criminal activity would be difficult, if not impossible. The best alternative, he suggests, depends on whether the cost of the goal of somewhat reducing certain kinds of consumption activity is outweighed by the costs of creating and maintaining a criminal industry.

Learning Objectives

After reading and discussing this selection, students should be able to

1. Recapitulate the different forms of criminal activity of potential interest to economists.
2. Describe what situations give rise to criminal organizations and contribute to their continued success.
3. Explain the complexities of understanding criminal activity as economic activity.
4. Explain the importance of black markets in maintaining criminal organizations.
5. Describe how other tools of economic analysis can be used to study criminal activity.

Question Clusters

1. What, according to Schelling, are the benefits of thinking about crime as an economic activity?

a. Why have economists given this topic so little attention?
b. What, according to Schelling, are the consequences of this neglect?
c. Why have 'indictment and conviction' been the dominant public policy approaches to crime?

2. What differentiates the different kinds of crime described in Schelling's typology?
a. What are the different forms he discusses?
b. What is the origin or motivating factor underlying these different forms of criminal activity?
c. What, in economic terms, are the common factors linking most kinds of crime?

3. What conditions give rise to the creation of criminal organizations to carry out crime?
a. Of what importance is size?
b. Of what importance are 'externalities'?
c. Of what importance are 'external economies'?
d. Of what importance is the 'corporate state' mentality?

4. Why, according to Schelling, is it so important to analyze 'market adjustments' in trying to understand the economics of crime?
a. In what sense can we view the costs of crime as a 'tax'?
b. What dictates the kind of 'tax' used in different sectors of the criminal industry?
c. What kinds of redistribution of benefits and costs occur as a result of these taxes, and how do these redistributions vary within the criminal industry?
d. Does Schelling suggest the magnitude of these transfers? Explain.

5. What makes it important, asks Schelling, to think about the 'tradeoffs among different costs and losses resulting from crime, and...in the different ways that government can approach the problem of crime'?
a. How does Schelling suggest these tradeoffs be evaluated?
b. To what degree does evaluating these tradeoffs depend on identifying the 'evils' of crime?
c. How do choices about the costs and losses of crime, and the methods chosen to attack them, generate new incentives that may change these costs and losses and alter the desirability of current methods of fighting crime?

6. In the final page of the reading selection, why does Schelling discuss the costs of black markets without mention of the cost of maintaining them?

Discussion Suggestions

The purpose of this reading selection is to reveal to students how economic analysis can be applied to what might seem to be the most unlikely activities, in this case to criminal activity. Students should be pressed to show the economic incentives that give rise to criminal activity and that sustain it. They should also be asked to think about what other aspects of their learning in economics can be applied to aid in understanding crime as an economic activity. The discussion can be particularly illuminating in discussing the criminal activity that students know best, such as faking ID cards, underage drinking, drug dealing, and so on.

'A THEORY OF NON-MARKET FAILURE', CHARLES WOLF, JR.

Writing in 1979, Wolf, of the RAND Corporation, attempts to remedy what he sees as the asymmetry that exists in thinking about the role of government in remedying market failure. Whereas a well-articulated theory of market failure exists, there is no comparably developed theory of non-market, or government, failure. Wolf, in this well-known paper, tries to fill this gap.

Wolf begins with a succinct summary of the four traditionally cited types of market failure. He then discusses why non-markets fail, going into both supply and demand side considerations, as well as the absence of any kind of market discipline. Based on this background, he then develops a parallel set of non-market failures, matching the categories of market failure with his categories of non-market failure. In assessing the results of his work, Wolf recognizes that the parallelism is not as neat as he had hoped. He also recognizes the greater difficulties of assessing the costs and benefits on non-market failure. He concludes that while it may be impossible to quantify these effects, the direction of these effects can be easily identified. Despite this shortcoming, he argues that awareness of non-market failure will force policy makers to consider more carefully the costs of intervention to correct market failures.

Learning Objectives

After reading and discussing the Wolf selection, students will be able to

1. Explain the nature and sources of market failure.
2. Describe the uniqueness of the sources of non-market failure.

3. Recapitulate Wolf's characterization of non-market failures and their parallels with market failures
4. Explain the advantages and limitations of Wolf's 'corrective' theory.

Question Clusters

1. How can the parallelism Wolf establishes between the traditional sources of market failure and the sources of non-market failure be sharpened?
   a. What are the benchmarks against which economists measure market failure?
   b. What are the benchmarks against which Wolf would measure non-market failure?
   c. Why is it easier to identify and quantify market failure than non-market failure?
2. How does Wolf define his categories of non-market failure?
   a. What does he mean by the terms 'internalities' and 'private' goals?
   b. How do 'internalities' manifest themselves?
   c. What defines the extent to which 'internalities' in non-market output are greater than the externalities in market outputs?
   d. What is the meaning of the non-market failures he characterizes as 'redundant and rising costs', 'derived externalities', and 'distributional equity in non-markets'?
3. What does Wolf mean when he says, 'These parallel categories are suggestive, but should not be misunderstood. The inadequacies or "failures" of non-market activities are not exact analogues of those associated with market activities.'?
   a. What is the source of possible confusion between equating 'internalities' and 'externalities'?
   b. How can this possible confusion be resolved?
4. What accounts for economists' lag in conceptualizing the sources of non-market failure and developing a theory that encompasses them?
   a. How does the quotation from John Maynard Keynes explain the lack of attention to non-market failure?
   b. What role does the work of political scientist Charles E. Lindblom play in responding to this question?
   c. If it were generally recognized by economists and others that there were 'incompetencies' in both the market system and the non-market system, how might this explain what prompted the development of Wolf's concept in the late 1970s?

Discussion Suggestions

The Wolf selection assumes an understanding of markets, the concept of market failures, and the implications of market failure for public policy. Because of the complexity of the subject, this paper is most appropriate for intermediate level classes. This does not mean that the concept of non-market failure should not be introduced in economics principles courses. It should be described there, but not in the detail present in the Wolf reading. This selection offers a unique opportunity to enlist students to consider Wolf's key question: how to further develop the parallelism among the four categories of market and non-market failure. The question is truly an interpretive one, to which there is no clear answer. But, through discussion students may develop some ideas about how to reconcile the two lists. If that is the case, they should communicate their thoughts to the author, Charles Wolf, Jr. He would most assuredly be interested in making 'these parallel categories' more than 'suggestive'.

'THE PERFECT DEMOGRAPHIC STORM: ENTITLEMENTS IMPERIL AMERICA'S FUTURE', LAURENCE J. KOTLIKOF AND SCOTT BURNS

In an excerpt from their recent book, *The Coming Generational Storm: What You Need to Know about America's Economic Future*, Kotlikoff and Burns describe the results that emerge from applying the concept of 'generational accounting' to the financing of federal entitlement programs – Social Security, Medicare, and Medicade. In brief, this relatively new concept involves comparing the present value of the future benefits people are scheduled to receive under these programs with the tax payments required to finance them. The result is a $51 trillion 'fiscal gap' between federal obligations under these entitlement programs and its current ability to finance these entitlements.

The authors focus on the factors that have contributed to the growth of the fiscal gap, the impact of several programs to reduce the costs of these entitlement programs, and the implications of these reform plans. The fiscal gap is largely the result of two factors. One is the tendency of politicians to shift the costs of current entitlement expenditures to future generations. The other is the nation's changing demography. As the baby boom population retires, the number of entitled beneficiaries relative to the work force whose taxes will be required to finance these entitlement benefits will greatly increase. The result is the large fiscal gap.

Kotlikoff and Burns offer several packages of reforms and present their effects to reduce the fiscal gap. These reforms will require either substantial reductions in entitlement benefits, large increases in taxes, or some combination of the two. They argue that the longer the delay in dealing with the fiscal gap, the larger that gap will become. To protect future generations of Americans, action must be taken now. Whether our politicians are willing to face the issue is the big question.

Learning Objectives

After reading and discussing this selection, students will be able to

1. Explain the meaning of generational accounting and the 'fiscal gap'.
2. Describe how the fiscal gap is calculated and the assumptions required to make that calculation.
3. Explain the differences in the relative contribution of the three major entitlement programs in accounting for the fiscal gap and in reducing its size.
4. Illustrate the importance of time in estimating the size of the fiscal gap.
5. Describe what other options may be available to control the growth of the fiscal gap.

Question Clusters

1. What is the meaning and significance of the concept of generational accounting?
   a. How can the concept of generational accounting be used?
   b. How is the concept used in this article in identifying and measuring the generational 'fiscal gap'?
   c. How might this concept be applied to an individual rather than to a national economy?
2. Why do the authors refer to entitlements as 'the perfect demographic storm'?
   a. What is the significance of using the words 'the perfect...storm' which comes from the title of a 1999 best seller, *The Perfect Storm*, by Jungar? The book describes the sinking of a Boston fishing boat off the coast of Massachusetts in 1995. (Responding to this questions requires knowledge of the book; if nobody is acquainted with the book, the instructor should explain the connection.)
   b. In what sense does this article undermine the accuracy of its own title?
   c. In what sense did the decision not to publish the Smetters–Gokhale study in the official 2004 budget document contribute to the appropriateness of the above article's title?

3. What accounts for the long, steady growth in the generational fiscal gap, which in 2004 reached a total of $51 trillion?
   a. What does it mean to say that much of the growth in the fiscal gap is demographic in origin?
   b. What do the authors mean when they say that '. . . each postwar generation, starting with Eisenhower's, picked the pockets of children and those coming in the future to benefit current taxpayers'?
   c. What recent economic decisions have contributed to a sharp increase in the fiscal gap's size?
4. How does the absence of decisions about reform contribute to the size of the fiscal gap?
   a. What is the mechanism that leads to this increase?
   b. What other factors contribute to increasing the fiscal gap?
   c. In what ways can the size of the gap be manipulated?
5. What options may be available to slow the growth of the fiscal gap?

Discussion Suggestions

This reading offers the possibility of engaging students in an issue that has direct importance to them, to their parents, and to their own future families. The selection can also lead to interesting discussions about the capacity to make long-range forecasts of the kind that come out of generational accounting. It can also reveal the power of the particular assumptions used to estimate the size of the fiscal gap, including the discount rate used, economic growth rate, tax rates, and a host of other variables. None of this undermines the Kotlikoff–Burns argument that what we have before us is the 'perfect demographic storm'.

OVERVIEW

The articles in this chapter are less focused on a specific theme than those in the other chapters, and thus it is less likely that instructors would assign all of them in a single course. Nevertheless, there are common themes running through them that students should investigate. We suggest several lines of investigation.

The first theme is the power of incentives. A second is the conditions under which markets fail to allocate goods efficiently. A third is the fact that attempts to correct market failures often create their own inefficiencies, which are called non-market failures. Underlying all of these questions is an examination of attempts to balance the effects of market and non-market failures and the effectiveness of remedies for them.

1. Economists believe that people respond to the incentives they face in their economic lives. Each of the authors has much to say about the power of incentives. What evidence would you cite from each of the reading selections – Akerlof, Barnett and Kaserman, Galbraith, Smith, Schelling, and Wolf – that shows individuals responding, and perhaps in some cases not responding, to economic incentives?

2. Policy makers sometimes enact policies that produce consequences they did not intend and do not like. What would each of the authors in this chapter say about the connection between incentives and the unintended consequences of policy?

3. Economists believe that normally markets are the most efficient way to allocate goods. They acknowledge, however, that market failures sometimes occur and result in the mis-allocation of goods. What would each of the authors have to say about the conditions under which markets fail to allocate goods efficiently?

4. Economists also believe that often government attempts to remedy market failures are inefficient because they do too much or too little. What would each of the authors have to say about the conditions under which assumed remedies for market failures give rise to non-market failures?

15. Labor Economics

The status and rewards people receive for their labor are of enduring interest to economists. This fact is not surprising. Of the three principal factors of production, namely, labor, land, and capital, labor has a human face. Labor power plays a crucial role in any economic system. It accounts for the largest share of national income, and its welfare is important in assessing the effectiveness of an economic system. To the extent that those who comprise the labor force are not treated fairly, efforts have been launched to improve the status of labor through public policy measures. Some of these measures have been successful, others much less so. Debate on these measures continues today and will continue well into the future.

This chapter offers a wide variety of selections. Because some of the clearest and most perceptive analyses of labor, regarding what it does and how it is rewarded, have come from the Classical economists, we include selections by both Adam Smith and Karl Marx. We follow with three recent policy-oriented selections.

The first two selections come from Adam Smith's *Wealth of Nations*. Both are classics, and are often assigned in labor economics courses because they are so clearly written, and continue to offer valuable insights about wages levels and wage differences. The first selection, Smith's Chapter 8, deals with the determinants of wages and fluctuations in wages resulting from changing economic conditions. The second selection, Smith's Chapter 10, examines what accounts for differences in the wages of people engaged in the various occupations, focusing on what we now call compensating wage differentials. What makes these analyses so interesting and valuable is that they arise from Smith's careful observation of labor markets and the conditions under which people work.

The next paper, by Hoffman and Reed, deals with the contemporary issue of wage discrimination against females. The authors have done more than run a few wage regressions to identify male-female wage differences, which are so often taken to represent the impact of wage discrimination. Instead, they carefully examined the labor practices of the XYZ corporation to find out why women's wages were lower than those of men. They conclude that male-female wage differences appear to be due not to wage discrimination, but rather to what can be viewed as differences in preferences between men and women. These differences stem from the quite different and important roles women play, particularly married women, in their families. The authors indicate that simply discovering wage differences is not sufficient to conclude that women suffer from wage discrimination in the labor market.

The next paper, by Warner and Asch, reports on the effectiveness of the all-volunteer military force, which replaced conscription in 1973. They discuss the reasons for the shift to an all-volunteer force, and the problems and issues that have been encountered. They then focus on the sustainability of the all-volunteer force in the years ahead. However, their analysis may require reconsideration, in light of this country's involvement in the war in Iraq at this writing in 2004, depending on how long the war continues, its costs, the resulting casualties, and the persistence of terrorist threats.

The final paper by Galston questions whether there may not be a need to reinstate a military draft in view of the war in Iraq. In discussing this issue, Galston expresses concern about equity: the uneven representation across economic classes in the all-volunteer force. He calls for greater social and economic class equity regarding the sacrifices required of those who serve in the military.

'OF THE WAGES OF LABOUR', ADAM SMITH

Having described the determinants of the natural and market prices of commodities in Chapter 7, Smith moves on in Chapter 8 to consider the determinants of the wages of labor. He begins by discussing how 'in the original state of things' those who labor enjoy the whole of its produce, because none of it has to be shared with a landlord or master. When land becomes private property, and in the absence of accumulated savings, the laborer must pay ground rent for using the land and pay the costs of maintenance (food and shelter) received while growing his crops. The exact level of wages depends on the bargain reached between the owners and laborers, and that in turn depends on the relative bargaining power of the two groups. Though wages cannot fall below the level required to maintain the worker and his family, wages can rise above that level depending on whether the economy is growing, stable, or declining. Smith then describes the forces giving rise to wage fluctuations in Great Britain. He notes the advantages of higher wages, tracing their impact on population size, population quality, and individual work effort. Finally, he focuses on the impact of prosperity and depression on wage levels. Throughout, Smith provides abundant examples that enliven his analysis.

Learning Objectives

After reading and discussing this selection, students should be able to

1. Describe the forces that determine the level of wages.
2. Explain how both short-run and long-run forces affect wage levels.
3. Clarify the importance of distinguishing between differences in wage levels and changes in wage levels.
4. Explain the effects of low wages and high wages on procreation, 'industry', productivity, and prices.

Question Clusters

1. How do changes in 'that original state of things' alter the extent to which 'the produce of labour constitutes the natural recompense or wages of labor'?
   a. What is the meaning of the 'whole produce of labor'?
   b. Under what conditions will wages not equal the 'whole produce of labor'?
2. What explains the range of wages paid by employers?
   a. In what sense do wages depend on the contract between laborers and employers?
   b. How does the strength of employers and laborers differ?
   c. What limits are imposed on the bargaining process?
3. What does Smith mean in suggesting the wage level must be 'consistent with common humanity'?
   a. How difficult is it to determine what wage level is 'consistent with common humanity'?
   b. Is Smith's conclusion that the wage level 'consistent with common humanity' at odds with his statement that 'a man must live by his work, and his wages must at least be sufficient to maintain him'? Why or why not?
   c. What is the relevance of slavery to Smith's discussion of the wages of labor?
4. Why does Smith take pains to distinguish the impact on wages of differences from changes in national wealth? How do his illustrations (from England, North America, China, East Indies) support his point?
5. What is the effect of lower versus higher wages on procreation, industry, productivity, and prices?
   a. Why does Smith devote so much attention to the number and welfare of children?
   b. How do economic forces affect population growth?

    c. How does population growth affect wage rates?

    d. How do wage rates affect the health, ability, and willingness of people to work hard?

6. What does Smith mean when he says that increases in wages increase prices, but also that the cause of increased wages tends to diminish prices?

Discussion Suggestions

This selection is broad in scope, detailed in its analysis, and filled with concrete examples. In view of its subject, this selection is most appropriate for labor economics courses. There it can be used in two different ways. One is to have students read it after they have learned the essentials from their textbook; in this case the selection will build upon what they already know and help demonstrate the reasonableness of the textbook approach. The other way is to use it to stimulate interest in understanding wage differences through the rich illustrations provided by the author. At the same time, students can be encouraged to use the selection to develop their own conceptual approach to the determinants of wages. Before beginning the discussion, it may prove useful to be certain there is a common understanding of Smith's terminology, including such terms as the whole produce of labor, maintenance, combinations, profit, masters, lowest species of labor, national wealth. It should be noted that the selection from Marx on the wages of labor builds on Smith's Chapter 8.

'INEQUALITIES ARISING FROM THE NATURE OF THE EMPLOYMENTS THEMSELVES', ADAM SMITH

In this selection, Smith analyzes the determinants of disparities in wages and profits in England, and in so doing introduces the concept of 'compensating' wage differentials. He begins by describing what would happen under conditions of 'perfect liberty', meaning that individuals would be freely able to choose their occupations and subsequently free to change their occupations. In this situation, he asserts that every individual would 'seek the most advantageous, and . . . shun the most disadvantageous employment' (p. 114). This leads him to focus on 'inequalities arising from the nature of the employments themselves'.

Smith catalogs five circumstances that make some occupations more attractive and others less attractive. These conditions lead in turn to relatively lower wages in some occupations and higher wages in others. His discussion is filled with concrete examples that illustrate the direction, and to some extent, the magnitude of these differing circumstances on wage levels. He then considers the profits associated with different occupations, cataloguing the factors that account for differences in profits, providing abundant examples to make his case. Finally, he enumerates the factors that are essential to 'perfect liberty' and help determine the flow of workers into different employments.

Learning Objectives

After reading and discussing this chapter from *The Wealth of Nations,* students will be able to

1. Explain the concept of compensating wage differentials and relate it to Smith's discussion of 'differences in pecuniary wages and profit'.
2. Elaborate on how each of the five 'principal circumstances' discussed by Smith give rise to wage differentials.
3. Explain the relationship between inequality in wages and inequality in profit.
4. Describe the meaning and implications of the three conditions Smith believes are necessary for 'perfect liberty'.

Question Clusters

1. What, according to Smith, determines differences in wage levels among different types of employment?
2. How are each of the 'five circumstances' discussed by Smith likely to lead to 'a small pecuniary gain in some [employments], and counter-balance a great one in others . . .'?
3. What does Smith mean when he says, '[t]he greater part of men have an overweening conceit of their abilities'? Where is evidence of this characteristic most visible?
4. Why is it that 'young people are particularly prone to over-value the chance of gain and under-value the risk of loss.'?
   a. What does Smith mean by this statement?
   b. In what types of employment would this tendency reveal itself most dramatically?
   c. Does Smith's statement still hold today?
5. Explain what factors account for differences in profits. Why are profits generally more equitable than wages?

Discussion Suggestions

Labor economics students should find this selection particularly interesting because current economics textbooks have not added much to the discussion of 'compensating wage differentials' since Smith developed the concept more than two centuries ago. Students should be urged to provide current examples of jobs where compensating wage differentials exist, those that result in both higher and lower relative wage rates. Students might also be asked to compare the understandability of Smith's presentation compared to that of their textbook. As in Smith's Chapter 8, the discussion will proceed more smoothly and effectively if there is a common understanding of Smith's terminology, including the following: 'advantageous' and 'disadvantageous' employments, 'the different employments of labor and stock', 'the whole of the advantages and disadvantages of different employments of labor and stock', 'pecuniary wages and profits', 'make a small pecuniary gain in some [employments], and counter-balance a great one in others...'

'SEX DISCRIMINATION? THE XYZ AFFAIR', CARL HOFFMAN AND JOHN SHELTON REED

The authors of this paper investigate why there are still differences in the occupational success of men and women despite almost two decades of equal rights legislation. Do these persistent differences result, as many would argue, from continuing biases and discrimination by employers, and from such practices as the use of seniority systems or irrelevant requirements of prior experience and education? Or do these imbalances persist, as others argue, because a significant portion of women workers do not share the career aspirations of the majority of men or the minority of women? Answers to these questions are important, for they largely determine whether or not employers can or should be held responsible for existing circumstances that disadvantage women in the workplace.

Learning Objectives

After reading and discussing this paper, students should be able to

1. Explain the meaning of discrimination, equality of opportunity, and equality of result.
2. Spell out what actions by employers are consistent with nondiscrimination.
3. Explain what accounts for differences between men and women workers in their aspirations and motivations; their resource commitment and career plans; and the impact of marriage and parenthood.
4. Describe the connection between gender-based wage discrimination and 'compensating wage differentials'.

Question Clusters

1. Why, according to Hoffman and Reed, is it difficult to understand the extent to which male–female wage differences are the result of wage discrimination?
   a. What kind of evidence is indicative of discrimination?
   b. What does the lack of wage parity say about discrimination?
   c. What would wage parity say about discrimination?
2. Who is responsible for the persistent differences in wage levels and occupational success between men and women workers?
   a. To what extent do the XYZ company's actions reflect a policy of discrimination in wages and in occupational advancement?
   b. To what extent do the actions of female workers contribute to differences in earning and career paths between female and male workers?
3. What do you conclude about the XYZ company's responsibility for the persistence of male–female differences in wages and career paths?
4. Do you believe that eventually wage and career path parity between men and women will emerge? Explain your reasoning.

Discussion Suggestions

This paper always generates lively discussion because it forces students to go beyond the stereotypical thinking about wage discrimination against women workers. The careful reasoning of the authors and the abundant evidence they provide transforms what might be an ill-informed argument into an evidence-based discussion. Students are quick to see the issue is more complex, that on average men and women have different preference patterns and these may give rise to persistent differences in wage and career paths. This leads to a still deeper question: whether women's preferences reflect what some observers would view as the product of a male-dominated culture, and whether that culture can or will change over time. On this point sharp differences of opinion emerge between men and women students, and there is probably no firm answer to this question. It should be noted that in discussing this selection Smith's Chapter 10 on 'compensating' wage differentials may be helpful.

'THE RECORD AND PROSPECTS OF THE ALL-VOLUNTEER MILITARY IN THE UNITED STATES', JOHN T. WARNER AND BETH J. ASCH

The all-volunteer military has been an established fact for more than 30 years. That is about the same duration as the military draft, which began in 1940 and continued until 1973. Few young college students will know much about either the military draft, upon which the nation relied in World War II, the Korean War, and the Vietnam War, or the all-volunteer force. The nation relied on the latter in the Gulf War, our military involvement in the former Yugoslavia, several brief national-building and humanitarian campaigns in the 1980s and 1990s, and most recently and importantly, the war in Iraq in 2004.

Warner, a former Secretary of the Navy, and Asch, a senior economist at the Rand Corporation, take a close look at the all-volunteer force. They begin by examining the economic implications of shifting from the draft to an all-volunteer force. This shift has increased economic efficiency by making better use of military labor, and has increased equity by paying people in the service closer to the wage they could earn as civilians. The authors go on to describe how the military has had to adapt to compete effectively in meeting its manpower requirements. The authors speculate on whether the all-volunteer force is sustainable and what must be done to sustain it.

Learning Objectives

After reading and discussing this paper, students should be able to

1. Recount what considerations doomed the military draft and led to creation of an all-volunteer force.
2. Describe the efficiency and equity considerations that accompany the shift to an all-volunteer force.
3. Explain what accounts for the problems encountered in maintaining the all-volunteer force.
4. Explain what must be done to ensure that the all-volunteer force is sufficient to provide for our common defense.
5. Evaluate how the prospects of active combat affect the willingness of young men and women to join the military and make it a career.

Question Clusters

1. What considerations and events of the early to mid-1960s were most conducive to stimulating interest in creating an all-volunteer force: demographic, economic, political, social, etc?

2. According to Asch, which factors are most important in analyzing the economic effects of an all-volunteer force?
   a. What kinds of economic effects must be considered?
   b. How is the concept of opportunity cost relevant to examining these economic effects?
   c. In what sense did conscription result in an excess 'opportunity cost' of acquiring military personnel?
   d. What equity issues are raised by the draft compared to an all-volunteer force?
3. What social costs and benefits are connected with a military draft? With an all-volunteer force?
   a. How are social costs and benefits defined?
   b. How would these costs and benefits be estimated in analyzing the effects of shifting away from conscription?
4. To ensure that the all-volunteer force continues to work effectively, what factors should guide development and implementation of compensation levels, dictate who will be 'hired' into the all-volunteer force, guide decisions about training requirements, and influence related decisions that are required to maintain a fully-prepared military force?
5. What issues may be problematic in maintaining and sustaining an all-volunteer force over the coming five years? Why would these matters concern you?

Discussion Suggestions

This topic has always been of enormous interest, certainly to young men years ago who anticipated or worried about being drafted. With the opening of the military services to women under the all-volunteer force, women are much more likely than ever before to take an interest in this subject. With the Iraq War and the extended policing it may require, will the appeal of joining the armed services diminish? Will National Guard enlistments and reenlistments decline? What will the Department of Defense have to do to maintain or even strengthen its military forces? These are interesting questions that are no doubt being analyzed at this very moment in 2004. One good way to examine them is by debate for and against resumption of the military draft.

'THINKING ABOUT THE DRAFT', WILLIAM A. GALSTON

Professor of Public Policy at the University of Maryland and a first-term adviser to President Clinton, William Galston questions the nation's shift more than 30 years ago from military conscription to an all-volunteer military force. He raises his questions immediately in the context of likely increases in the need for military personnel in Iraq. However, he is even more concerned about what the absence of conscription says about the civic responsibility we cultivate in our democracy. In particular, he questions why there should not be greater equity across social and economic class lines in the sacrifices demanded of those who perform military service.

Learning Objectives

After reading and discussing this essay, students should be able to

1. Contrast the differing views about the obligations of citizenship in a democracy.
2. Explain the differing views about substituting market for non-market services, as occurs with an all-volunteer force.
3. Describe the polarization of society that Galston believes has been occurring since the nation shifted to an all-volunteer force.
4. Explain the contrast in the problems described by Galston and those described in the Warner–Asch reading selection about the all-volunteer force.

Question Clusters

1. Why do people hold such wide-ranging views about how we staff our military forces?
   a. What does Galston mean by his phrase 'the end of citizenship'?
   b. In what sense is compulsory military service like slavery?
2. What is the difference between what Galston describes as 'optional citizenship', 'spectatorial citizenship', and what might be called a 'lack of military experience citizenship'?
   a. What does he mean by 'duty-free understanding of citizenship'?
   b. What does he see as the reason for and the danger arising from 'optional citizenship'?
3. Why have others contended that conscription 'would represent an abuse of state power'?
   a. What is the nature of the debate that centers around the 'Millian center'?
   b. What is the relationship between slavery and military conscription?
4. What are the dangers, according to Galston, of the 'commodification of social and civic life'?
   a. What does 'commodification' mean?

b. What are some examples of 'commodification', both those mentioned by Galston and others that come to mind?
c. What does Galston mean when he says that 'compensation as the key incentive or motive implies wrongly, that military service is something to be bought and sold in the market, not part of the fundamental social contract'?
d. In what sense does military conscription carry dangers analogous to those cited by Galston in his discussion concerning the hiring of foreigners or other citizens to do our fighting?
5. What role does compulsory military service play in 'expanding mutual awareness across cultural lines'?
a. What are the 'civic dividends' Galston talks about in his final paragraph?
b. Are there ways of achieving 'mutual awareness' other than through conscription?
c. What are the likely difficulties of achieving this goal through other means?

Discussion Suggestions

This reading selection can be paired profitably with the Warner–Asch selection. Taken together, these two selections pose contrasting views about what might be called 'equity' of conscription and the 'efficiency' of an all-volunteer force. If there is time to discuss only one of the two papers, this selection is likely to generate more active participation because it deals with the question of fairness. By contrast, the Warner–Asch selection offers an opportunity to reinforce student understanding of economic efficiency.

OVERVIEW

These five selections are more closely connected than they may initially seem. The connection is provided by the chapters from Smith that deal with wages and wage differences. The Hoffman–Reed selection seeks to explain the role of wage discrimination in accounting for male–female wage differences. The Warner–Asch paper deals in part with the wage levels that must be offered to attract young men and women into the all-volunteer force; this matter is especially pertinent during war-time. The Galston paper, by favoring resumption of the military draft, ignores the opportunity cost of those who serve in the absence of 'perfect liberty'.

1. Is the Hoffman–Reed selection more closely related to Smith's Chapter 8 or Chapter 10?
2. What is the connection between the Warner–Asch selection and Smith's two chapters?
3. What is the connection between the Galston selection and Smith's two chapters?

16. Income Distribution

A perennial concern among economists and the general public is the inequality of income and wealth that occurs under capitalism. Typically, a small fraction of the population receives a substantial fraction of the national income; an even smaller fraction of the population controls an even more substantial fraction of the national wealth. This inequality of wealth generates inequality of income; the inequality of income generates further inequality of wealth; and the cycle repeats itself. While this situation is not surprising, a generalized expectation developed that some other form of economic organization was needed to moderate these inequalities of capitalism. Proponents of socialism, supported by the vigorous criticisms of capitalism launched in *The Communist Manifesto* gave voice to these concerns, which persist to this day. Indeed, these concerns have been heightened in the 1990s with the development of the 'widening gap' between the incomes of those at the top of the US income distribution and those at the bottom representing those people officially classified as poor.

We present here a group of reading selections that address this important and nagging issue. We begin with some of the classics and then move to modern arguments.

Adam Smith describes the factors influencing the distribution of income in his Book I, Chapters 5 and 6. Though Smith espouses the labor theory of value in Chapter 5, he recognizes in Chapter 6 that the price of commodities reflects the combined value of the labor, the capital, and the land used to produce these commodities. Smith also explains why the returns to each of these resources – wages to labor, profit and interest to capital, and rents to land – vary, and the circumstances giving rise to these differences.

Marx, through his extensive research on the Industrial Revolution in England, continues the discussion started by Smith, but comes to strikingly different conclusions. In his 'Wages of Labor', he describes how workers steadily lose as capitalists benefit from their work, and the resultant 'social misery' that is produced. In his 'On Estranged Labour', Marx points out the implications of this process, the 'alienation' it produces, and the enslavement of the worker that results. Both of these essays were written before *The Communist Manifesto*.

Tawney approaches the subject of inequality in a more detached way. He attempts to clarify the meaning of the term, and discusses the benefits of greater equality. He goes on to outline how to deal with inequality by increasing opportunities for people based on their 'circumstances, institutions, and manner of life'. Though not included in this essay, elsewhere in his book Tawney provides illuminating data on the distribution of income and wealth in the UK in the early part of the twentieth century

Writing in the mid-1970s, Okun offers a fresh analysis of income inequality and the difficulties of using redistribution policies to promote greater equality of opportunity and the greater equality of income that together are needed to create what he calls a humane society. In Chapter 3, he examines the nature and scope of economic inequality and inequality of opportunity in the 1970s, suggesting that taking informed steps to increase equality can be both efficient and equitable. In Chapter 4, he discusses the kinds of policies that can be efficient and equitable and explains policy flaws that weaken redistributive effects.

Haveman provides a detailed analysis of changes in the rate of poverty from the early 1960s to the end of the twentieth century. He offers an impressive body of evidence. He also explains why the poverty rate failed to decline as much and as fast as promoters of the 1964 War on Poverty predicted and expected. At the same time, he describes the many new programs that have been initiated to restrain if not reduce the poverty rate. He also notes some important social changes that have hampered the nation's effort to reduce poverty.

The final selection by Hansen and Lampman takes an early look at the expected impact of the 1972 Basic Educational Opportunity Grant program, and then provides an assessment of the program as of 1980. The authors find that while the goal of introducing need-based grants was to help low income students overcome the financial barriers to college attendance, the BEOG program did little to narrow the gap in enrollment rates between students from higher and lower income families. They note the practical difficulties associated with implementing redistributive programs intended to be both efficient and equitable.

'ON THE REAL AND NOMINAL PRICE OF COMMODITIES, OR OF THEIR PRICE IN LABOUR, AND THEIR PRICE IN MONEY', AND 'OF THE COMPONENT PARTS OF THE PRICE OF COMMODITIES', ADAM SMITH

In these two chapters, Smith lays out his labor theory of value as a basis for the prices of commodities, and the role of wages as well as other factors in determining prices. In the first few pages of Chapter 5, Smith presents his labor theory of value. He argues that the real value of a commodity is the quantity of labor that may be commanded by the possession of it. He goes on to say that 'the real price of everything, what everything really costs to the man who wants to acquire it, is the toil and trouble of acquiring it' (p. 33). Figuring out the value of goods in terms of labor is difficult because the nature of the work people do varies so much. No absolute figure exists, so the matter is resolved 'by the higgling and bargaining of the market'.

Inasmuch as the quantity of labor is not easy to estimate, the prices of commodities are expressed in terms of other commodities. But doing so requires stating the value of each commodity in terms of each of the many other commodities that are exchanged in a barter economy, thus creating an unmanageable situation. The solution is provided by inventing money and expressing the value of all commodities in terms of its currency. Thus, the real price of any commodity always reflects its labour value whereas its money price is called the nominal price.

In Chapter 6, Smith explains how the price of every commodity is accounted for by the sum of the three components of price – the wages of the labor that produces the commodity, the profit of the entrepreneur who owns the capital (including raw materials and advance payment of wages) used to produce the commodity, and the rent going to the owner of the land used to produce the commodity. Smith explains that profit is different from the wages of the person who oversees and directs production. He argues that profit is determined by the market rate of return and is proportional to the amount of the stock invested by the entrepreneur. Smith allows that some commodities, such as ocean fish, have prices that resolve only into wages and profits. He also points out that a gardener who owns his own garden receives compensation for labor, rent, and profit even though common usage would confound the three and describe them all as the gardener's wages.

Learning Objectives

After reading and discussing these two reading selections, students should be able to

1. Clarify the difference between the real and nominal price of a commodity.
2. Explain why Smith believed that 'labour . . . (is) the only standard by which we can compare the values of different commodities at all times and at all places'.
3. Identify the component parts of the 'whole price of any commodity'.
4. Describe how the mix of the rewards going to these component parts varies among individuals.

5. Explain the relationship between the component parts of price and the concept of opportunity cost.

Question Clusters

1. How does Smith reconcile the following two statements. What is the meaning of each and the significance of Smith's use of 'value' and 'price'?
   a. 'The value of any commodity...is equal to the quantity of labour which it enables him to purchase or command. Labour, therefore, is the real measure of the exchangeable value of all commodities'.
   b. 'The commodity is then sold for precisely what it is worth or what it really costs to the person who brings it to market.'?
2. What does Smith mean when he says, 'labour, therefore, it appears evidently, is the only universal, as well as the only accurate measure of value, and the only standard for which we can compare the values of different commodities at all times and in all places'?
3. If labor is indeed the real price of everything, what is the relevance of Smith's discussion of the several 'parts' of the price of commodities?
   a. What are the 'parts' of the price, and why does Smith emphasize them?
   b. How do we reconcile Smith's statement: 'The commodity is then sold for precisely what it is worth, or what it really costs to the person who brings it to market', when in reality, the price may be affected by the 'higgling and bargaining of the market . . .'?
   c. What does Smith mean when he says that 'labour, like commodities, may be said to have a real and a nominal price'?
4. What does Smith mean when he says, 'The market price of every particular commodity is regulated by the proportion between the quantity which is actually brought to market and the demand of those who are willing to pay the natural price of the commodity, or the whole value of the rent, labour, and profit, which must be paid in order to bring it thither'?
   a. What does Smith mean by 'the ordinary rate of profit'?
   b. Why does Smith say that some people can be called 'a loser by trade'?
   c. What does Smith mean when he inserts the phrase, 'at least where there is perfect liberty'?
5. How is Smith's description of how markets operate consistent with his notion of the 'invisible hand'?
   a. What does Smith mean by the 'invisible hand'?
   b. How does the 'invisible hand' operate?
6. To what extent is Smith's analysis appropriate to today's economy?
   a. Would there be any disagreement about the distinction between 'value' and 'price'?

b. Where would you observe in today's economy the 'higgling and bargaining of the market'?

c. What language do modern economists use to characterize the behavior of prices, as well as temporary and permanent differences in prices, as described by Smith?

d. How would modern economists identify who experiences the gains when market price differs from the natural price, both when the differences are temporary and when they are long-lasting?

e. What reservations might economists have today about the extent to which market prices tend toward natural price?

Discussion Suggestions

A discussion assignment based on Chapters 5-6, Book I of the *Wealth of Nations*, fits best into a labor economic course. These two chapters have a somewhat esoteric flavor but provide the essential underpinning for understanding what Marx has to say in the following two selections. These two chapters are also interesting because they require a focus on interpretation.

'WAGES OF LABOUR', KARL MARX

Marx's analysis of the wages of labor focuses on the plight of landless laborers who are dependent for their livelihood on capitalists who own the land on which they work. The laborers' wage is the amount that remains after the ground rent is paid to the capitalist. The normal wage paid is that which provides for the worker's subsistence and the costs of raising a family. Marx, picking up on Smith's discussion of wages, describes what happens to wages as economic conditions change, concluding that whatever happens, the workers come out short while the capitalists profit from their work. Marx then considers how the conditions within society affect workers in the following situations: (1) when the wealth of society is diminishing, (2) when wealth is increasing, and (3) when wealth is static. After tracing the effects on labor, all of which are disadvantageous, he concludes that 'social misery is the goal of the economy'.

Learning Objectives

After reading and discussing this selection, students should be able to

1. Explain why Marx believes the normal wage received by labor is likely to decline.

2. Detail how the worker loses when the market price gravitates to the natural price.
3. Analyze why there is a lack of close correspondence between wage changes and the gains of the capitalist.
4. Explain how wages change in the face of economic growth, economic stability, and economic decline.

Question Clusters

1. Why, according to Marx, are workers more vulnerable to changing economic conditions than capitalists?
   a. What does Marx mean when he says, 'where worker and capitalist both suffer, the worker suffers in his existence while the capitalist suffers in the profit on his dead mammon.' ?
   b. How does the worker suffer?
   c. How does the capitalist suffer?
   d. How does their suffering differ?
2. Why is the worker 'sure to lose and to lose most from the gravitation of the market price toward the natural price'?
   a. How does the division of labor affect the situation for laborers?
   b. What does Marx mean when he says 'the demand, upon which the worker's life depends, is determined by the whims of the wealthy and the capitalists.'?
   c. Why does Marx give little or no attention to the situation in which demand for labor exceeds its supply?
3. How does Marx explain the stability of wages even when the capitalist gains and the cost of provisions varies?
4. In his discussion of the 'three conditions in which society may find itself' how does Marx reach his conclusion, which reads: 'So, in a declining state of society, we have the increasing misery of the worker; in an advancing state, complicated misery; and in the terminal state, stationary misery'.
   a. What is the meaning of the three terms: declining, advancing, terminal state?
   b. Why is it that even when wealth is increasing, workers do not benefit?
   c. Why is it that even when prosperity is increasing, workers do not benefit?
5. What does Marx mean when he says, 'social distress is the goal of the economy' and how does he arrive at this conclusion?
6. How do Marx's views differ from Smith's with respect to the price of labor and the effects of the division of labor?

Discussion Suggestions

Marx's analysis of the wages of labor is presented here because it offers an early and widely-held view about how income is distributed in a capitalist economy, not to mention how it contributes to the concept of worker alienation. Marx's analysis in both of these selections is closely linked to his reading and understanding of not only Smith's Chapters 1-3 on the division of labor and Smith's Chapter 7 on the natural and market prices of commodities, but also of Chapters 5 and 6, which immediately precede this selection. What makes this selection so interesting is the sharp contrast it provides with Smith's Chapter 8 on the wages of labor. Because of its difficulty, this selection is probably best reserved for an intermediate course, such as labor economics. On the other hand, introductory economics students have risen to the challenge of discussing this selection, and with it the closely related selection of alienated labor. For an assignment, students might be asked to contrast the view of Marx on wages with Smith's Chapter 6 on the component parts of the prices of commodities.

'ESTRANGED LABOUR', KARL MARX

Having set the stage earlier by describing what determines the wages of labor, Marx here describes the somewhat elusive concept of alienated labor. The alienation of labor is a distinct characteristic of capitalism rising out of the division of labor and specialization, the facts of private property, and the motivating force of capitalism, avarice. Marx describes the condition of labor and argues that as the worker produces more, he becomes devalued as a person According to Marx, the worker becomes a commodity, an alien being that reflects the *objectification of labor*. This condition Marx describes as *alienation*. As a result of alienation, the worker loses his identity so that his life is no longer his own. Because labor is the means to his existence, the worker becomes a slave who can only maintain himself as a worker. In the end, the worker is 'freely active only in his animal functions'. Marx explains that the root cause of alienation is private property. Private property is both the result of alienated labor and the means by which labor is alienated.

Learning Objectives

After reading and discussing this selection, students should be able to

1. Explain the concept of 'alienated labor'.
2. Detail the process by which labor becomes alienated.

3. Explain the consequences of alienation.
4. Elaborate upon the relationship between alienation and private property.
5. Give contemporary examples of worker alienation.

Question Clusters

1. How do we interpret Marx's statement: 'The externalization [alienation] of the worker in his product means not only that his labour becomes an object, an external existence, but that it exists outside him, independently of him and alien to him, and begins to confront him as an autonomous power; that the life which he has bestowed on the object confronts him as hostile and alien'.
   a. What is the meaning of 'alienation'?
   b. What does Marx mean in saying, 'his labour becomes an object' and assumes 'an external existence'?
   c. What does Marx mean by saying that his labor 'exists independently, outside of himself, and alien to him, and that it stands opposed to him as an autonomous power'?
2. What is your interpretation of this statement: 'We arrive at the result that man (the worker) feels himself to be freely active only in his animal functions – eating, drinking, and procreating, or at most also in his dwelling and in personal adornment – while in his human functions he is reduced to an animal. The animal becomes human and the human becomes animal.'?
3. What is the meaning of the term 'species-being' as contrasted to 'species-life'?
4. What is your interpretation of the following paragraph: 'The alienation of the worker in his object is expressed as follows in the laws of political economy: the more the worker produces the less he has to consume; the more value he creates the more worthless he becomes; the more refined his product the more crude and misshapen the worker; the more civilized the product the more barbarous the worker; the more powerful the work the more feeble the worker; the more the work manifests intelligence the more the worker declines in intelligence and becomes a slave of nature.'?
5. If Marx is correct about alienated labor, what kinds of evidence in today's world would be consistent with his view? What kinds of behavior would provide evidence of alienation?
6. What, according to Marx, is the relationship between 'alienated labor' and 'private property'?
   a. What is the meaning of the statement: '*Private property* thus derives from an analysis of the concept of *alienated labour*, i.e. *alienated man*, estranged labour, estranged life, *estranged man*.'?
   b. Why does Marx regard this link as so important to his analysis?

7. Do you think many contemporary workers feel alienated by the 'external character of labor', which is, according to Marx, 'demonstrated by the fact that it belongs not to him but to another, and that in it he belongs not to himself but to another'?

Discussion Suggestions

This reading is difficult. At one level, it seems appropriate for a labor economics course. But it can also be used to good effect in an introductory course, even though discussing it will stretch the skills of first year students. However, there is nothing wrong with doing so, because it is important that students gain some understanding of what Marx is all about and learn to deal with challenging material. As in the prior selection, Marx uses terminology that will be unfamiliar and perhaps even frustrating to readers. For that reason, a number of the questions above are designed to interpret particular sentences rather than ideas that emerge from reading the selections. In discussing this selection, students should be asked to contrast the views of Marx and Smith regarding what Marx refers to as the 'only motive forces which political economy recognizes are avarice and the war between the avaricious, competition'. What would Smith say to this? Students might also be asked what evidence, if any, would indicate that contemporary workers feel alienated by 'external labor', which 'is shown by the fact that it is not his own work but work for someone else, that in work he does not belong to himself but to another person'. Finally, students might be asked why this reading selection is paired with others dealing with income distribution.

'EQUALITY', R. H. TAWNEY

Tawney argues against economic inequality. He begins by trying to clarify the meaning of equality. Among the distinctions he makes is that conveyed by the statement, 'The equality which all thinkers emphasize as desirable is not equality of capacity or attainment but of circumstances, institutions, and manner of life'. He goes on to criticize the fallacy of supposing that inequalities of circumstances or opportunity are justified because of differences in personal qualities unless these latter differences are relevant to the former differences. He also talks about what we would now call the societal benefits of reduced inequality and what measures might increase equality of incomes and wealth.

Learning Objectives

After reading and discussing the Tawney selection, students should be able to

1. Summarize different concepts of inequality.
2. Explain differences in inequality of circumstances, institutions, and opportunities as compared to differences in personal qualities.
3. Describe how greater equality leads to societal benefits.
4. Indicate how Tawney's concepts are used in contemporary discussions of inequality.

Question Clusters

1. What does Tawney mean by this statement: 'the well-being of a society is likely to be increased if it so plans its organization that whether their powers are great or small, all its members may be equally enabled to make the best of such powers as they possess.'?
   a. If people are naturally unequal, why should there be any concern about equality?
   b. What does Tawney mean in saying that 'social institutions should be planned, as far as possible, to emphasize and strengthen, not the class differences which divide, but the common humanity which unites, them.'?
   c. Why does Tawney invoke the phrase 'common humanity' and what does it mean?
   d. What different kinds of equality does Tawney discuss (e.g., 'capricious inequalities') and what do they mean?
2. Why do those people who dread a dead-level of income or wealth seem not to dread a dead-level of law and order, and of security of life and property?
3. In what sense, according to Tawney, are opportunities for upward mobility limited?
   a. Of what importance is the fact that 90 percent of the population is comprised of wage earners?
   b. Does this imply there can be no upward mobility within the wage earning sector?
4. How does Tawney view the possibility that redistribution can make substantial numbers of people better off?
   a. What is the basis for Tawney's statements that 'no redistribution of wealth would bring general affluence' and that 'the equalization of incomes would make everyone right'?
   b. What does he mean by 'general affluence'?
   c. What does he mean by 'would make everyone right'?

5. In what sense is the well-being of society enhanced by reduced inequality?
   a. What is the meaning of the phrase 'well-being of society'?
   b. What IS the significance of the frequent references to the term 'common humanity'?
6. What are the mechanisms for reducing inequality?
   a. What mechanisms does Tawney discuss and/or recommend? What mechanisms does he neglect to mention?
   b. What mechanisms would you recommend for England at the time he published his book (1931) and for the US today?

Suggestions for Discussion

Tawney's book is the first major treatment of inequality since Marx. Because Tawney takes a much broader approach, it will be useful to ask students to contrast the views of these two writers. Students also profit from the quantitative information Tawney presents on income inequality in England during the early part of the twentieth century. Students can use Tawney's data to show the effect of redistribution on average incomes of the 'non-rich' and 'poor'. The same exercise can be carried out for the United States drawing on income and wealth data compiled by the US Census Bureau and the Federal Reserve System. Finally, this essay provides a starting point for discussing the so-called 'widening gap' in US incomes and the significance of this gap in the context of Tawney's essay.

'EQUALITY OF INCOME AND OPPORTUNITY', ARTHUR OKUN

In this third chapter of his book, *Equality and Efficiency: The Big Tradeoff*, Okun examines in some detail the magnitude and character in the distribution of economic inequality. He proceeds to describe some of the underlying causes of inequality, as well as the role of choice and chance in producing both high and low incomes. He next considers the relationship between inequality of income and inequality of opportunity in the United States. Finally, he highlights inequalities of opportunity and their consequences for both economic efficiency and equality of income. He concludes with the optimistic view that in social welfare policy the usually assumed tradeoff between equality and efficiency can be averted. The secret is to attack inequalities of opportunity, such as sexual discrimination in jobs and barriers in access to capital, rather than trying directly to equalize incomes.

Learning Objectives

After reading and discussing this chapter, students should be able to

1. Explain the various dimensions of economic inequality and of inequality of opportunity.
2. Explain what kinds of policy measures can create greater equality of opportunity.
3. Describe how to evaluate the potential for greater economic equality through measures that intend to provide greater equality of opportunity.

Question Clusters

1. What is the nature of the conflict, as Okun sees it, between the goals of economic efficiency and the achievement of greater equity and/or income equality?
   a. Why are these goals assumed to conflict with one another?
   b. Under what circumstances might these goals not conflict with one another but instead be complementary?
2. What complexities arise in measuring the distribution of economic welfare?
   a. How can the distribution of economic welfare be measured?
   b. Why might strict equality of income fail to produce equality in economic welfare?
   c. What does Okun mean when he discusses 'cafeterias' and 'casinos'?
3. What, according to Okun, are the dimensions of equality of opportunity?
   a. What types of unequal opportunity does Okun dislike, and why?
   b. What types of equal opportunity does Okun seem to favor, and why?
4. What does Okun mean by the following statements: 'the political process rather than the marketplace must judge the legitimacy of some preferences'? and 'political decisions about fair play' can result in the 'general possibility that what is good for equality may be good for efficiency.'?
5. What does Okun see as the potential for greater equality of opportunity?
   a. What are the likely benefits?
   b. What are the likely costs?
   c. How can the likely benefits and costs be compared?

Discussion Suggestions

It is important to make certain that students firmly grasp the difference between equality of opportunity and equality of income, and the extent to which equality of opportunity is likely to produce equality of income.

Comparing the views of Okun and Tawney will be helpful because important parts of their messages are the same, even though their language differs. This reading selection also offers an opportunity to introduce the concept of cost-benefit analysis even though quantifying these costs and benefits of policies to achieve greater equality of opportunity or greater equality of income is difficult.

'INCREASING EQUALITY IN AN EFFICIENT ECONOMY', ARTHUR OKUN

In this final chapter of his book, Okun evaluates the potential of various measures to increase economic equality. He sees progressive taxation, transfer payments to low-income groups, and jobs programs as means of narrowing the disparities in living standards among Americans and of eliminating the economic deprivation that violates the principles of democracy. At the same time, he uses the 'leaky bucket' metaphor to emphasize the need to be efficient in implementing redistribution policies. Put simply, he asks readers to think of using a bucket to redistribute resources from taxpayers in general to the poor. But, if the bucket has holes in it, some fraction, perhaps a large fraction, of the contents of the bucket will leak out before the bucket reaches the poor. In other words, to be effective, redistribution programs must be targeted and efficient.

Learning Objectives

After reading and discussing this selection, students should be able to

1. Explain the concept of the 'leaky bucket' in understanding how to deal with income inequality.
2. Explain the sources of revenue to finance redistribution programs.
3. Explain costs and benefits of redistribution programs for different population groups.
4. Explain how you would determine the tradeoff between redistribution programs and efficiency.

Question Clusters

1. When equality and efficiency conflict with one another, how can the conflict be resolved?
2. What is the importance of the 'leaky bucket' metaphor used by Okun?

    a. What is put into the 'leaky bucket'?

    b. Why does the bucket leak?

    c. How much leakage can or should be tolerated?

    d. What mechanisms are available to plug these leaks?

    e. Is it possible to find buckets that do not leak? If so, describe what they might be like.

3. How effective are transfer payments likely to be in lifting people out of poverty when a 'leaky bucket' is used?

    a. How important to their effectiveness is the targeting of anti-poverty programs?

    b. What is the connection, if any, between targeting and the 'leaky bucket'?

    c. What forces are at work to weaken the targeting of programs designed to help the poor?

4. What does Okun mean by these statements: 'The society that stresses equality and mutual respect in the domain of rights must face up to the implications of these principles in the domain of dollars.' and 'The market needs a place, and the market needs to be kept in its place' and '... I cheered the market; but I could not give it more than two cheers'?

5. According to Okun, what is the contradiction between the domain of dollars in capitalism and the domain of rights in a democracy?

Discussion Suggestions

This selection is suitable for students at any level, but its length, unless edited, may render it less appropriate for the principles course. It would fit easily into a labor or public finance course. Because students may be unfamiliar with the redistribution programs of the 1970s, they need to be acquainted with current redistribution programs so they can apply Okun's analysis. The instructor can prepare this information, or students can be asked to assemble a list of comparable current redistribution programs. The important point is to enable them to understand how these programs work as well as their limitations. Finally, at the end of the discussion, after the issues have been discussed, it may be instructive to ask students how they view the tradeoff between equality and efficiency. Why do they favor or not favor increased redistribution? What accounts for their differing viewpoints?

'POVERTY AND THE DISTRIBUTION OF ECONOMIC WELL-BEING SINCE THE 1960S', ROBERT HAVEMAN

In 1964, when President Lyndon B. Johnson declared 'an unconditional War on Poverty' approximately one fifth of the American population could be classified as 'poor', which means in current terms a family of four with an income of roughly $17,000 or less. The expectation was that the War on Poverty would substantially reduce if not eliminate poverty. A host of new anti-poverty programs was quickly initiated, and during the following decade, the poverty rate dropped by more than half. But, since then it has risen somewhat and remained roughly constant in the 10-12 percent range through the 1990s and into the twenty-first century.

Haveman, who has made a life-long study of the causes and consequences of poverty, reviews four decades of effort to fight poverty. He begins by reviewing the trends in poverty for different population groups. He then examines how the views of economists slowly changed, particularly as efforts to reduce poverty stagnated in the late 1970s and early 1980s. Next, he describes the effects of a variety of public policies, particularly those targeted toward helping the poor. Finally, he examines the relationship between economic growth and its effects on the poor population. Unlike the general treatment by Tawney, for example, Haveman employs a blend of history, data, and analysis to examine why the nation's efforts to reduce the poverty rate have not been more successful.

Learning Objectives

After reading and discussing this selection, students should be able to

1. Describe the trends in the poverty rate over the past four decades.
2. Explain the changing variety of programs mounted to fight poverty.
3. Explain the relationship between economic growth and poverty.
4. Recount how the views of economists about how to reduce poverty changed and what gave rise to these changes.
5. Summarize what you see as the main challenges in fighting poverty.

Question Clusters

1. Why, according to Haveman, has there been such unexpected difficulty in reducing the poverty rate and altering the conditions that give rise to poverty?
   a. What were the expectations of economists about the nation's ability to reduce the poverty rate?
   b. What accounted for the rapid reduction in poverty from the early 1960s to the late 1970s?
   c. What forces slowed the reduction in the late 1970s and 1980s?
2. What is the meaning and significance of 'poverty' in what we think of as an affluent nation?

    a. What is the meaning of the term 'poverty rate'?
    b. How is the poverty rate measured, and what are some of the difficulties in measuring it?
    c. What has been the trend in the rate of poverty?
    d. How has the poverty rate responded to changing levels of affluence in the US?

3. What factors seemed to contribute to the success of the early anti-poverty programs?
    a. What kinds of programs were established?
    b. What seemed to be their major failings?
    c. What steps were taken to overcome these failings?
    d. How successful did these programs prove to be?

4. What does Haveman have to say about the future prospects of reducing the poverty rate?
    a. What does he mean when he refers to the weakness of the nation's equalizing institutions?
    b. What does he mean by saying that 'the nation needs now to place on its agenda the strengthening of institutions and policies that are able to cushion the impact of a reversal of fortunes on those who are already disadvantaged.'?

5. What is your assessment of the comments on the Haveman paper by the two appointed discussants?
    a. The comments by Burtless?
    b. The comments by Katz?
    c. What new ideas do they inject into the discussion?

Discussion Suggestions

This selection differs substantially from the selections in all other modules. Rather than developing a closely reasoned discussion of an issue, this paper is crammed full of data on poverty, descriptions of programs to deal with poverty, explanations about why things didn't work, new targeting that is more effective, and so on. What students should see is Haveman's systematic and evidence-filled attempt to evaluate the nation's progress in the challenging effort to reduce poverty. This paper is probably most appropriate in a public finance or labor course simply because of it length and comprehensiveness.

'BASIC OPPORTUNITY GRANTS FOR HIGHER EDUCATION: GOOD INTENTIONS AND MIXED RESULTS', W. LEE HANSEN AND ROBERT J. LAMPMAN

This paper was written early in 1973 shortly after the 1972 reauthorization of the Higher Education Act of 1965 went into effect. That reauthorization established a new method of financing higher education through creation of a federal need-based grant program for students attending college. The grants, first named Basic Educational Opportunity Grants (BEOG) and much later renamed as Pell Grants, sought to provide a basic level of student support which would be augmented by federal work-study funds and subsidized federal loans, as dictated by student financial need. The objective of the BEOG program was to raise college attendance among academically able young people from low income families who otherwise would not have been able to finance and attend college.

It became apparent to the authors that the BEOG program had attributes similar to a negative income tax program, which was then seen as an important weapon to use in the War on Poverty. While the negative income tax was designed to offset the effects of poverty, there had been much concern about the incentive effects such a program would create. Similarly, with BEOG a new set of incentives would be created. The authors try to show how the low-income targeting of the program would be eroded as students sought independent student status, meaning their financial need would be based on their own income rather than that of their parents.

In a 1982 supplement to their original paper, the authors offer evidence that the low income targeting of the BEOG program was indeed eroded, and the impact of BEOG grants did little to equalize enrollment rates for students from low income families. However, the program did help ensure the financial viability of private colleges and universities by making it possible for students attending higher cost private colleges to qualify for larger grants than they would have received by attending public institutions.

Learning Objectives

After reading and discussing this selection, students should be able to

1. Explain the workings of a negative income tax and the importance of its key parameters.
2. Describe the parallels between negative income tax payments and student need-based grants.

3. Identify the incentive effects created by each of these programs and the likely alterations in the behavior of program participants and potential program recipients.
4. Describe the effects of these incentives over the first decade of the BEOG program.

Question Clusters

1. Why is it that public programs such as BEOG, which were designed to cope with market failures, often fail to overcome these market failures and instead produce other effects (unintended effects) few people had anticipated?
   a. What failures in higher education was the BEOG program expected to address?
   b. In what sense were the goals of the BEOG program matched to the sources of market failure?
2. What factors determine the extent to which BEOG could overcome market failures?
   a. Of what importance are such matters as the 'guarantee', definition of family unit, definition of income and of deductions, income accounting period, BEOG tax rate, and 'break even' income level in affecting the cost of the BEOG program?
   b. How important are these same items in achieving the goals set for the BEOG program?
3. How important is the distinction between 'dependent' and 'independent' student status?
   a. How clear-cut is the distinction between these two types of student status?
   b. How important is this distinction for students from families with different income levels?
   c. How enforceable is this distinction for decisions about the size of financial aid awards?
4. What explains the failure of the BEOG program to concentrate need-based grants on students from low income families and to increase the enrollment rate for this group of students?
   a. What role was played by Congress in altering the program?
   b. What role was played by students and their parents in adapting to the program?
   c. Is it possible to separate the effects of these two influences on enrollments?
5. What steps are required to ensure that a program such as this one, the Pell grant program, achieves its stated goals or objectives?

Discussion Suggestions

This selection appeals to students. Not only does it deal with a topic that affects many of them – how to provide equal opportunity in financing higher education – but also because it applies economics to a program they are all familiar with. In addition, this program provides a living example of an effort to overcome market failure, which in turn leads to non-market failures that undercut the expected effects by intervening in the market for higher education. This selection can be juxtaposed with the Adam Smith reading on education, to show that some issues never go away. They simply reappear in different guises.

OVERVIEW

Whether to leave the distribution of income to the play of market forces or redistribute income through government actions has always been and will continue to be the subject of endless debate. Adam Smith's early interest in the distribution of income among labor, capital, and land occupied economists and social commentators until the early postwar period. Then, with the availability of detailed data on the size distribution of earnings and of income, which included wages, rent, and interest, the concern about the factor shares that had been much discussed by Smith and others who followed him largely disappeared. The focus now is almost exclusively on the size distribution. Recognizing the shift of attention, we nonetheless suggest consideration of the following questions:

1. How did Smith and Marx come to such different understandings of the implications of the distribution of income among the owners of land, labor, and capital?
2. Why has it taken so long, or so it appears, to move to the concept of providing equal opportunity as a means of dealing with income distribution problems as an alternative to targeted redistribution programs?
3. How does the availability of data on the size distribution re-orient people's thinking about both the efficiency and equity of the distribution of income?
4. What is the link between the position taken by Okun in his two selections and that taken by Haveman in his selection?
5. If income is regarded as too unevenly distributed, how would the shape of the size distribution change if the 'excess' incomes of those at the top of the distribution were reallocated, either across the board (in equal dollar amounts to earners in each income interval, or in equal percentage increments (in equal percentage amounts to earners in each income

interval)? How satisfactory to the public would be the outcome of these two redistribution schemes?

17. Whither Economics?

The economics profession carries on a continuous dialogue regarding what economics and economists are doing and should be doing. How these questions are framed and answered greatly depends on the time and circumstances that cause them to be discussed. Typically, these questions are raised when some new paradigm emerges. It is regarded by its proponents as an alternative to the dominant status quo and by its opponents as an attack on what they hold dear. The very fact that these questions are posed tests the contending view while at the same time sharpens the arguments of those who support the dominant approach.

We present here one such encounter. It took place in 1970 at a time when considerable numbers of younger economists were complaining about economists' lack of relevance, and were offering an alternative approach called 'radical' economics. In retrospect, this battle can be viewed in classic terms. The small group of radical economists attacked the citadel of economics, but were repulsed by mainline economists. Though the beleaguered attackers retreated, they nonetheless left an impact. The profession did begin to respond. And so it goes. The contestants in this case are two well-known economists, Robert Heilbroner, author of *The Worldly Philosophers*, and the future Nobel Laureate, Robert Solow.

Heilbroner begins by challenging the relevance of economics and economists to the modern world. He contends that economics pretends to be a science, but in fact is driven by ideology. He argues that economics should give more attention to real world problems and the uncertainties that surround those problems. In addition, he calls for a shift toward 'instrumentalism' in which economists would join with others in seeking to articulate goals and then apply their 'scientific' procedures of economic analysis to describe the various ways of achieving these goals.

Solow responds by arguing that the attention of economists is shifting toward some of the concerns he mentions, that many of the questions he raises are complex and difficult to study and understand, that the way economists approach their subject does indeed reflect their interests, ideologies, and values, but not enough to skew their results. Like Heilbroner, he despairs of advancing knowledge through interdisciplinary research, and finally argues that in advancing knowledge there is need for a balanced approach that neither claims too much for its scientific approach nor is unduly influenced by ideology that is impervious to analysis and evidence.

The third selection is quite different. In it, Charles R. Morris, a professional writer, focuses on the popular slogan used in the 1992 presidential campaign: 'It's the Economy, Stupid'. The idea behind this slogan was that should Clinton be elected as the next president, he could and would take decisive action to boost the economy, which in the early 1990s had slid into a mild recession. Morris makes it clear, however, that presidents have little power to manage the economy. He takes readers through a tour of modern economics, which reveals that the economy is even less predictable than most economists may have realized. On this sober note, Morris concludes by offering to candidates and presidents a set of 'guidelines for sound stewardship' of the economy. Equally important, he cautions the public to drop its expectation that presidents can exert much control over the economy.

'ON THE LIMITED RELEVANCE OF ECONOMICS', ROBERT L. HEILBRONER

As part of a symposium entitled, 'Capitalism and the Economics', Robert L. Heilbroner raises some unsettling questions about the relevance of economics as a science. His questions came on the heels of an effort in the late 1960s by a group of younger economists to create what it called 'radical economics'. While this effort was short-lived, questions about the relevance of economics both preceded and followed this 1970 exchange between Heilbroner and the future Nobel Laureate, Robert M. Solow, whose essay follows this selection.

Heilbroner stresses not the accomplishments of economics, which he admires, but rather what it has failed to do. He points to the ineffectiveness of economists in dealing with pressing current problems. He suggests that since economists are at or near the top of the income distribution, they naturally tend to be conservative in their outlook and the subject they study. More importantly, he criticizes economists for emulating physical scientists by depicting the economic process as a series of interconnected mathematical equations. He criticizes them further for their reliance on behavioral assumptions that frequently fail to hold and that cannot be verified, as in the case of firms maximizing profits. At another level, Heilbroner is concerned that because economists ignore the political system within which the economy is embedded, their conclusions must be partial, incomplete, and often erroneous; their models distort reality. Heilbroner concludes by arguing that economists should be an instrument of social science, focused less on describing how the economy behaves and more on how society should behave. If economics became an instrument of change, he argues, it could confer upon the discipline the relevance that it needs so people could achieve those ends they value.

Learning Objectives

After reading and discussing this Heilbroner selection, students should be able to

1. Explain Heilbroner's catalog of criticisms of economics and economists.
2. Explain what Heilbroner sees as the virtues of economics and economists.
3. Explain what Heilbroner sees as the science of economics.
4. Describe Heilbroner's concept of 'instrumentalism' and its implications for economics.

Question Clusters

1. Is it possible, according to Heilbroner, for economics to be relevant and also a science?
2. What does Heilbroner mean by 'relevance'?
   a. Why does Heilbroner put quotation marks around the word in the title?
   b. Does his definition of 'relevance' change during the course of the article? Explain the change.
   c. Why do economists avoid certain topics that Heilbroner would consider relevant?
3. What does Heilbroner mean by 'science'?
   a. Why does Heilbroner put quotation marks around the word in the title?
   b. What characteristics of work in economics would give rise to it being thought of as a science?
   c. Does being scientific require expressing economic relationships in mathematical terms?
   d. Does being scientific also require 'severity of language', abstractions, concepts, and formulas?
4. Do both 'relevance' and 'science' require the construction of behavioral assumptions?
   a. What assumptions are involved in being 'relevant' and in being 'scientific'?
   b. Is there any conflict between the assumptions required to be 'relevant' as contrasted to 'scientific'?
   c. Would a more relevant economics dispense with the behavior assumptions of economics as a science?
   d. If economics were placed on a more pragmatic basis, would this diminish the need for abstractions?

5. What does Heilbroner mean by 'instrumentalism'?
   a. How would 'instrumentalism' overcome the penchant of economists to be scientific?
   b. Does 'instrumentalism' obviate the need for making behavioral assumptions?
   c. Does an instrumental approach to economics eliminate the need to make predictions?
   d. According to Heilbroner, is it more important for economists to be able to explain or to predict?
6. If economics moved in the direction Heilbroner proposes, would students find the subject more interesting and immediately relevant?
   a. Freshman students? Economics majors?
   b. How might each group be affected by this shift?
   c. Based on your knowledge of economics, has the shift that Heilbroner proposed already occurred?

Discussion Suggestions

While this selection might be discussed toward the end of an introductory principles course, it is much more suitable for intermediate courses, in which students have already acquired a deeper understanding of economics. By then, students will have become sufficiently immersed in economics to assess its potentialities to be both relevant and scientific. The Heilbroner reading should be paired with the Solow selection to ensure that students are exposed to both sides of the issue.

'SCIENCE AND IDEOLOGY IN ECONOMICS', ROBERT M. SOLOW

In his gentle but amusing style, Solow takes on Heilbroner point by point while claiming not to do so. He indicates that students should master the foundations of the discipline even if they won't use everything they learn. He suggests that the focus of economics shifts toward the relevant but with a lag. He argues that economists are in the middle of the liberal – conservative spectrum – to the right of other social sciences and humanities but to the left of the sciences. And he points out that some issues that economists are accused of avoiding are vague, hard to define, and difficult to resolve.

Solow directs his strongest statements to the subject of economics as a 'value-free social science'. While admitting that economists are influenced by their interests, ideologies, and values, he dismisses the notion that economists are unduly influenced by unstated value premises. He argues that if social science is as value-laden as Heilbroner charges, the challenge is to find ways to make it value-free. Like Heilbroner, Solow is not optimistic about the prospects for an interdisciplinary economics; it most often involves taking a qualitative rather than quantitative approach. This means sacrificing the rigor, precision and hypothesis testing that characterizes a scientific approach in the search for answers. He is also concerned about how to think about the varied effects of economic policies: whose welfare is affected, that of the individual or of the larger society?

Solow concludes that the scientific approach of economics is essential in helping society deal with its problems. Economists should not give up in the face of the difficulties pointed out by Heilbroner. Instead, they should work harder. Solow believes that economic science can provide a helpful framework for philosophical and ideological discussions of economic institutions.

Learning Objectives

After reading and discussing the Solow selection, students should be able to

1. Explain the meaning of economics as a science.
2. Explain the criticisms of economics as a science and how these criticisms are answered.
3. Assess the implications of pursuing Heilbroner's recommendations.
4. Reconcile the conclusions of Heilbroner and Solow on the role of economics as a science.

Question Clusters

1. How does Solow view the possibilities of resolving the conflict between science and ideology?
   a. How does Solow define science? Ideology?
   b. In what sense is 'scientism' the same as science?
   c. How do Solow's and Heilbroner's conceptions of science differ?
2. Can economics be value-free or must it be biased?
   a. What is the meaning of value-free as seen by Solow?
   b. How does Solow deal with the views expressed by Myrdal on the role of value judgments in economics?
   c. Why, according to Solow, is the distinction between qualitative and quantitative thinking so important in discussing value-free social science?
   d. How should and do economists deal with the infiltration of value judgments into economic analysis?

3. Why do Solow and Heilbroner agree that prospects are dim for creating an interdisciplinary economics?
   a. What do Heilbroner and Solow mean by 'interdisciplinary economics'?
   b. Do efforts to make economics 'quantifiable' rule out the possibilities of it being interdisciplinary?
   c. Why, according to Solow, is it so difficult to develop what Heilbroner calls 'interdisciplinary economics'?
4. What is the value for economists, and particularly for economics students, of the Heilbroner–Solow exchange?
   a. Aside from the time-based examples cited by both authors, how does their exchange capture contemporary concerns about the nature and direction of the work in economics?
   b. On what basis do you believe the issues they discuss are more or less important now than they were more than 30 years ago?

Discussion Suggestions

As noted above for the Heilbroner selection, this article is more appropriate for students toward the end of an intermediate theory course. By this time, they will have been sufficiently exposed to a variety of methical issues in economics, enough for them to appreciate the Heilbroner–Solow exchange. Students, particularly economics majors, are likely to be more comfortable with Solow's analysis. However, it is important for them to understand both the critique issued by Heilbroner and the defense offered by Solow.

'IT'S *NOT* THE ECONOMY, STUPID', CHARLES R. MORRIS

This *Atlantic Monthly* article by Charles Morris, written shortly after the 1992 national election, uses the popular campaign slogan, 'It's the economy, stupid'. Presidential candidate Clinton's criticisms of the economy's performance under President George H. Bush promoted Clinton's victory and Bush's defeat. Morris argues that the power of the presidency to manage the economy is vastly exaggerated, and that, in fact, presidents can do little. In developing his thesis, Morris takes his readers through an illuminating survey of economics, circa 1992.

Learning Objectives

After reading and discussing this selection, students should be able to

1. Describe the direct and indirect powers that the president can use to manage the economy.
2. Explain why the economy would be difficult to manage even if the President did have greater power to do so.
3. Explain why presidents have been forced into the position of appearing to manage the economy.
4. Elaborate the dangers of maintaining this pose.

Question Clusters

1. Why according to Morris is there so much emphasis on the President's power and responsibility to manage the economy?
   a. What does it mean to 'manage' the economy?
   b. In what sense is the economy manageable?
   c. What power does the President have to manage the economy? To give direction to the economy?
2. What is the meaning of Morris' statement: 'The resemblance, in fact, is no accident, for both the image of the President as button-pusher in the economic engine room and the heavily psychologized tactics in Vietnam are squarely in a peculiarly American tradition of thinking about society and the economy.'?
   a. What is the origin of the images of 'button-pusher' or 'pulling levers'?
   b. What was the role of Keynesianism in helping to shape these images?
   c. What, according to Morris, is the current status of economic forecasting, and how does it influence the image of 'button pusher' or 'pulling levers'?
   d. In what sense can the economy be 'managed' in the short run but not in the long run? Why? Why not?
3. Of what relevance to this subject is the 1990s surge of interest in 'complexity' and its offshoot, 'chaos' theory?
   a. How does complexity affect our ability to understand the economic system? To predict its course?
   b. How does the idea of an 'adaptive system' affect our ability to understand and predict the economy?
4. What are the consequences of the pervasive belief that the President can manage the economy?
   a. What is the role of the press in promoting the idea that presidents can manage the economy?
   b. What additions would you add to the list of cautionary guidelines proposed by Morris?
5. How do we elevate the level of economic literacy within the press corps and among the general public?

   a. By insisting on more economics training for reporters and newspaper columnists?

   b. By cautioning politicians to temper their remarks and promises about economics?

   c. By increasing the number of economics majors?

   d. By requiring all high school students to take a full year of economics?

   e. In any other way?

Discussion Suggestions

This reading selection can be used together with the Heilbroner-Solow exchange because it examines recent developments in economics and how they may affect the ability of a President to predict, much less manage, the economy. This reading selection can also be used in conjunction with the macroeconomic readings in Part Three. This selection can best be understood by students who have a firm grounding in economics, namely economics majors. However, the powerful message in this article is something that should be included as a part of introductory courses, even if this means editing the selection. In addition, Question 5 can lead to an open-ended discussion about how to increase economic literacy and also how politicians might rethink the economic promises they make with an eye to the actual likelihood of their realization.

OVERVIEW

Taken together, these three selections raise important questions about the role of economists and the work they do. As already noted, the Heilbroner and Solow selections should be paired. These readings are most appropriate for senior economics majors enrolled in a capstone course or senior seminar. By then they will be well-grounded in economics and able to understand and appreciate the Heilbroner–Solow exchange. Here are some questions that merit consideration after completing the modules:

1. How might one verify whether, and by how much, the economics profession has moved to embrace the instrumentalism proposed by Heilbroner?

2. What kinds of evidence would indicate that economics has become more scientific in the manner suggested by Solow?

3. If Heilbroner and Solow were to update their papers, do you think their positions would change to any significant degree?

PART FIVE

Discussing Financial Economics

18. The Evolution of Money

Most citizens and many economists take fiat-money for granted. How societies evolved from collections of largely detached and self-sufficient family units to highly interdependent networks that use sophisticated financial arrangements is interesting and informative. In this chapter, we present four readings that students can discuss to better their understanding of the evolution of monetary arrangements.

We begin with Chapter 4 of the *Wealth of Nations* in which Adam Smith argues that the evolution of money, trade, and the division of labor are three facets of the same stage of economic development. Smith argues that a society cannot take advantage of specialization unless it can trade widely, and that it cannot trade at reasonable cost unless it agrees on a medium of exchange. Smith provides an overview of the evolution of money from commodity forms through the coinage that was widely in use in 1776.

The chapters from Bray Hammond's *Banks and Politics in America from the Revolution to the Civil War* provide insights into the monetary and banking arrangements chosen by the United States immediately after the ratification of the Constitution. The choices were controversial. Some wanted only gold as money, fearing the inflation that paper money might bring. Others wanted paper money, fearing that reliance on gold and the requirement that taxes be paid in specie amounted to a scheme to cheat them from their land holdings.

Banking arrangements were also controversial. Jefferson thought the nation was comprised of self sufficient yeoman-farmers who would have little need of banks. Others feared that banks would become perpetual and powerful institutions. Conversely, Hamilton believed that the future of the United States involved the growth of commerce, and that banks were necessary to make commerce flourish.

In 'Anchors Away', Angela Redish explains how the 1973 US decision to leave the gold standard was the culmination of a centuries long process. She explains how the gold standard involved tradeoffs. On one hand, tying money to gold assured that the supply of money would not grow rapidly, avoiding the chance of runaway inflation. On the other hand, tying money to gold constrained economic growth when the supply of gold did not grow as rapidly as output might require. Redish explains that the creation of gold-backed notes and the Bretton Woods Agreement were both attempts to maintain the

253

anchor – the connection of money to gold – while lengthening the anchor chain.

Finally, Radford, in his account entitled, 'Economic Organization of a P.O.W. Camp', explains that the transaction efficiencies available through the use of money are so great that money became an institution in prisoner of war camps. Radford argues that camp experience with its monies – both cigarettes and a paper currency called the Bully Mark – paralleled events that happened over time in the larger world. Economic forces, Radford claims, were as important in the camps as in the outside world. The article provides insights into the connection between the supply of money and inflation, and into the workings of Gresham's law. It even provides insights into dual currency arrangements such as that experienced in the US in the late nineteenth century.

CHAPTER 4, *THE WEALTH OF NATIONS*, ADAM SMITH

In Chapter 4, Adam Smith argues that because the division of labor greatly increases trade among individuals, it gives rise to the use of money. He provides an overview of the evolution of money from commodity forms, through the use of metals in bar form, to the types of coinage that were used in his era. He explains that coinage obviates the need to weigh and assay metal money, but creates an incentive for 'princes and sovereign states' to diminish the real quantity of metal contained in coins.

Learning Objectives

After reading and discussing Chapter 4, students should be able to

1. Explain the connection between the division of labor and the use of money.
2. List the costs and benefits to individuals of an economy with coined money.
3. Explain how 'inflation' is the modern equivalent of the debasement of coins by princes and sovereign states. Explain who benefits from inflation and who loses.
4. Explain how money has evolved from something that had value in use to something that has little value in use but great value in exchange.

Question Clusters

1. Why, according to Smith, does the division of labor lead to the use of money? Do you agree with Smith that the division of labor accounts for the use of money?
2. What, according to Smith, are the costs and benefits to society of money use?

a. Why, according to Smith, do metals make better money than other commodities?
b. What, according to Smith, gives rise to coinage?
c. What does Smith mean when he says, '[t]he inconvenience and difficulty of weighing those metals with exactness gave occasion to the institution of coins...(which) were received by tale as at present, without the trouble of weighing.'?
d. What does Smith mean when he says that the '... avarice and injustice of princes and sovereign states, abusing the confidence of their subjects, have by degrees diminished the real quantity of metal, which had been originally contained in their coins.'?
3. According to Smith, does money have 'value in use' as well as 'value in exchange'? What is the difference between value in use and value in exchange?
4. How, according to Smith, has the value of money evolved over time?

Discussion Suggestions

Chapter 4 of Smith works as a stand-alone assignment if it comes after students have studied specialization. Interesting background reading on commodity money is available in Paul Einzig, *Primitive Money*, Second Edition, Pergamon Press, Oxford, 1966, pp. 332-88, and Edwin W. Kemmerer, *Money*, The Macmillan Company, NY, 1935, pp. 3-16. The Federal Reserve Bank of Richmond has a virtual museum of commodity money on the web site at http://www.rich.frb.org/econed/museum/index.html.

BANKS AND POLITICS IN AMERICA FROM THE REVOLUTION TO THE CIVIL WAR, BRAY HAMMOND, CHAPTERS 5-6

Chapters 5 and 6 tell the story of banks and banking in the United States in the period immediately before and after the Constitution was ratified. The story focuses on the Bank of the United States that was proposed by Alexander Hamilton, opposed by James Madison and Thomas Jefferson, and chartered in February of 1791 when President Washington signed the act incorporating the Bank rather than vetoing it as he had been preparing to do.

The history of the first bank is the story of competing visions of America. Jefferson envisioned a nation of self-sufficient yeomen farmers whose existence might be threatened by the Bank. Other agrarians feared the Bank would become like the 'perpetual monopolies' of England, which their forefathers had fled. Hamilton believed the Bank was necessary to promote trade and commerce and to provide for growth in the young country. Madison believed that the Bank was not constitutional, specifically because the Constitution had not authorized it.

Closely tied to the debate about the Bank was a debate about fiat-money. To fight the Revolution, the colonists had permitted their fledgling government to issue unbacked 'Continental' dollars, which had rapidly depreciated during the war. Many feared new inflation if unbacked paper money was issued by the Bank, and believed that the money supply should be limited to gold and silver. But gold and silver were so scarce that many were unable to obtain what they needed to pay taxes and debts even though their farms and handicrafts were productive. Many of those who favored paper money feared that defining legal tender to be gold and silver amounted to a scheme to seize their lands.

Chapters 5 and 6 of Hammond provide students with an opportunity to discuss the forces that competed for directional control of early US economic development. Few students will know before reading Hammond that the nation's early banking arrangements were so hotly debated, and that the subject generated a near crisis of Constitutional principles.

Learning Objectives

After reading and discussing the chapters from Bray Hammond's book, students should be able to

1. State the arguments for and against the constitutionality of the Bank of the United States.
2. Explain the tradeoffs involved in allowing the Bank of the United States to issue unbacked fiat-money.
3. Identify the different interest groups that took positions on the Bank; explain their positions and why they held them.
4. Discuss the connection between the creation of the Bank and the facilitation of interstate trade.
5. Argue for or against the chartering of the Bank of the United States with well-formed economic arguments.
6. Argue for or against the issuance of fiat-money with well-formed economic arguments.

Question Clusters

1. What, according to Hammond were the most important arguments against establishment of a Bank of the United States?

   a. According to Hammond, did the Constitution authorize establishment of national banks?

   b. According to Hammond, why were certain interest groups opposed to the Bank?

2. What, according to Hammond were the most important arguments for establishment of a Bank of the United States?

   a. According to Hammond, what interest groups favored establishment of the Bank?

   b. Why, according to Hammond, was a system of state banks insufficient to meet the commercial needs of the United States?

3. What, according to Hammond, is the connection between the establishment of the Bank of the United States and the creation of fiat-money for the US?

   a. What groups favored creation of fiat-money?

   b. What groups opposed creation of fiat-money?

4. According to Hammond, did the Constitution authorize the government to establish the Bank of the United States?

   a. Why did Madison believe the Bank was unconstitutional?

   b. Why did Hamilton believe that the Constitution permitted creation of the Bank?

5. In your own view, did Congress and President Washington act wisely by establishing the Bank of the United States in 1791?

Discussion Suggestions

The material in sections V through VIII of Chapter 5 concerns institutional details about Bank operations. Many instructors will want to de-emphasize these sections. It is important for students to read Chapter 4 in order to understand why the Bank was controversial and who the stakeholders were. To supplement discussion of Hammond, we sometimes have students conduct 'Mock Congressional Hearings', using the following scenarios to create role players.

Mock Congressional Hearings

It is December, 1790. Congressional Hearings are being held to determine whether Congress should approve two resolutions. The first resolution grants a charter to the Bank of the United States. The second resolution grants legal tender status to paper dollars that the bank will issue, and permits the Bank to hold whatever gold backing it deems prudent.

    Five speakers are scheduled. Students will be assigned to the staffs of one of the five speakers. Each staff will research the position of its speaker before class and then testify on behalf of the speaker in the Mock Hearings. Each speaker is allotted ten minutes for testimony. After all have spoken, a final debate on each resolution will be held. Congress will then vote.

Speaker one is Caleb Strong. Strong is a member of the committee that will deliberate these resolutions. He is appearing at these hearings to provide Congress with a background report about the colonies' experience with issues of 'continental' paper dollars during the period of the revolution. Speaker two is Alexander Hamilton, who has submitted a plan for the Bank to Congress. Hamilton favors the establishment of the Bank and will testify that the Bank is necessary for the growth of commerce in the United States. Speaker three is James Madison who opposes the creation of the Bank. Madison opposes the Bank, largely on Constitutional grounds. However, at the hearing he will represent all those voices that oppose the creation of the Bank. Speaker four is Albert Gallatin, who represents those in the United States who favor the issuance of paper money. Speaker five is William Findley, who represents those in the United States who oppose the issuance of paper money.

'ANCHORS AWEIGH: THE TRANSITION FROM COMMODITY MONEY TO FIAT MONEY IN WESTERN ECONOMIES', ANGELA REDISH

The United States left the gold standard in 1973 when President Nixon permanently suspended convertibility of the United States dollar into gold. Since then, the developed world has had pure fiat-money. In this article, Angela Redish argues that the transition from commodity money to fiat-money was a gradual process that took centuries rather than decades to accomplish. She suggests that the relationship between money and gold is like the relationship between a ship and its anchor. Over several centuries, the world experienced rising seas and sought ever more ingenious ways to lengthen the anchor chain. Finally, in 1973, the chain was broken.

Redish begins her story in the late Middle Ages when it was customary for kings and princes to proclaim coins to be legal tender 'for a given unit of account values' (p. 779). The monarch had the right both to run the mint and to define the unit of account. Redish provides an example of this arrangement for England using the equation $M = (pg)G$ where G is gold measured in ounces and pg is the pound sterling value of an ounce of gold as specified by the King. She uses the equation to illustrate what happened when Henry VIII raised the mint price of silver from 2.43 to 2.64 pounds sterling.

Europe began substituting paper notes for coin as early as the seventeenth century. By the end of the eighteenth century, note-issuing banks became increasingly common. At the same time, Redish points out, there developed a system of central banks whose notes were legal tender. Redish suggests that the emergence of central banks was another strategy for lengthening the anchor chain. Once central bank notes could be held as backing for private bank notes, the equation linking money and gold became $M = k\,(pg)G$, where k was inversely related to the reserve ratio.

The gold standard was suspended in both World War I and II, as it typically was when nations urgently required seigniorage. In 1925, it was resumed by Great Britain in part because postwar hyperinflation had dramatically demonstrated the perils of inconvertible currencies. After World War II, it was resumed as the result of the Bretton Woods Agreement, which specified that the US dollar would be convertible into gold at $35.00 per ounce and that other nations would fix the value of their currencies to the dollar. As Redish explains, Bretton Woods lengthened the anchor chain once more and for the last time. The fundamental problem that finally caused the failure of the Bretton Woods arrangement was the same as the problem that had required an ever lengthening chain for over a hundred years: the rate of economic growth was greater than the rate of increase in the gold supply.

Learning Objectives

After reading and discussing Redish's article, students should be able to

1. Explain why the title of the article is 'Anchors Aweigh'.
2. Describe the benefits and costs of the gold standard.
3. Identify and evaluate the evidence that Redish uses to support her claim that the suspension of the gold standard was a very gradual process.
4. Use the data from Table 1 to explain why Henry VIII earned revenue for the Crown by raising the mint price of silver in 1542.
5. Explain why the emergence of central banks amounted to a lengthening of the anchor chain.
6. Interpret what Redish means when she says that policy makers have done a poor job of 'finding an alternative (cheaper) anchor and making it credible'.

Question Clusters

1. In 1971, president Nixon suspended the convertibility of the US dollar into gold. Why, according to Redish, was the transition from commodity money to fiat-money a far more gradual process than this definitive action by the US would suggest?
   a. What does Redish mean by commodity money?
   b. What, according to Redish, are the milestone events along the road to fiat-money? How long did the process take?

    c. Why, according to Redish, was the Bretton Woods agreement an important step in the transition?

    d. Why, according to Redish, was it no longer possible in the late twentieth century to 'lengthen the chain further'?

2. According to Redish, is a commodity money system or a fiat-money system superior?

    a. What, according to Redish, are the advantages of a fiat-money system? Of a commodity money system?

    b. What, according to Redish, is the role of hyperinflation in explaining the transition from commodity money to fiat-money?

    c. What does Redish mean when she says that the money stock is anchored by a natural resource constraint? Is such an anchor an advantage or a disadvantage of commodity money?

    d. Why, according to Redish, did the British go off the gold standard during World War I? Why did they return to the gold standard after the war?

3. Why, according to Redish, did the monetary authority play a role in the commodity money standard?

    a. What does Redish mean when she says that coins were traded by their value in a unit of account which differed from the medium of exchange? How can the unit of account be different than the medium of exchange?

    b. What is a central bank and what role did it play in the transition?

4. Should the US reinstate convertibility of the dollar into gold?

    a. What does Redish mean when she says that policy makers have done a bad job of 'finding an alternative (cheaper) anchor and making it credible'?

    b. What is more important, opportunities for seigniorage or the assurance that the money supply cannot grow too rapidly?

Discussion Suggestions

In principles courses, instructors often explain that money arrangements begin with commodity money, pass through a period where precious metals are coined, and end with inconvertible fiat-money. Seldom are the details of the process spelled out. Discussion of the Redish article provides a valuable opportunity for students to think about how monetary arrangements evolve and to consider the costs and benefits of tying money to gold. The article would also provides a good introduction to the money section of a Money and Banking course.

'THE ECONOMIC ORGANISATION OF A P.O.W. CAMP', R. A. RADFORD

We provide a more complete abstract of the Radford article in Chapter 13. Here we focus on the aspects of the reading that detail with the creation and use of commodity monies in the P.O.W. camps.

In Radford's camp cigarettes functioned like money and were held and accepted by smokers and non-smokers alike. Radford explains why the intrinsic usefulness of cigarettes was a disadvantage to their use as money. Smokers persistently lowered the stock of money. When delivery of Red Cross parcels was interrupted and the stock of cigarettes not replaced, prices tended to fall. Right after delivery of parcels, prices would rise. Camp members had to contend with inflation and deflation that made holding inventories and timing purchases risky. Radford points out that a fall in the supply of cigarettes not only lowered prices generally, but also changed the price structure. When parcels were quite scarce, basic foodstuffs such as bread rose in value relative to less essential items.

Radford reports that the camp entertainment committee organized a store that bought foodstuffs at market prices and used them to produce snacks and meals sold at a companion restaurant. The store issued a paper currency, called the 'Bully Mark', that was backed by food rather than cigarettes. As long as parcels were delivered regularly, the restaurant and store flourished and camp prices remained stable. When parcel delivery was disrupted, the shop suffered from a change in relative prices and became glutted with the goods that prisoners valued less in hard times. The shop, restaurant, and Bully Mark ultimately failed. 'Prices moved', says Radford, 'with the supply of cigarettes, and refused to stay fixed in accordance with a theory of ethics'.

Learning Objectives

After reading and discussing the Radford article, students should be able to

1. Make the case that cigarettes functioned as money in the P.O.W. camps.
2. Explain what Radford means when he says that cigarettes had a disadvantage as money because they were intrinsically useful.
3. Provide an explanation of the failure of the Bully Mark.

Question Clusters

1. According to Radford, did cigarettes function well as money in the P.O.W. camp?

    a. Was it important to their use as currency that cigarettes had intrinsic value?

    b. Why would individuals re-roll their machine-rolled cigarettes?

    c. What is the significance of the fact that a reduction of Red Cross parcels changed prices?

2. What, according to Radford, accounts for the failure of the 'Bully Mark'?

    a. Why, according to Radford, were cigarettes acceptable as money even after the Bully Mark failed?

    b. What does Radford mean when he says that 'prices moved with the supply of cigarettes, and refused to stay fixed in accordance with a theory of ethics.'?

Discussion Suggestions

Students find it interesting to realize that the efficiency gains from transacting with money are sufficiently large to lead to the creation of money even in a short-duration society like Radford's camp. The article provides a good example to help students to understand what Smith means when he links specialization to the extent of the market and the use of money in exchange.

OVERVIEW

Several themes tie the articles of this chapter together. Here we suggest discussion strategies that instructors might use to help students investigate these themes.

One theme that runs through all four articles is the connection between trade and the use of money. We suggest that instructors invite students to consider how the authors of the other articles would react to Adam Smith.

In Chapter 4 of the *Wealth of Nations,* Adam Smith says, '...every prudent man in every period of society, after the first establishment of the division of labour, must naturally have endeavoured to manage his affairs in such a manner, as to have at all times by him, besides the peculiar produce of his own industry, a certain quantity of some one commodity or other, such as he imagined few people would be likely to refuse in exchange for the produce of their industry' (pp. 24-5).

1. Would Radford agree with Smith? Why or why not?
2. Would Bray say that Hamilton agreed with Smith? Why or not?
3. Would Bray say that Jefferson agreed with Smith? Why or why not?
4. Would Redish agree with Smith? Why or why not?

A second theme that runs through the articles are the tradeoffs between the use of gold and fiat-monies. We suggest these avenues of discussion:

1. The articles we have read describe the evolution from commodity money through coinage to fiat-money. What do each of the authors have to say about the costs and benefits to society of breaking the 'anchor chain' and adopting fiat-money?
2. What evidence do the authors provide for the superiority of fiat-money over gold?
3. What evidence do the authors provide that inflation is more likely when fiat-money is adopted?
4. Do you agree that fiat-money is a superior alternative to gold coins?

Finally, students might investigate the importance of the development of money to development of the economic life of society. Instructors might ask

1. How important, according to each of the authors we have read, is the development of money to the economic life of society?
2. How important, in your view, is the social institution of money?

19. The Theory of Interest

In a 1967 essay, Paul Samuelson described Irving Fisher as 'perhaps the greatest single name in the history of American economics' (p. 17), and goes on to praise the *Theory of Interest* by saying that 'it is hard to imagine a better book to take with you to a desert island' (p. 18). Later in the same essay, he says that the *Theory of Interest* gives a supply and demand determination of interest rates that is neither circular nor superficial in its reasoning, but 'a formulation that analyzes these to their ultimate source in taste and technology'.

For Fisher, the rate of interest is determined jointly by the patience of a population and the productivity of its capital. To understand Fisher's idea requires careful thought. First, Fisher is talking about the real rate of interest, the ratio at which individuals may trade goods today for goods tomorrow. Second, there is not a monetary authority in Fisher's theory that raises the important question of whether and for how long a change in monetary policy can change the real rate of interest. Third, for Fisher the rate of interest is no different from any other trading ratio. Fisher would argue that lending at the real rate of interest is no different from trading apples for oranges at market prices. Fisher forces his readers to rethink the meaning of usury. Finally, the equilibrium interest rate, like all equilibrium prices, coordinates the behavior of diverse economic agents. In equilibrium, all agents adjust their internal measures of impatience and their interest measures of the productivity of capital to the rate determined by the market. By interacting in a market, borrowers and lenders confront everyone with the market price of goods today for goods tomorrow.

Students can better understand why the interest rate gravitates toward an equilibrium by discussing the *Theory of Interest*. Fisher writes clearly, and builds his theory in several stages. In our experience, the early chapters are accessible to pre-principles students provided the instructor prepares the ground by explaining discounting and capitalization. In our view, Fisher's chief insights are available in the first approximation, so that discussing Chapters 1 through 5 would be adequate in many courses. In financial market courses, however, students will gain important additional insights from discussing Fisher's second and third approximations, and we include discussion suggestions for Chapters 6 through 8 and for Chapter 9.

THE THEORY OF INTEREST, IRVING FISHER, CHAPTERS 1-5

Irving Fisher begins the *Theory of Interest* with an intriguing sentence: 'Income is a series of events'. According to Fisher, what ultimately matters is the psychic income that derives from enjoyable events such as consumption. Enjoyment can be approximated by accounting for the cost of real activities that produce enjoyment, which Fisher terms the cost of one's 'living'. Money income is money received that can be used either to pay for one's current living or invested to help meet the cost of living in future years.

Fisher emphasizes that while capital goods are the source of future services, the value of capital is accounted for by the value placed on those future services. The value of capital derives from the value of income produced by the capital and not the other way around. Fisher calls the rate of interest the bridge between income and capital because it is used to compute the present value of a future stream of income. Capital gains are not properly income, but rather revaluations of future income.

In Chapter 2, Fisher explains that there can be as many interest rates as there are goods, since one can exchange any good now for another at a later date. A practical definition of the real rate is the nominal rate adjusted by the cost of living.

In Chapter 3, Fisher rebuts the view that collection of interest is immoral, paying particular attention to the claim that payment of interest denies labor the full value of its product. He debunks several misperceptions about what determines the interest rate, and emphasizes that the interest rate is not a simple translation of the physical productivity of land or capital.

In Chapter 4, Fisher defines human impatience. By a value of human patience of five percent, Fisher means that an individual asked to give up a bundle of consumption goods today must receive an additional five percent goods next year in order to be equally well satisfied with the two bundles. Fisher explains that human impatience depends on personal traits and on the size, time-distribution, composition, and riskiness of the income stream that an individual possesses. He suggests that an individual with an increasing income profile will tend to have a high level of impatience and be inclined to borrow while an individual with a decreasing profile will have a low level of impatience and be inclined to lend. Fisher discusses the effect of riskiness and different attitudes toward risk on an individual's impatience. He also suggests that different types of persons tend to have different levels of impatience.

In Chapter 5, Fisher provides his first approximation to the theory of interest. He assumes a simple world where all income streams are certain, the loan market is competitive, no limits to borrowing exist beyond the requirement that loans be repaid, and the loan market is the only vehicle through which individuals may change the time/shape of their income streams. In such a world, individuals with high rates of impatience borrow from individuals with low rates of impatience until, reaching equilibrium, all impatience rates equal the rate of interest. The equilibrium rate of interest exists where demand to borrow current income in exchange for income next year is just equal to supply of current income in exchange for income next year. Fisher says, 'The rate of interest is equal to the degree of impatience upon which the whole community may concur in order that the market for loans be exactly cleared' (p. 120).

Learning Objectives

After reading and discussing Chapters 1-5 of Fisher, students should be able to

1. Explain what Fisher means when he says that 'income is a series of events'.
2. Explain how psychic income, real income, and money income are different.
3. Provide an example that illustrates how the value of a capital good depends on the value of the income produced by the capital good.
4. Provide an intuitive explanation of discounting.
5. Explain how Fisher would counter the claim that the collection of interest is immoral.
6. Define human impatience and provide examples of individuals with high levels of impatience and with low levels of impatience.
7. Explain the sense in which the equilibrium rate of interest coordinates levels of impatience among the members of a society.

Question Clusters

1. What does Irving Fisher mean when he says, 'Income is a series of events.'?
   a. What does Fisher mean by enjoyment income? By real income? By money income?
   b. Why does Fisher believe that enjoyment income is fundamental?
2. What, according to Fisher, is the relationship between the value of an apple orchard and the value of the apples the orchard produces?
   a. What, according to Fisher, would be the difference in value between an orchard with mature trees and an orchard with juvenile trees if the orchards were otherwise the same?
   b. How, according to Fisher, does the rate of interest help determine the value of the orchard?

    c. Why, according to Fisher, do past costs of developing the orchard have no direct influence on the orchard's value?

3. What, according to Fisher, is the relationship between money interest and real interest?

    a. Why does Fisher describe the rate of interest as a '...premium on present goods over future goods of the same kind'? What is to be gained by describing the rate of interest in this way?

    b. What, according to Fisher, is the relationship among foresight, money interest, and real interest?

4. How would Fisher rebut the claim that charging interest is unfair to the debtor?

    a. How would Fisher answer the Marxian claim that to charge interest is to withhold from labor a portion of its product?

    b. How would Fisher answer Thomas Aquinas who argued that the collection of interest is wrong because it is a payment for time which God alone may give and take away?

5. What, according to Fisher, is the relationship between human impatience and the rate of interest?

    a. What does Fisher mean by 'human impatience'?

    b. Why, according to Fisher, is there a relationship between the time/shape of the income stream and human impatience? Between the uncertainty of the income stream and human impatience?

    c. Would Fisher believe that the typical college student has a high or low rate of impatience? Why?

6. What, according to Fisher, determines the rate of interest in the first approximation?

    a. In what sense does a market for loans produce coordination among individuals with different degrees of impatience?

    b. How do Charts 5 and 6 illustrate coordination among individuals with different degrees of impatience?

    c. If all humans are impatient, could the rate of interest in an economy ever be negative?

    d. In what sense does an individual maximize when he coordinates his rate of impatience to the market interest rate?

    e. What, according to Fisher, is wrong with the theory that states that the real rate of interest must equal the rate of productivity of the capital stock?

7. In your view, does Fisher's first approximation describe a theory that is relevant in today's economy? Why or why not?

Discussion Suggestions

Instructors of different courses will assign *The Theory of Interest* with different objectives in mind. Principles instructors may want students to discuss Fisher's ideas about the forces that determine the interest rate, since students may come to economics with the naïve view that interest rates are somehow set by banks and other financial institutions without regard to borrowers and lenders. Intermediate macro instructors may also want students to discuss Fisher's ideas about income, since these are fundamental to our system of national accounts and to standard definitions of the cost of living and the real rate of interest. For instructors in financial markets courses, discussion of the chapters provides an introduction to capitalization and discounting. All may want students to discuss Fisher's rebuttal to the claim that interest is immoral.

To completely discuss Chapters 1 through 5, instructors should allow at least two 50-minute class periods. To save time, we sometimes de-emphasize Chapter 1 by assigning it as background reading and focus discussion on Chapters 2 through 5. Intermediate theory and financial market instructors will probably want to have students read and discuss the 'second approximation' in Chapter 6.

One warning: Some of the racial and ethnic characterizations made by Fisher in Chapter 4 are inappropriate by modern standards. We tell students directly that we consider these characterizations to be wrong and inappropriate. We ask them to focus instead on Fisher's ideas about interest rates.

THE THEORY OF INTEREST, IRVING FISHER, CHAPTERS 6-8

In Chapter 5, Fisher assumes that only by loans can one change the time/shape of an income stream. In Chapter 6, Fisher weakens this assumption by acknowledging that individuals may choose among various investment opportunities, each offering a different income stream. An individual may alter the time shape of an income stream both through investment and through loans.

By way of example, Fisher assumes that a land owner has three uses for his land: farming, forestry, and mining. Farming provides a constant stream of income, forestry provides low income in early years and higher income later. Mining provides high income in early years and low income later. How should the land owner use the land?

Fisher explains that the land owner's problem may be divided into two parts. First, the land owner should choose the land use that maximizes the present value of the net income stream produced by the land. Next, the land owner should lend or borrow to provide himself with the income stream he most prefers. Because the interest rate will affect both the optimal use of land and the land owner's borrowing and lending, Fisher says that both investment opportunities and human impatience determine the equilibrium rate of interest.

In Chapter 6, Fisher introduces the concept of 'rate of return over cost'. Rate of return over cost is essentially the same as the internal rate of return of an investment opportunity. Fisher defines the rate of return over cost as the discount rate, such that the present value of the cash outlays required by the investment just equals the present value of the income to be realized from the investment. Later in the chapter, Fisher considers a broader set of investment opportunities where the investor is free to adjust continuously the amount of investment, or put another way, the intensity with which he uses the investment technology. The relevant internal rate, given continuous investment opportunities, is the marginal rate of return over cost, the discount rate such that the present value of outlays equals the present value of income for the last bit of investment effort. With continuous investment opportunities, optimality requires using an investment technology until the marginal rate of return over cost falls to the market rate of interest.

In Chapter 8, Fisher explains why both investment opportunities and human impatience are important determinants of the market rate of interest. To illustrate why investment opportunities are important, Fisher considers 'island' economies for which the return on investment opportunities is determined by nature. On such islands, the rate of interest and human impatience would equal the natural rate of return. He points out that the most important way in which an entire society can alter the shape of its income stream is by altering its use of labor. Using labor to produce capital goods provides society with later income at the cost of earlier income. Using labor to produce consumption goods does the opposite.

Learning Objectives

After reading and discussing Chapters 5-8, students should be able to

1. Explain why the investment opportunities available to a society affect the equilibrium rate of interest.
2. Explain why it is optimal for an individual to first choose an investment that provides the largest possible present value of net income, and then to borrow and lend to provide the most preferred income stream.

3. Given a table of outlays and incomes associated with investment projects, compute the present value of outlays, the present value of incomes, and the project that maximizes present value all as functions of the market rate of interest.
4. Explain what Fisher means by the rate of return over cost and the marginal rate of return over cost.
5. Provide examples that show that both human impatience and investment opportunities combine to determine the market rate of interest.

Question Clusters

1. Why, according to Fisher, do the investment opportunities available to a society help determine the equilibrium rate of interest?
   a. What, according to Fisher, would be the effect on the equilibrium interest rate of a new invention, such as the cell phone, or the computer, or a new automobile technology, such as the hybrid engine?
   b. How does Fisher's 'hard tack' illustration make clear that investment opportunities are important determinants of the interest rate?
2. Why, according to Fisher, can an investor's problem be broken into two parts?
   a. What are the two parts of the investor's problem?
   b. Why does Fisher claim that the investor need not concern himself with the time/shape of the income stream afforded by an investment?
   c. Fisher claims that an investor nearing retirement should invest in a new forest if that is the highest present value investment available, even though the forest will yield no income until after the investor dies. How would Fisher resolve this apparent puzzle?
3. What does Fisher mean by the marginal rate of return over cost?
   a. How does Fisher use the marginal rate of return over cost to characterize an optimal investment decision?
   b. How does Chart 16 illustrate the use of the marginal rate of return over cost? How would Chart 16 change if the market rate of interest rose?
4. What does Fisher mean when he says that '...borrowing and lending, the narrower method of modifying income streams, cannot be applied to society as a whole...'?
   a. Why can't society modify its income stream through borrowing and lending?
   b. How, according to Fisher, can society modify its income stream?

Discussion Suggestions

Chapters 6 through 8 will be of most interest to instructors teaching financial markets courses because students must understand present value in order to understand Fisher's second approximation. Because these chapters provide more explanation and illustration than the standard textbook, instructors may wish to use them to introduce optimal investment decisions. The idea that the real rate of interest is determined jointly by human impatience and investment opportunities is powerful, in part, because it argues that there is a 'natural level' of the real rate of interest that no central bank can alter in the long-run.

THE THEORY OF INTEREST, IRVING FISHER, CHAPTER 9

In Chapter 9, Fisher modifies the theory of interest to account for uncertainty. He quickly concludes that there may be many interest rates representing many different rates of exchange between income this year and income next year because of the risk that income next year may not be paid in full. He argues that it is useful to think of normal interest as the return on a fairly safe loan and to think of different rates of interest as the sum of normal interest and compensation for risk bearing.

Uncertainty compels collateral, and the necessity to offer collateral may limit a person's ability to borrow. It may be then that an investor, because of restrictions on borrowing, will not be able to bring the marginal rate of return over cost down to the market rate of interest. Likewise, an impatient individual may not be able to bring the rate of impatience down to the market rate of interest.

Fisher points out that an increase in the riskiness of current income relative to later income will tend to raise human impatience and the market rate of interest. An increase in the riskiness of later income relative to current income will have the opposite effect. He also points out that stocks may not be more risky than bonds because bond holders bear more inflation risk, while stock holders may lower risk through diversification.

At the end of the chapter, Fisher summarizes how uncertainty affects the principles of investment, impatience, and market clearing. He argues that investors will maximize expected present values, that individuals will choose the income stream that they expect will be most preferred, and that the market for loans will clear.

Learning Objectives

After reading and discussing Chapter 9, students should be able to

1. Explain the difference that uncertainty makes to the principles of optimal investment and optimal impatience.
2. Explain why uncertainty may leave an investor with a marginal rate of return over cost above the market interest rate.
3. Provide an example of an individual who is unable to bring his rate of impatience down to the market rate of interest.
4. Discuss whether the existence of uncertainty invalidates the first and second approximations to the theory of interest.

Question Clusters

1. What, according to Fisher, are the most important ways that income stream uncertainty affects the theory of interest?
   a. Why does uncertainty give rise to collateral?
   b. How is an investor affected by uncertainty?
   c. How is an impatient consumer affected by uncertainty?
2. Why does Fisher believe that stocks may not be much riskier than bonds?
   a. What does Fisher mean by diversification?
   b. What evidence does Fisher cite to support his claim?
3. Do you believe that uncertainty invalidates Fisher's first and second approximations to the theory of interest or leaves those conclusions largely intact?

Discussion Suggestions

This short chapter makes a nice introduction to decision making under uncertainty, which could serve to introduce that topic in a financial markets course. It would only make sense to assign this chapter to students who have read at least Chapters 5 and 6.

OVERVIEW

Full comprehension of the three sections of Fisher's book is less challenging than achieving an overview through articles written at different times by authors with different perspectives. What we suggest is simple. If students discuss both the first and second approximations, instructors should ask them at the end what important insights the second approximation provides to the theory of interest that the first does not. They can also ask what additional concepts and ideas are important for understanding the second approximation that do not come into play in the first. This same strategy can be employed a second time if students read and discuss all three approximations.

20. International Financial Institutions

Globalization of financial markets is a two-edged sword. While global financial markets can channel funds from savers in one nation to the most productive capital projects in the world, increased globalization has also made nations and their financial institutions more vulnerable to shocks that originate outside their borders. In this chapter, we suggest three readings and discussion strategies through which students can examine these issues.

In the first, Maurice Obstfeld examines the costs and benefits of the global capital market. He points out that only recently has the world begun to approximate the levels of financial openness common in the nineteenth century. The benefits of openness are several. Global financial markets channel savings to the most productive projects in the world. Global markets permit citizens of different nations to share risks. Openness disciplines domestic policy makers with the threat of capital outflows.

But there are also costs of openness. Open markets constrain domestic policy – a nation cannot simultaneously maintain fixed exchange rates, domestic monetary policy goals, and open capital markets. It must give up one of the three. Openness is also costly because it limits a country's ability to tax capital when it can move across borders to avoid taxes.

In the second article, Frederic Mishkin examines global financial crises such as the one that swept through Asia in the late 1990s. For Mishkin, a crisis occurs when shocks to the system so interfere with information flows that financial institutions are no longer able to channel funds from savers to investors. Mishkin first examines how asymmetric information problems grow worse during a crisis, and then looks for common symptoms among the Asian nations that experienced a crisis in 1997 and 1998. He concludes that the common element was too rapid credit expansion.

Mishkin concludes his article by asking what might have been done to stem the crisis. He argues that central banks in the crisis countries were powerless to help distressed financial firms because expanding liquidity might have triggered expectations of worsening inflation. He suggests liquidity from a foreign source such as the IMF could possibly help stem the crisis.

In the third paper, Kenneth Rogoff assesses the many proposals for new institutions that have been made in the wake of the Asian crisis. He argues that there is a parallel between domestic bank runs and international financial crises, but doubts that what we know about reducing the risks of bank runs within a country can be applied internationally. He fears that creation of a 'deep pockets' international lender would result in lax oversight and moral hazard problems. He doubts that nations are willing to cede sufficient authority to allow for the creation of either an international bankruptcy court or a global financial regulator. He also believes that there are serious limits to what developing nations can do on their own. In the end, Rogoff argues that his favorite solution is for nations to revise their laws so that they can rely more on equity financing and less on debt.

'THE GLOBAL CAPITAL MARKET: BENEFACTOR OR MENACE?', MAURICE OBSTFELD

In 1998, the *Journal of Economic Perspectives* published Obstfeld's paper as part of a symposium on globalization. In the paper, Obstfeld asks why global financial transactions have grown rapidly, why financial crises have been frequent, and whether or not the benefits of global financial markets outweigh the costs.

As Obstfeld explains, the benefits of global financial trading arise from several sources. Global financial markets permit residents of different countries to share risks. They allow countries with small domestic savings flows to finance productive investment projects. They promote efficiency by channeling savings to its most productive uses world-wide. They discipline domestic policy makers by threatening to respond to unwise policies with capital outflows. While benefits may be hard to quantify, Obstfeld argues that they are substantial.

Obstfeld suggests that recent increases in global financial activity are moving the world back to levels of financial openness common in the nineteenth century. He provides data on net capital flows between 1870 and 1996 that show that the world is still less open today than it was before World War I. He charts the standard deviation of New York–London interest rate differences that document a lack of convergence for most of the twentieth century. Only recently, Obstfeld argues, are New York and London rates displaying the same degree of convergence as they did prior to World War I.

One of the costs of global financial openness is revealed by what Obstfeld calls the open-economy 'trilemma': a country cannot simultaneously maintain fixed exchange rates, domestic monetary-policy goals, and open capital markets. It may choose two of the three. Obstfeld uses the trilemma to interpret the evolution of global financial markets, and concludes that the recent explosion of international financial activity began with the return to floating exchange rates in 1973.

Global financial openness is also costly because it places limits on a country's fiscal policy. Capital is hard to tax when it can move freely across borders. Openness becomes a threat where available social services are paid for by labor or consumption taxes. So far, this situation has yet to materialize. Obstfeld argues that there are still substantial cross-country differences in levels of social services and capital taxation rates.

Obstfeld next returns to an assessment of the benefits of financial openness. He first observes a paradox. Thus far citizens of the world are not taking full advantage of opportunities to diversify their portfolios by holding foreign assets. Next, he provides a brief assessment of recent capital market crises where capital inflows quickly turn to capital outflows. He concludes that private mismanagement and insufficient financial supervision are largely to blame for recent crises, but that root causes of crises may remain even if management and supervision are improved. The problem is information and the propensity of individuals to remain uninformed, and, therefore, susceptible to panic. Finally, Obstfeld comments on the IMF as an emergency lender of last resort. Under Bretton Woods, the role of the IMF was to support the exchange rate mechanism. The IMF has sought to broaden its role as emergency lender and to take on the additional role as promoter of capital market openness. Obstfeld observes that the benefits of expanded IMF lending are somewhat offset by the moral hazard problem that lending creates.

Obstfeld concludes that despite crises, globalization of financial markets is unstoppable and conveys significant net benefits to the growing world.

Learning Objectives

After reading and discussing the article, students should be able to

1. Explain why Obstfeld believes that world financial markets were less open for most of the twentieth century than they were just before World War I.
2. Interpret Table 1 and Figure 1 and use them to support the claim that financial markets were less open for most of the twentieth century than they were before World War I.
3. Define the 'openness trilemma' and explain how Obstfeld uses it to discuss the costs and benefits of open financial markets.
4. Explain why financial market openness places restrictions on domestic fiscal policy.
5. Explain Obstfeld's view on the changing role of the IMF since the collapse of the Bretton Woods exchange rate mechanism.
6. Decide whether the benefits of financial openness outweigh the costs.

Question Clusters

1. How does Obstfeld use the data contained in Table 1 and Figure 1 to demonstrate that economic integration is on the rise?
   a. In what sense is it true that economic integration has not quite reached the level that it had reached in the nineteenth century?
   b. What, according to Obstfeld, accounted for the decline in integration that occurred between 1900 and 1970?
2. In what sense, according to Obstfeld, does international integration involve a fundamental compromise?
   a. How would Obstfeld explain the provisions of the Maastricht Treaty that required convergence of member inflation rates and federal fiscal deficits to levels achieved by Germany?
   b. How would Obstfeld explain the fact that the EMU will have a single central bank rather than independent central banks for each member?
   c. Why might Obstfeld agree that Britain's tentative decision not to join the EMU might be in that nation's best interest?
3. Why, according to Obstfeld, does international integration tend to reduce the ability of nations to tax capital?
   a. In what sense does international openness threaten to end generous social programs in European nations?
4. What, according to Obstfeld, are the most important market failures associated with international financial integration?
   a. What does Obstfeld mean by the 'international diversification puzzle'?
   b. In what sense does integration make capital market crises more likely?
5. In your own view, do the benefits of international capital market integration outweigh the costs? What should US managers do to take advantage of the benefits of integration while not overexposing their companies to the risks associated with integration?

Discussion Suggestions

Students at several levels can benefit from reading and discussing the Obstfeld article. Principles instructors might assign the article as part of a module on globalization, a topic which has generated more heat than light in recent years. More advanced students might read the article as part of a module on financial market integration and/or financial market crises.

'GLOBAL FINANCIAL INSTABILITY: FRAMEWORK, EVENTS, ISSUES', FREDERIC MISHKIN

Mishkin's article is the introduction to a *Journal of Economic Perspectives* symposium on global financial instability organized in the aftermath of the Asian financial crises of the late 1990s. Mishkin begins with the fact that the essential function of financial markets and institutions is channeling funds from savers to individuals and firms that can most productively use them. Financial instability occurs when 'shocks to the financial system interfere with information flows so that the financial system can no longer do its job' (p. 6). Financial firms process information that influences the creditworthiness of investment opportunities. Assessing creditworthiness is hard because borrowers have more information than lenders – the classic problem of asymmetric information. During a crisis, shocks make it difficult to separate the investment wheat from the chaff.

Mishkin argues that four factors lead to worsening of asymmetric information problems during a crisis. First, during a crisis, banks and other financial institutions frequently experience loss of capital as asset values fall. Because it is difficult to raise new capital during a crisis, they typically reduce lending. If the crisis is bad enough, a panic may occur because depositors can not tell the difference between weak and strong loan portfolios. Second, during a crisis, interest rate increases lead to credit rationing because banks understand that low-risk borrowers are less likely to remain in the borrowing pool when interest rates increase. Interest rate increases undermine a bank's capital. Banks lend long and borrow short so that unforeseen increases in interest rates raise their costs more than their revenues. Third, uncertainty increases during a crisis, making it harder to separate good risks from bad risks. Fourth, during a crisis, the balance sheets of non-financial firms deteriorate, providing firms an incentive to take greater risks with borrowed funds. The effect is reinforced by declines in the value of assets posted as collateral.

Mishkin next looks for factors that crisis economies had in common. After ruling out several of the usual suspects, such as inflation and fiscal deficits, Mishkin notes that most economies that experienced a crisis in 1997 and 1998 were experiencing large capital inflows, high rates of credit growth, a high incidence of non-performing loans, and low liquidity levels in the pre-crisis years. Given these conditions, financial firms were like tinder-dry forests vulnerable to any spark.

While the root cause of the crises was the excessive risk-taking that accompanied the rapid growth of credit expansion, what sparked the panic was the combination of stock price decreases and news of financial-firm failures.

This flared into speculative attacks on the currencies and dramatically lower exchange rates.

Mishkin argues that the currency crises turned into full-fledged financial crises for two reasons. First, lower exchange rates caused higher debt service for the crisis countries because many foreign loans were denominated in hard currencies. Second, lower exchange rates quickly translated into higher costs for imports, higher inflation rates, and higher short-term interest rates.

As financial firms failed, central banks in the crisis countries were powerless to help them. They were caught on the horns of a dilemma: if they provided liquidity, investors would fear that the central bank was no longer committed to curtailing inflation and interest rates would soar. If they raised interest rates to fight inflation, financial firms would find themselves in even worse positions.

Mishkin closes his article by observing that a foreign source of liquidity, such as that provided by the IMF, might be successful when a domestic source of liquidity would not. He reviews several of the policy issues related to the crises and introduces other symposium papers that deal with them.

Learning Objectives

After reading and discussing the Mishkin article, students should be able to

1. Define a financial crisis.
2. Explain why financial firms are particularly vulnerable to asymmetric information problems.
3. Reconstruct Mishkin's case that the root cause of the financial crises of 1997 and 1998 was excessive risk-taking fostered by a too rapid growth in credit.
4. Explain the mechanisms whereby the failure of some financial firms turn into full-blown financial crises.
5. Explain why Mishkin believes that an international financial institution such as the IMF is in a better position than individual central banks to provide liquidity during a financial crisis.

Question Clusters

1 How, according to Mishkin, did adverse selection and moral hazard contribute to the financial crises that occurred in Mexico and East Asia in the mid- to late- 1990s?
   a. What does Mishkin mean by adverse selection? Moral hazard? How are these two problems the same? How are they different?
   b. What, according to Mishkin, caused the financial crises?

    i. Does Mishkin believe there was a common cause? Why or why not?

    ii. Were the crises caused by irresponsible monetary and fiscal policies? Why or why not?

    iii. What does Mishkin mean by deterioration of balance sheets? How did such deterioration contribute to the crises?

  c. Why, according to Mishkin, were banks in the crisis nations unable to recover from non-performing loans that occurred in the wake of an increase in bank lending in the 1990s?

  d. How, according to Mishkin, did the fact that many crisis-nation loans were denominated in dollars accelerate the crisis?

  e. Why, according to Mishkin, did the central banks of crisis nations err when they increased credit to troubled banks?

2. Why, according to Mishkin, can an international lender, such as the IMF, succeed in helping to end the crisis when a domestic central bank cannot?

  a. Why can't a domestic central bank supply the liquidity needed to avoid widespread failure of financial firms?

  b. According to Mishkin, should the IMF be liberal in lending to nations facing a financial crisis?

3. What lessons should US policy makers learn from the financial crises in Mexico and East Asia?

Discussion Suggestions

Although it is meant to be read as part of the symposium on global financial instability, we find that Mishkin's piece works well as a free-standing analysis of the causes of international financial crises. We have also successfully paired it with the Rogoff article that appeared in the symposium and which is covered below.

Whether or not they have previously studied economics, students will be aware of the many criticisms that have been directed at the IMF. It is useful for students to realize that the IMF was designed to function as an international lender of last resort and to consider its value in that context.

'INTERNATIONAL INSTITUTIONS FOR REDUCING GLOBAL FINANCIAL INSTABILITY', KENNETH ROGOFF

In the wake of the Asian financial crisis, the *Journal of Economic Perspectives* published a symposium on global financial instability which included Rogoff's essay. In the essay, Rogoff assesses the many proposals that have been made for new institutions designed to reduce financial instability resulting from the interconnectedness of financial markets. Rogoff points out that proposals for change are being promoted more vigorously than at any time since Bretton Woods.

First, Rogoff considers whether or not there is a crisis in global capitalism. He argues that global finance has permitted the US to lever a small domestic saving rate into a large increase in capital. For developing nations, the benefits are not so clear. Sudden withdrawals of short-term funds have caused financial crises and substantial decreases in growth in many developing nations in the 1990s. Still, Rogoff argues that the benefits from capital market integration are potentially very great. Globalization allows long-run efficiency gains by channeling saving to projects with the highest returns. It also allows small countries to diversify risks associated with specialization in production of a narrow range of goods.

Next, Rogoff considers the parallel between internal bank runs and international financial panics. Banks are vulnerable to runs because they lend long and borrow short. Diamond and Dybvig (1983) argue that a run is one possible banking equilibrium: when an agent believes others will withdraw their funds, it is optimal for the agent to follow suit whenever liquidation of bank assets is costly. Rogoff argues that the parallel is valid. In many countries, bank runs lead to government bailouts, increased issuance of government securities, and flight from country debt. Also, many investments in developing countries are long-term projects financed by short-term liabilities. The question is, can policy remedies that avoid bank runs be applied to avoid international financial crises?

Rogoff goes on to consider several institutional remedies for global financial instability. He concludes that creation of a 'deep pockets' international lender of last resort would lead to more lax oversight by domestic financial authorities. He argues that the G-7 nations are not likely to provide the IMF with sufficiently deep pockets. Rogoff points out that central banks frequently function as crisis managers as the Fed did in the rescue of Long-Term Capital Management, but concludes that the IMF and G-7 already play this role. He considers prospects for establishment of an international bankruptcy court that would permit an orderly temporary suspension of payments by institutions that are under attack. He concludes, however, that an international bankruptcy court would probably not be able to seize assets or take over financing decisions as a domestic court can. Rogoff also considers a global financial regulator, and a world monetary authority. He presents arguments against each.

Next, Rogoff considers steps that developing nations could take themselves to reduce their vulnerability to sudden outflows of capital. He concludes that restrictions on capital outflows would probably scare off investors and that restrictions on capital inflows might prove workable for some countries, but would likely be suspended if a developing country faced a shortage of funds. Rogoff also points out that countries can act to strengthen their own financial regulations, but that doing so is not proof against a bank run or a panic.

Finally, Rogoff takes his own turn at 'playing Keynes'. In Rogoff's view, global financial stability would be greatly increased if nations depended less on debt financing and more on equity. He explains that current laws and institutional practices create bias in favor of debt financing. Eliminating those biases would be difficult, Rogoff argues, but highly effective in reducing financial instability.

Learning Objectives

After reading and discussing the Rogoff article, students should be able to

1. Explain the parallel between domestic bank runs and international financial crises.
2. State and explain the costs and benefits of the institutional solutions that Rogoff studies.
3. State and explain the costs and benefits to developed and developing countries of global financial markets.
4. Explain why Rogoff believes that more equity financing would reduce international financial instability.
5. Reconstruct Rogoff's argument in favor of removal of the legal and institutional biases toward debt financing.

Question Clusters

1. According to Rogoff, is the status quo in international lending arrangements tenable or untenable?
   a. What are the most important problems associated with the status quo? How were these illustrated by the crises in Mexico and Asia?
   b. According to Rogoff, is the IMF capable of handling international financial crises? Why or why not?
2. What, according to Rogoff, is wrong with the grand plans that have been presented to save the global financial system?
   a. A 'deep pockets' lender of last resort?
   b. An international financial crisis manager?
   c. An international bankruptcy court?
   d. A global financial regulator?
   e. An international deposit insurance corporation?
   f. A world monetary authority?

3. According to Rogoff, can developing countries handle the problem of vulnerability to speculative capital flows on their own?
   a. Why is global financial instability a consequence of 'speculative capital flows'?
   b. What steps can developing countries take?
   c. Are the available steps adequate in Rogoff's view? Why or why not?
4. Why does Rogoff believe that the long run solution to global financial instability requires a larger role for equity financing of developing country projects?
   a. How would equity financing help solve the problems of financial crises?
   b. Why does Rogoff believe that the scale is tilted in favor of debt financing?
5. Do you believe that the International Monetary Fund will play an increasing or decreasing role in future international financial arrangements? Why?

Discussion Suggestions

Students today frequently encounter criticism of the IMF in the media. By reading and discussing the Rogoff article, students have an opportunity to consider whether or not an institution such as the IMF is essential for international financial stability. Like Rogoff, they have an opportunity to 'play Keynes' by contemplating alternative institutional arrangements and choosing those that they believe can work. Discussion here will improve student understanding of problems that result when financial institutions create liquidity by financing long-term loans with short-term borrowing. It will also give students a better appreciation of a fundamental tradeoff – providing assistance to a nation in crisis increases the likelihood of future crises.

OVERVIEW

There are quite a few issues that readers of all three article might investigate after discussing each individually. The first is the costs and benefits of financial openness. We suggest these questions:

1. Obstfeld, Mishkin, and Rogoff all have ideas about the costs and benefits of financial globalization.
   a. What, according to the three authors, are the most important benefits of financial openness?
   b. What, according to the three, are the most important costs of openness?
   c. Would the three authors agree on strategies for diminishing the costs of openness? Why or why not?

A second issue is the role of international financial institutions in lowering the likelihood and seriousness of international financial crises. We suggest these questions:

2. Would Obstfeld, Mishkin, and Rogoff agree that there is need for an international institution to lower the likelihood and provide remedies for international financial crises?
   a. Why, according to the authors, might an international institution succeed when domestic institutions cannot?
   b. What would an international institution do in a crisis?
   c. What benefits would an international institution provide to the global financial community?
   d. What are the disadvantages of creating a strong international financial institution to help with financial crises?

A third issue is why international crises occur. We suggest these questions:

3. Would Obstfeld, Mishkin, and Rogoff agree about the causes of the Asian financial crisis?
   a. Would the authors agree that asymmetric information problems become worse during a financial crisis? Why or why not?
   b. Would the authors agree that falling asset prices deepen and accelerate financial crises? Why or why not?
   c. Would the authors agree on the connection between exchange rate crises and financial crises?

References

Abercrombie, M. L. Johnson (1960), *The Anatomy of Judgment: An Investigation into the Process of Perception and Reasoning*, New York: Basic Books.

Adler, Mortimer J. and Charles Van Doren (1972), *How to Read a Book: The Classic Guide to Intelligent Reading*, Revised and Updated Edition, New York: Simon & Schuster.

Bartlett, Robin (1998), 'Making Cooperative Learning Work in Economics Classes', in William E. Becker and Michael Watts (eds), *Teaching Economics to Undergraduates: Alternatives to Chalk and Talk*, Cheltenham, UK and Lyme, USA: Edward Elgar, 11-34.

Bartlett, Robin and Marianne Ferber (1998), 'Humanizing Content and Pedagogy in Economics Classrooms', in William. B. Walstad and Phillip Saunders (eds), *Teaching Undergraduate Economics: A Handbook for Instructors*, New York: Irwin McGraw Hill, 109-25.

Becker, William E. and Michael Watts (1996), 'Chalk and Talk: A National Survey on Teaching Undergraduate Economics', *American Economic Review*, **86** (2), 448-53.

Becker, William E. and Michael Watts (1998), *Teaching Economics to Undergraduates: Alternatives to Chalk and Talk*, Cheltenham, UK and Lyme, USA: Edward Elgar.

Becker, William E. and Michael Watts (2001), 'Teaching Economics at the Start of the 21st Century: Still Chalk and Talk', *American Economic Review*, **91** (2), 446-51.

Bligh, Donald (ed.) (1986), *Teach Thinking by Discussion*, University of Surrey, Guildford, UK: Society for Research in Higher Education and NFER-Nelson.

Bloom, Benjamin S. (ed.) (1956), *Taxonomy of Educational Objectives: The Classification of Educational Goals: Handbook I, Cognitive Domain*, New York: Longmans Green.

Bonwell, Charles C. and James A. Eison (1991), *Active Learning: Creating Excitement in the Classroom*, ASHE-ERIC Higher Education Report No. 1, Washington, DC: The George Washington University, School of Education and Human Development.

Bransford, John D (ed.) (2000), *How People Learn: Brain, Mind, Experience, and School*, Committee on Developments in the Science of Learning, and

Committee on Learning Research and Educational Practice, Commission on Behavioral and Social Sciences and Education, Washington, DC: National Research Council.

Chickering, Arthur W. and Zelda F. Gamson (1987), 'Seven Principles for Good Practice', *AAHE Bulletin*, 39, 3-7.

Chizmar, John F. and Anthony L. Ostrosky (1998), 'The One-Minute Paper', *Journal of Economic Education*, **29** (1) , 3-10.

Christensen, C. Roland, with Abby J. Hansen (1987), *Teaching and the Case Method: Text, Cases, and Readings*, Boston: Harvard Business School Press.

Christensen, C. Roland, David A. Garvin and Ann Sweet (eds) (1991), *Education for Judgment: The Artistry of Discussion Leadership*, Boston: Harvard Business School Press.

Clerici-Arias, Marcelo, Mark Maier and Scott Simkins (2002), 'Using Just-in-Time Teaching Techniques in Principles of Economics Course: A Preliminary Report', unpublished Manuscript presented at the 2003 Allied Social Science Association Meetings.

Denby, David (1996), *Great Books*, New York: Simon & Schuster.

Diamond, Douglas W. and Philip H. Dybvig (1983), 'Bank Runs, Deposit Insurance and Liquidity', *Journal of Political Economy* **91** (3), 401-19.

Hansen, W. Lee (1978), 'Improving Classroom Discussion in Economics Courses', in Phillip Saunders, Arthur L. Welsh, and W. Lee Hansen (eds), *Resource Manual for Teacher Training Programs in Economics*, New York: National Council on Economic Education, 127-67.

Hansen, W. Lee (1986), 'What Knowledge Is Most Worth Knowing – For Economics Majors?' *American Economic Review*, **76** (2), 149-52.

Hansen, W. Lee (2001), 'Expected Proficiencies for Undergraduate Economics Majors', *Journal of Economic Education*, **32** (3), 231-42.

Hansen, W. Lee and Michael K. Salemi (1998), 'Improving Classroom Discussion in Economics Courses', in William B. Walstad and Phillip Saunders (eds), *Teaching Undergraduate Economics: A Handbook for Instructors*, New York: Irwin McGraw-Hill, 207-26.

Hansen, W. Lee, Michael K. Salemi and John J. Siegfried (2002), 'Use It or Lose It: Teaching Literacy in the Economics Principles Course', *American Economic Review*, Papers and Proceedings of the American Economic Association, **92** (2), 463-72.

Hume, David (1970), *Writings on Economics*, Eugene Rotwein (ed), Madison: University of Wisconsin Press.

Johnston, Carol G. et al. (2000), 'An Evaluation of the Introduction of Collaborative Problem Solving for Learning Economics', *Journal of Economic Education*, **31** (1), 13-29.

Krueger, Anne O. (1991), 'Report of the Commission on Graduate Education in Economics', *Journal of Economic Literature*, **29** (3), 1035-53.

Light, Richard J. (1992), 'The Harvard Assessment Seminars, Second Report,' Cambridge, MA, USA: Harvard University Graduate School of Education and Kennedy School of Government.

Maier, Mark H. (2000), 'Reporting Out: Closure Without the Tedium', *Journal of Cooperation and Collaboration in College Teaching*, **10** (3), 117-21.

Mazur, Eric (1997), *Peer Instruction: A User's Manual*, Upper Saddle River, NJ, USA: Prentice Hall.

McGoldrick, KimMarie and Andrea L. Ziegert (eds) (2002), *Putting the Invisible Hand to Work: Concepts and Models of Service Learning in Economics*, Ann Arbor, MI, USA: The University of Michigan Press.

McKeachie, Wilbert J., et al. (2002), *Teaching Tips: Strategies, Research, and Theory for College and University Teachers, 11th edition*, Lexington, MA: D.C. Heath and Company.

Petr, Jerry L. (1998), 'Student Writing as a Guide to Student Thinking', in William B. Walstad and Phillip Saunders (eds), *Teaching Undergraduate Economics: A Handbook for Instructors*, New York: Irwin McGraw-Hill, 227-46.

Salemi, Michael K. (2002), 'An Illustrated Case for Active Learning', *Southern Economics Journal*, **68** (3), 721-31.

Samuelson, Paul A. (1967),'Irving Fisher and the Theory of Capital', in William J. Fellner, (ed.), *Ten Economic Studies in the Tradition of Irving Fisher*, New York: John Wiley, 17-37.

Siegfried, John J. et al. (1991), 'The Status and Prospects of the Economics Major', *Journal of Economics Education*, **22** (3), 197-224.

Smith, Donna M. and David. A. Kolb (1986), *The User's Guide for the Learning-Style Inventory: A Manual for Teachers and Trainers*, Boston, MA, USA: McBer and Company.

Taylor, Beck A. and Tisha L. N. Emerson (2004), 'Comparing Student Achievement Across Experimental and Lecture-Oriented Sections of a Principles of Microeconomics Course', *Southern Economic Journal*, **70** (3), 672-93.

Taylor, John B. (2000), 'Teaching Modern Macroeconomics at the Principles Level', *American Economic Review*, Papers and Proceedings of the American Economic Association, **90** (2), 90-4.

Walstad, William B. and Ken Rebeck (2002), 'Assessing the Economic and Economic Opinions of Adults', *Quarterly Review of Economics and Finance*, **42** (5), 921-35 .

Walstad, William B. and Phillip Saunders (eds) (1998), *Teaching Undergraduate Economics: A Handbook for Instructors*, New York: Irwin McGraw-Hill.

PART SIX

Appendix

The Economic Organisation of a P.O.W. Camp

By R. A. RADFORD

INTRODUCTION

AFTER allowance has been made for abnormal circumstances, the social institutions, ideas and habits of groups in the outside world are to be found reflected in a Prisoner of War Camp. It is an unusual but a vital society. Camp organisation and politics are matters of real concern to the inmates, as affecting their present and perhaps their future existences. Nor does this indicate any loss of proportion. No one pretends that camp matters are of any but local importance or of more than transient interest, but their importance there is great. They bulk large in a world of narrow horizons and it is suggested that any distortion of values lies rather in the minimisation than in the exaggeration of their importance. Human affairs are essentially practical matters and the measure of immediate effect on the lives of those directly concerned in them is to a large extent the criterion of their importance at that time and place. A prisoner can hold strong views on such subjects as whether or not all tinned meats shall be issued to individuals cold or be centrally cooked, without losing sight of the significance of the Atlantic Charter.

One aspect of social organisation is to be found in economic activity, and this, along with other manifestations of a group existence, is to be found in any P.O.W. camp. True, a prisoner is not dependent on his exertions for the provision of the necessaries, or even the luxuries of life, but through his economic activity, the exchange of goods and services, his standard of material comfort is considerably enhanced. And this is a serious matter to the prisoner : he is not " playing at shops " even though the small scale of the transactions and the simple expression of comfort and wants in terms of cigarettes and jam, razor blades and writing paper, make the urgency of those needs difficult to appreciate, even by an ex-prisoner of some three months' standing.

Nevertheless, it cannot be too strongly emphasised that economic activities do not bulk so large in prison society as they do in the larger world. There can be little production ; as has been said the prisoner is independent of his exertions for the provision of the necessities and luxuries of life ; the emphasis lies in exchange and the media of exchange. A prison camp is not to be compared with the seething crowd of higglers in a street market, any more than it is to be compared with the economic inertia of a family dinner table.

Naturally then, entertainment, academic and literary interests, games and discussions of the " other world " bulk larger in everyday life than they do in the life of more normal societies. But it would be

189

wrong to underestimate the importance of economic activity. Everyone receives a roughly equal share of essentials ; it is by trade that individual preferences are given expression and comfort increased. All at some time, and most people regularly, make exchanges of one sort or another.

Although a P.O.W. camp provides a living example of a simple economy which might be used as an alternative to the Robinson Crusoe economy beloved by the text-books, and its simplicity renders the demonstration of certain economic hypotheses both amusing and instructive, it is suggested that the principal significance is sociological. True, there is interest in observing the growth of economic institutions and customs in a brand new society, small and simple enough to prevent detail from obscuring the basic pattern and disequilibrium from obscuring the working of the system. But the essential interest lies in the universality and the spontaneity of this economic life ; it came into existence not by conscious imitation but as a response to the immediate needs and circumstances. Any similarity between prison organisation and outside organisation arises from similar stimuli evoking similar responses.

The following is as brief an account of the essential data as may render the narrative intelligible. The camps of which the writer had experience were Oflags and consequently the economy was not complicated by payments for work by the detaining power. They consisted normally of between 1,200 and 2,500 people, housed in a number of separate but intercommunicating bungalows, one company of 200 or so to a building. Each company formed a group within the main organisation and inside the company the room and the messing syndicate, a voluntary and spontaneous group who fed together, formed the constituent units.

Between individuals there was active trading in all consumer goods and in some services. Most trading was for food against cigarettes or other foodstuffs, but cigarettes rose from the status of a normal commodity to that of currency. RMk.s existed but had no circulation save for gambling debts, as few articles could be purchased with them from the canteen.

Our supplies consisted of rations provided by the detaining power and (principally) the contents of Red Cross food parcels—tinned milk, jam, butter, biscuits, bully, chocolate, sugar, etc., and cigarettes. So far the supplies to each person were equal and regular. Private parcels of clothing, toilet requisites and cigarettes were also received, and here equality ceased owing to the different numbers despatched and the vagaries of the post. All these articles were the subject of trade and exchange.

THE DEVELOPMENT AND ORGANISATION OF THE MARKET

Very soon after capture people realised that it was both undesirable and unnecessary, in view of the limited size and the equality of supplies, to give away or to accept gifts of cigarettes or food. " Goodwill " developed into trading as a more equitable means of maximising individual satisfaction.

We reached a transit camp in Italy about a fortnight after capture and received $\frac{1}{4}$ of a Red Cross food parcel each a week later. At once exchanges, already established, multiplied in volume. Starting with simple direct barter, such as a non-smoker giving a smoker friend his cigarette issue in exchange for a chocolate ration, more complex exchanges soon became an accepted custom. Stories circulated of a padre who started off round the camp with a tin of cheese and five cigarettes and returned to his bed with a complete parcel in addition to his original cheese and cigarettes ; the market was not yet perfect. Within a week or two, as the volume of trade grew, rough scales of exchange values came into existence. Sikhs, who had at first exchanged tinned beef for practically any other foodstuff, began to insist on jam and margarine. It was realised that a tin of jam was worth $\frac{1}{2}$ lb. of margarine plus something else ; that a cigarette issue was worth several chocolate issues, and a tin of diced carrots was worth practically nothing.

In this camp we did not visit other bungalows very much and prices varied from place to place ; hence the germ of truth in the story of the itinerant priest. By the end of a month, when we reached our permanent camp, there was a lively trade in all commodities and their relative values were well known, and expressed not in terms of one another—one didn't quote bully in terms of sugar—but in terms of cigarettes. The cigarette became the standard of value. In the permanent camp people started by wandering through the bungalows calling their offers—" cheese for seven " (cigarettes)—and the hours after parcel issue were Bedlam. The inconveniences of this system soon led to its replacement by an Exchange and Mart notice board in every bungalow, where under the headings " name ", " room number ", " wanted " and " offered " sales and wants were advertised. When a deal went through, it was crossed off the board. The public and semi-permanent records of transactions led to cigarette prices being well known and thus tending to equality throughout the camp, although there were always opportunities for an astute trader to make a profit from arbitrage. With this development everyone, including non-smokers, was willing to sell for cigarettes, using them to buy at another time and place. Cigarettes became the normal currency, though, of course, barter was never extinguished.

The unity of the market and the prevalence of a single price varied directly with the general level of organisation and comfort.in the camp. A transit camp was always chaotic and uncomfortable : people were overcrowded, no one knew where anyone else was living, and few took the trouble to find out. Organisation was too slender to include an Exchange and Mart board, and private advertisements were the most that appeared. Consequently a transit camp was not one market but many. The price of a tin of salmon is known to have varied by two cigarettes in 20 between one end of a hut and the other. Despite a high level of organisation in Italy, the market was morcellated in this manner at the first transit camp we reached after our removal to Germany in the autumn of 1943. In this camp—Stalag VIIA at Moosburg in Bavaria—there were up to 50,000 prisoners of all nationalities. French, Russians, Italians and Jugo-Slavs were free to move about within the camp : British and Americans were confined to their compounds, although a few cigarettes given to a sentry would always procure permission for one or two men to visit other compounds. The people who first visited the highly organised French trading centre, with its stalls and known prices, found coffee extract—relatively cheap among the tea-drinking English—commanding a fancy price in biscuits or cigarettes, and some enterprising people made small fortunes that way. (Incidentally we found out later that much of the coffee went " over the wire " and sold for phenomenal prices at black market cafés in Munich : some of the French prisoners were said to have made substantial sums in RMk.s. This was one of the few occasions on which our normally closed economy came into contact with other economic worlds.)

Eventually public opinion grew hostile to these monopoly profits—not everyone could make contact with the French—and trading with them was put on a regulated basis. Each group of beds was given a quota of articles to offer and the transaction was carried out by accredited representatives from the British compound, with monopoly rights. The same method was used for trading with sentries elsewhere, as in this trade secrecy and reasonable prices had a peculiar importance, but as is ever the case with regulated companies, the interloper proved too strong.

The permanent camps in Germany saw the highest level of commercial organisation. In addition to the Exchange and Mart notice boards, a shop was organised as a public utility, controlled by representatives of the Senior British Officer, on a no profit basis. People left their surplus clothing, toilet requisites and food there until they were sold at a fixed price in cigarettes. Only sales in cigarettes were accepted—there was no barter— and there was no higgling. For food at least there were standard prices : clothing is less homogeneous and the price was decided around a norm by the seller and the shop manager in agreement ; shirts would average say 80, ranging from 60 to 120 according to quality and age. Of food, the shop carried small stocks for convenience ; the capital was provided by a loan from the bulk store of Red Cross cigarettes and repaid by a small commission taken on the first transactions. Thus the cigarette attained its fullest currency status, and the market was almost completely unified.

It is thus to be seen that a market came into existence without labour or production. The B.R.C.S. may be considered as " Nature " of the text-book, and the articles of trade—food, clothing and cigarettes—as free gifts—land or manna. Despite this, and despite a roughly equal distribution of resources, a market came into spontaneous operation, and prices were fixed by the operation of supply and demand. It is difficult to reconcile this fact with the labour theory of value.

Actually there was an embryo labour market. Even when cigarettes were not scarce, there was usually some unlucky person willing to perform services for them. Laundrymen advertised at two cigarettes a garment. Battle-dress was scrubbed and pressed and a pair of trousers lent for the interim period for twelve. A good pastel portrait cost thirty or a tin of " Kam ". Odd tailoring and other jobs similarly had their prices.

There were also entrepreneurial services. There was a coffee stall owner who sold tea, coffee or cocoa at two cigarettes a cup, buying his raw materials at market prices and hiring labour to gather fuel and to stoke ; he actually enjoyed the services of a chartered accountant at one stage. After a period of great prosperity he overreached himself and failed disastrously for several hundred cigarettes. Such large-scale private enterprise was rare but several middlemen or professional traders existed. The padre in Italy, or the men at Moosburg who opened trading relations with the French, are examples : the more subdivided the market, the less perfect the advertisement of prices, and the less stable the prices, the greater was the scope for these operators. One man capitalised his knowledge of Urdu by buying meat from the Sikhs and selling butter and jam in return : as his operations became better known more and more people entered this trade, prices in the Indian Wing approximated more nearly to those elsewhere, though to the end a " contact " among the Indians was valuable, as linguistic difficulties prevented the trade from being quite free. Some were specialists in the Indian trade, the food, clothing or even the watch trade. Middlemen traded on their own account or on commission. Price rings and agreements were suspected and the traders certainly co-operated. Nor did they welcome newcomers. Unfortunately the writer knows little of the workings of these people : public opinion was hostile and the professionals were usually of a retiring disposition.

One trader in food and cigarettes, operating in a period of dearth, enjoyed a high reputation. His capital, carefully saved, was originally about 50 cigarettes, with which he bought rations on issue days and held them until the price rose just before the next issue. He also picked up a little by arbitrage ; several times a day he visited every Exchange or Mart notice board and took advantage of every discrepancy between prices of goods offered and wanted. His knowledge of prices, markets and names of those who had received cigarette parcels was phenomenal. By these means he kept himself smoking steadily—his profits—while his capital remained intact.

Sugar was issued on Saturday. about Tuesday two of us used to visit Sam and make a deal ; as old customers he would advance as much of the price as he could spare then, and entered the transaction in a book. On Saturday morning he left cocoa tins on our beds for the ration, and picked them up on Saturday afternoon. We were hoping for a calendar at Christmas, but Sam failed too. He was left holding a big black treacle issue when the price fell, and in this weakened state was unable to withstand an unexpected arrival of parcels and the consequent price fluctuations. He paid in full, but from his capital. The next Tuesday, when I paid my usual visit he was out of business.

Credit entered into many, perhaps into most, transactions, in one form or another. Sam paid in advance as a rule for his purchases of future deliveries of sugar, but many buyers asked for credit, whether the commodity was sold spot or future. Naturally prices varied according to the terms of sale. A treacle ration might be advertised for four cigarettes now or five next week. And in the future market " bread now " was a vastly different thing from " bread Thursday ". Bread was issued on Thursday and Monday, four and three days' rations respectively, and by Wednesday and Sunday night it had risen at least one cigarette per ration, from seven to eight, by supper time. One man always saved a ration to sell then at the peak price : his offer of " bread now " stood out on the board among a number of " bread Monday's " fetching one or two less, or not selling at all— and he always smoked on Sunday night.

THE CIGARETTE CURRENCY

Although cigarettes as currency exhibited certain peculiarities, they performed all the functions of a metallic currency as a unit of account, as a measure of value and as a store of value, and shared most of its characteristics. They were homogeneous, reasonably durable, and of convenient size for the smallest or, in packets, for the largest trans- actions. Incidentally, they could be clipped or sweated by rolling them between the fingers so that tobacco fell out.

Cigarettes were also subject to the working of Gresham's Law. Certain brands were more popular than others as smokes, but for currency purposes a cigarette was a cigarette. Consequently buyers used the poorer qualities and the Shop rarely saw the more popular brands : cigarettes such as Churchman's No. 1 were rarely used for trading. At one time cigarettes hand-rolled from pipe tobacco began to circulate. Pipe tobacco was issued in lieu of cigarettes by the Red Cross at a rate of 25 cigarettes to the ounce and this rate was standard in exchanges, but an ounce would produce 30 home-made cigarettes. Naturally, people with machine-made cigarettes broke them down and re-rolled the tobacco, and the real cigarette virtually disappeared from the market. Hand-rolled cigarettes were not homogeneous and prices could no ·longer be quoted in them with safety : each cigarette was examined before it was accepted and thin ones were rejected, or extra demanded as a make-weight. For a time we suffered all the inconveniences of a debased currency.

Machine-made cigarettes were always universally acceptable, both for what they would buy and for themselves. It was this intrinsic value which gave rise to their principal disadvantage as currency, a disadvantage which exists, but to a far smaller extent, in the case of metallic currency;—that is, a strong demand for non-monetary purposes. Consequently our economy was repeatedly subject to deflation and to periods of monetary stringency. While the Red Cross issue of 50 or 25 cigarettes per man per week came in regularly, and while there were fair stocks held, the cigarette currency suited its purpose admirably. But when the issue was interrupted, stocks soon ran out, prices fell, trading declined in volume and became increasingly a matter of barter. This deflationary tendency was periodically offset by the sudden injection of new currency. Private cigarette parcels arrived in a trickle throughout the year, but the big numbers came in quarterly when the Red Cross received its allocation of transport. Several hundred thousand cigarettes might arrive in the space of a fortnight. Prices soared, and then began to fall, slowly at first but with increasing rapidity as stocks ran out, until the next big delivery. Most of our economic troubles could be attributed to this fundamental instability.

PRICE MOVEMENTS

Many factors affected prices, the strongest and most noticeable being the periodical currency inflation and deflation described in the last paragraphs. The periodicity of this price cycle depended on cigarette and, to a far lesser extent, on food deliveries. At one time in the early days, before any private parcels had arrived and when there were no individual stocks, the weekly issue of cigarettes and food parcels occurred on a Monday. The non-monetary demand for cigarettes was great, and less elastic than the demand for food : consequently prices fluctuated weekly, falling towards Sunday night and rising sharply on Monday morning. Later, when many people held reserves, the weekly issue had no such effect, being too small a proportion of the total available. Credit allowed people with no reserves to meet their non-monetary demand over the week-end.

The general price level was affected by other factors. An influx of new prisoners, proverbially hungry, raised it. Heavy air raids in the vicinity of the camp probably increased the non-monetary demand for cigarettes and accentuated deflation. Good and bad war news certainly had its effect, and the general waves of optimism and pessimism which swept the camp were reflected in prices. Before breakfast one morning in March of this year, a rumour of the arrival of parcels and cigarettes was circulated. Within ten minutes I sold a treacle ration, for four cigarettes (hitherto offered in vain for three), and many similar deals went through. By 10 o'clock the rumour was denied, and treacle that day found no more buyers even at two cigarettes.

More interesting than changes in the general price level were changes in the price structure. Changes in the supply of a commodity, in the German ration scale or in the make-up of Red Cross parcels, would raise the price of one commodity relative to others. Tins of oatmeal, once a rare and much sought after luxury in the parcels, became a commonplace in 1943, and the price fell. In hot weather the demand for cocoa fell, and that for soap rose. A new recipe would be reflected in the price level : the discovery that raisins and sugar could be turned into an alcoholic liquor of remarkable potency reacted permanently on the dried fruit market. The invention of electric immersion heaters run off the power points made tea, a drug on the market in Italy, a certain seller in Germany.

In August, 1944, the supplies of parcels and cigarettes were both halved. Since both sides of the equation were changed in the same degree, changes in prices were not anticipated. But this was not the case : the non-monetary demand for cigarettes was less elastic than the demand for food, and food prices fell a little. More important however were the changes in the price structure. German margarine and jam, hitherto valueless owing to adequate supplies of Canadian butter and marmalade, acquired a new value. Chocolate, popular and a certain seller, and sugar, fell. Bread rose ; several standing contracts of bread for cigarettes were broken, especially when the bread ration was reduced a few weeks later.

In February, 1945, the German soldier who drove the ration waggon was found to be willing to exchange loaves of bread at the rate of one loaf for a bar of chocolate. Those in the know began selling bread and buying chocolate, by then almost unsaleable in a period of serious deflation. Bread, at about 40, fell slightly ; chocolate rose from 15 ; the supply of bread was not enough for the two commodities to reach parity, but the tendency was unmistakable.

The substitution of German margarine for Canadian butter when parcels were halved naturally affected their relative values, margarine appreciating at the expense of butter. Similarly, two brands of dried milk, hitherto differing in quality and therefore in price by five cigarettes a tin, came together in price as the wider substitution of the cheaper raised its relative value.

Enough has been cited to show that any change in conditions affected both the general price level and the price structure. It was this latter phenomenon which wrecked our planned economy.

PAPER CURRENCY—Bully Marks

Around D-Day, food and cigarettes were plentiful, business was brisk and the camp in an optimistic mood. Consequently the Entertainments Committee felt the moment opportune to launch a restaurant, where food and hot drinks were sold while a band and variety turns performed. Earlier experiments, both public and private, had pointed the way, and the scheme was a great success. Food was bought at market prices to provide the meals and the small profits were devoted to a reserve fund and used to bribe Germans to provide grease-paints and other necessities for the camp theatre. Originally meals were sold for cigarettes but this meant that the whole scheme was vulnerable to the periodic deflationary waves, and furthermore heavy smokers were unlikely to attend much. The whole success of the scheme depended on an adequate amount of food being offered for sale in the normal manner.

To increase and facilitate trade, and to stimulate supplies and customers therefore, and secondarily to avoid the worst effects of deflation when it should come, a paper currency was organised by the Restaurant and the Shop. The Shop bought food on behalf of the Restaurant with paper notes and the paper was accepted equally with the cigarettes in the Restaurant or Shop, and passed back to the Shop to purchase more food. The Shop acted as a bank of issue. The paper money was backed 100 per cent. by food ; hence its name, the Bully Mark. The BMk. was backed 100 per cent. by food : there could be no over-issues, as is permissible with a normal bank of issue, since the eventual dispersal of the camp and consequent redemption of all BMk.s was anticipated in the near future.

Originally one BMk. was worth one cigarette and for a short time both circulated freely inside and outside the Restaurant. Prices were quoted in BMk.s and cigarettes with equal freedom—and for a short time the BMk. showed signs of replacing the cigarette as currency. The BMk. was tied to food, but not to cigarettes : as it was issued against food, say 45 for a tin of milk and so on, any reduction in the BMk. prices of food would have meant that there were un-backed BMk.s in circulation. But the price of both food and BMk.s could and did fluctuate with the supply of cigarettes.

While the Restaurant flourished, the scheme was a success : the Restaurant bought heavily, all foods were saleable and prices were stable.

In August parcels and cigarettes were halved and the Camp was bombed. The Restaurant closed for a short while and sales of food became difficult. Even when the Restaurant reopened, the food and cigarette shortage became increasingly acute and people were unwilling to convert such valuable goods into paper and to hold them for luxuries like snacks and tea. Less of the right kinds of food for the Restaurant were sold, and the Shop became glutted with dried fruit, chocolate, sugar, etc., which the Restaurant could not buy. The price level and the price structure changed. The BMk. fell to four-fifths of a cigarette and eventually farther still, and it became unacceptable save in the Restaurant. There was a flight from the BMk., no longer convertible into cigarettes or popular foods. The cigarette re-established itself.

But the BMk. was sound ! The Restaurant closed in the New Year with a progressive food shortage and the long evenings without lights due to intensified Allied air raids, and BMk.s could only be spent in

Appendix

the Coffee Bar—relict of the Restaurant—or on the few unpopular foods in the Shop, the owners of which were prepared to accept them. In the end all holders of BMk.s were paid in full, in cups of coffee or in prunes.   People who had bought BMk.s for cigarettes or valuable jam or biscuits in their heyday were aggrieved that they should have stood the loss involved by their restricted choice, but they suffered no actual loss of market value.

PRICE FIXING

Along with this scheme came a determined attempt at a planned economy, at price fixing.   The Medical Officer had long been anxious to control food sales, for fear of some people selling too much, to the detriment of their health.   The deflationary waves and their effects on prices were inconvenient to all and would be dangerous to the Restaurant which had to carry stocks.   Furthermore, unless the BMk. was convertible into cigarettes at about par it had little chance of gaining confidence and of succeeding as a currency.   As has been explained, the BMk. was tied to food but could not be tied to cigarettes, which fluctuated in value.   Hence, while BMk. prices of food were fixed for all time, cigarette prices of food and BMk.s varied.

The Shop, backed by the Senior British Officer, was now in a position to enforce price control both inside and outside its walls.   Hitherto a standard price had been fixed for food left for sale in the shop, and prices outside were roughly in conformity with this scale, which was recommended as a " guide " to sellers, but fluctuated a good deal around it.   Sales in the Shop at recommended prices were apt to be slow though a good price might be obtained : sales outside could be made more quickly at lower prices.   (If sales outside were to be at higher prices, goods were withdrawn from the Shop until the recommended price rose : but the recommended price was sluggish and could not follow the market closely by reason of its very purpose, which was stability.)   The Exchange and Mart notice boards came under the control of the Shop : advertisements which exceeded a 5 per cent. departure from the recommended scale were liable to be crossed out by authority : unauthorised sales were discouraged by authority and also by public opinion, strongly in favour of a just and stable price.   (Recommended prices were fixed partly from market data, partly on the advice of the M.O.)

At first the recommended scale was a success : the Restaurant, a big buyer, kept prices stable around this level : opinion and the 5 per cent. tolerance helped.   But when the price level fell with the August cuts and the price structure changed, the recommended scale was too rigid.   Unchanged at first, as no deflation was expected, the scale was tardily lowered, but the prices of goods on the new scale remained in the same relation to one another, owing to the BMk., while on the market the price structure had changed.   And the modifying influence of the Restaurant had gone.   The scale was moved up and down several times, slowly following the inflationary and deflationary waves, but it was rarely adjusted to changes in the price structure. More and more advertisements were crossed off the board, and black market sales at unauthorised prices increased : eventually public opinion turned against the recommended scale and authority gave up the struggle. In the last few weeks, with unparalleled deflation, prices fell with alarming rapidity, no scales existed, and supply and demand, alone and unmellowed, determined prices.

PUBLIC OPINION

Public opinion on the subject of trading was vocal if confused and changeable, and generalisations as to its direction are difficult and dangerous. A tiny minority held that all trading was undesirable as it engendered an unsavoury atmosphere ; occasional frauds and sharp practices were cited as proof. Certain forms of trading were more generally condemned ; trade with the Germans was criticised by many. Red Cross toilet articles, which were in short supply and only issued in cases of actual need, were excluded from trade by law and opinion working in unshakable harmony. At one time, when there had been several cases of malnutrition reported among the more devoted smokers, no trade in German rations was permitted, as the victims became an additional burden on the depleted food reserves of the Hospital. But while certain activities were condemned as anti-social, trade itself was practised, and its utility appreciated, by almost everyone in the camp.

More interesting was opinion on middlemen and prices. Taken as a whole, opinion was hostile to the middleman. His function, and his hard work in bringing buyer and seller together, were ignored ; profits were not regarded as a reward for labour, but as the result of sharp practices. Despite the fact that his very existence was proof to the contrary, the middleman was held to be redundant in view of the existence of an official Shop and the Exchange and Mart. Appreciation only came his way when he was willing to advance the price of a sugar ration, or to buy goods spot and carry them against a future sale. In these cases the element of risk was obvious to all, and the convenience of the service was felt to merit some reward. Particularly unpopular was the middleman with an element of monopoly, the man who contacted the ration wagon driver, or the man who utilised his knowledge of Urdu. And middlemen as a group were blamed for reducing prices. Opinion notwithstanding, most people dealt with a middleman, whether consciously or unconsciously, at some time or another.

There was a strong feeling that everything had its " just price " in cigarettes. While the assessment of the just price, which incidentally varied between camps, was impossible of explanation, this price was nevertheless pretty closely known. It can best be defined as the price usually fetched by an article in good times when cigarettes were plentiful. The "just price" changed slowly; it was unaffected by short-term variations in supply, and while opinion might be resigned to departures from the "just price", a strong feeling of resentment persisted. A more satisfactory definition of the "just price" is impossible. Everyone knew what it was, though no one could explain why it should be so.

As soon as prices began to fall with a cigarette shortage, a clamour arose, particularly against those who held reserves and who bought at reduced prices. Sellers at cut prices were criticised and their activities referred to as the black market. In every period of dearth the explosive question of "should non-smokers receive a cigarette ration?" was discussed to profitless length. Unfortunately, it was the non-smoker, or the light smoker with his reserves, along with the hated middleman, who weathered the storm most easily.

The popularity of the price-fixing scheme, and such success as it enjoyed, were undoubtedly the result of this body of opinion. On several occasions the fall of prices was delayed by the general support given to the recommended scale. The onset of deflation was marked by a period of sluggish trade; prices stayed up but no one bought. Then prices fell on the black market, and the volume of trade revived in that quarter. Even when the recommended scale was revised, the volume of trade in the Shop would remain low. Opinion was always overruled by the hard facts of the market.

Curious arguments were advanced to justify price fixing. The recommended prices were in some way related to the calorific values of the foods offered : hence some were overvalued and never sold at these prices.   One argument ran as follows :—not everyone has private cigarette parcels : thus, when prices were high and trade good in the summer of 1944, only the lucky rich could buy. This was unfair to the man with few cigarettes. When prices fell in the following winter, prices should be pegged high so that the rich, who had enjoyed life in the summer, should put many cigarettes into circulation. The fact that those who sold to the rich in the summer had also enjoyed life then, and the fact that in the winter there was always someone willing to sell at low prices were ignored. Such arguments were hotly debated each night after the approach of Allied aircraft extinguished all lights at 8 p.m.   But prices moved with the supply of cigarettes, and refused to stay fixed in accordance with a theory of ethics.

CONCLUSION

The economic organisation described was both elaborate and smooth-working in the summer of 1944. Then came the August cuts and deflation. Prices fell, rallied with deliveries of cigarette parcels in September and December, and fell again. In January, 1945, supplies of Red Cross cigarettes ran out : and prices slumped still further : in February the supplies of food parcels were exhausted and the depression became a blizzard. Food, itself scarce, was almost given away in order to meet the non-monetary demand for cigarettes. Laundries ceased to operate, or worked for £s or RMk.s: food and cigarettes sold for fancy prices in £s, hitherto unheard of. The Restaurant was a memory and the BMk. a joke. The Shop was empty and the Exchange and Mart notices were full of unaccepted offers for cigarettes. Barter increased in volume, becoming a larger proportion of a smaller volume of trade. This, the first serious and prolonged food shortage in the writer's experience, caused the price structure to change again, partly because German rations were not easily divisible. A margarine ration gradually sank in value until it exchanged directly for a treacle ration. Sugar slumped sadly. Only bread retained its value. Several thousand cigarettes, the capital of the Shop, were distributed without any noticeable effect. A few fractional parcel and cigarette issues, such as one-sixth of a parcel and twelve cigarettes each, led to momentary price recoveries and feverish trade, especially when they coincided with good news from the Western Front, but the general position remained unaltered.

By April, 1945, chaos had replaced order in the economic sphere : sales were difficult, prices lacked stability. Economics has been defined as the science of distributing limited means among unlimited and competing ends. On 12th April, with the arrival of elements of the 30th U.S. Infantry Division, the ushering in of an age of plenty demonstrated the hypothesis that with infinite means economic organisation and activity would be redundant, as every want could be satisfied without effort.

Index